Colette: The Woman, The Writer

COLETTE:
The Woman, The Writer

Edited by
ERICA MENDELSON EISINGER
and
MARI WARD McCARTY

The Pennsylvania State University Press
University Park and London

The following articles were previously published in slightly different form in the following periodicals:

"Discours de Mme Françoise MALLET-JORIS," Brussels: *Bulletin de l'Académie Royale de Langue et de Littérature Françaises*, 51 (1973) ("Pour le centenaire de Colette: Séance publique du 15 décembre 1973"), pp. 157–173. Reprinted as "Une Vocation feminine?" in *Cahiers Colette*, no. 1 (1977), pp. 41–60.

Donna Norell, "Belief and Disbelief: Structure as Meaning in Colette's *La Lune de pluie*," *L'Espirit Créateur*, 18, no. 2 (summer 1978), pp. 62–75.

Joan Hinde Stewart, "Colette: The Mirror Image," *French Forum*, 3, no. 3 (Sept. 1978), pp. 195–205.

Library of Congress Cataloging in Publication Data
Main entry under title:

Colette: the woman, the writer.

    Includes bibliographical references and index.
    Contents: Genesis: A womanly vocation / Françoise Mallet-Joris. The first steps in a writer's career / Michèle Blin Sarde. Colette and the enterprise of writing / Anne Duhamel Ketchum. — [etc.]
    1. Colette, 1873–1954—Criticism and interpretation—Addresses, essays, lectures. I. Eisinger, Erica Mendelson, 1944-   . II. McCarty, Mari Ward, 1946-
PQ2605.028Z633   848'.91209   81-47169
ISBN 0-271-00286-7   AACR2

The editors dedicate this book to their parents:

Helen Gottlieb Mendelson
Arthur I. Mendelson
Vera Bantz Ward
Donald B. Ward

Contents

III Generation: The Production and Texture of Writing

Foreword: Celebrating Colette

Modes of celebration expose the desire of the celebrants. In 1973 France celebrated the one hundreth anniversary of the birth of Gabrielle Sidonie Colette. Events included lectures; "soirées Colette" at the Comédie Française; a Colette stamp; a homage to Colette at the Royal Belgian Academy of Letters with the participation of the Goncourt Academy (she had been a member of both); radio and television programs; the publication of a volume of correspondence, *Lettres à ses pairs*; a sixteen-volume edition of her complete works; and an exhibit of manuscripts, letters, photographs, and other memorabilia at the Bibliothèque Nationale. Colette was enjoying almost as much popularity as her character Claudine who, in the early 1900's, lent her name to ice creams, perfumes, hats, body lotions, cigarettes, and collars. Colette had become a fictional character generated by her own texts and by the texts of the critics and biographers who told her story over and over again.

The character "Colette" embodies a series of myths that range from the eternal feminine to the exemplary woman writer, from the sensuous French woman to the wise survivor. Special interest groups representing the patriarchy or counter systems such as matriarchy or androgyny have used these myths to their advantage. Myths do more than tell us something about the cultures in which they flourish; they also tell us something about the materials through which they are structured. What is there in the more than sixty texts written by Colette — novels, short stories, plays, fictionalized reminiscences, animal dialogues, prose poems, theatre criticism, newspaper articles, journals, and letters — that has encouraged this kind of mythologizing? What is happening in these texts that might explain the hectic coming and going, in the minds of most readers (the least as well as the most sophisticated), between Colette's written words and the representation of Colette's life?

One approach might be sought in such words as heterogeneity, hybrid, or mongrel. There is a crossing, a mixing in all Colette's texts of genders (male and female), of social classes (the demi-monde, the marginals, and the bourgeoisie), of cultures (learned and popular), and most importantly of genres (narrative and dramatic fiction, autobiography, biography). Attempts to situate Colette in relation to the women authors of the turn of the century whom she frequented (Renée Vivien, Natalie Clifford-Barney, Lucie Delarue-Mardrus, Anna de Noailles) or to women authors of other cultural traditions (Gertrude Stein, Virginia Woolf), or attempts to relate her to the "classical generation of 1870" (Marcel Proust, André Gide, Charles Péguy, Paul Valéry, Alain) fail and for the same reasons. Neither sexual identity nor contemporaneity can cope with the difference between the texts of the best-known French woman writer of the first half of the twentieth century and those of other writers. Their texts function within the protocols of a group and hers do not. Where then is she located, and how does this peripheral location account for the heterogeneity within her texts?

By refusing to abide by the rules that govern the production of accepted and expected meanings, Colette alters the rules of literary play. She thereby confuses the reader, even the reader steeped in formalist ideology who knows that the gulf between words and things is, in reality (if not in fancy), unbridgeable. These rules are fairly simple. They require that the signs identifying male and female, fiction and biography or autobiography, social classes, and levels of style be unambiguous. The point is that these signs are ambiguous in the Colette corpus from *Claudine à l'école* (1900, the year Nietzsche died) to *Le Fanal bleu* (1949, the year of Simone de Beauvoir's *Le Deuxième Sexe* and the Communist victory in China).

For example ... Men are usually represented as weak (physically and morally) in Colette's texts and women as strong. The descriptions of male and female body language to which we are accustomed are sometimes reversed. The social class of the characters is difficult to establish and unfamiliar to middle class readers. Colette's characters are neither high nor middle nor low. They are often *dé-classés*, as is the narrator, Colette. They are everywhere and nowhere. Their mobility has its source in sexual promiscuity which is itself a powerful conveyor of ambiguity. The reader's confusion is increased by the odd blend of popular and learned cultures. An oral and a written tradition have come together. The rituals and ceremonies of village life transmitted from mother to daughter impose their order on the conventions of the *fin-de-siècle* salacious novel and on sophisticated urban life. The richness and the coherence of this popular culture — of village culture to be more precise — provide a documentation that augments the reader's sense of a repository of wisdom and reality beyond and behind the text. This repository is represented once again by "Colette" and her nostalgia for a dying past.

Almost any moment of any of Colette's first person texts may serve to illustrate still further this ambiguity. The first person narrator always claims to be writing about something that happened in a more or less distant past. Because this first person narrator is an observer as well as a writer, a distance is maintained that reinforces the illusion of reality. The narrator has been there where it happened, or is there while it is happening. And, of course, the narrator is often called "Colette" or "Madame Colette." It is the repeated use of the name more than any other narrative or stylistic device that sustains the reader's conviction of "real" events outside the texts and that suggests the labels autobiography-biography. Conventional fiction requires that writer and character have different names. When they do not, the texts are not read as fictions. Colette has gone a step beyond Proust who went a step beyond Balzac. Balzac juxtaposed names of "real" and invented characters, but never used his own name in a text. Proust called his narrator, on two lonely occasions, "Marcel," but never Proust. Colette, who chose to have only one name — a convenient patronymic that was also a woman's name — used it constantly.

What she did that had never been done before with the same vigor was to write in fiction her own biography. As early as 1931 adoring disciples were transforming biography into hagiography. The transformation was completed by her third husband, Maurice Goudeket, in his two volumes *Près de Colette* (1956) and *La Douceur de vieillir* (1965). His description of Colette's deathbed behavior, his insistence on Colette's texts as miracles hint at the possibility of elevating Colette to the status of a lay saint. Her fictions and his have merged in the mind of the reader. To his emphasis on miracles we add her reiteration of renunciation, to his account of her deathbed word "Regarde!" we add her accounts of the lost paradise of childhood and the jealous inferno of a first marriage. Biography and hagiography together have overwhelmed the texts, making it difficult to read and write outside the moral, Manichean universe of the hagiographical structure.

We celebrate, at the opening of this volume, the desire to go beyond the myths, to forget for a time (we may come back to her) the representative of female wisdom, the embodiment of France. We celebrate an introduction to new ways of reading literature that come from the developing area of feminist critical theory and from semiotics. It is at the points of articulation between the two that the most exciting texts are being produced. We celebrate the new directions in Colette criticism.

Elaine Marks

Madison, Wisconsin
January 1981

Introduction

ERICA EISINGER and MARI McCARTY

Colette's work is a celebration of woman, of her strength and elasticity, of her gift for endurance. In a literary career which spans a half-century and includes more than sixty titles, Colette speaks continuously of the female art of survival. "What a solid creature is woman!" she proclaims.

Colette's stories of female durability have particular relevance in our contemporary search for the female presence and the female voice in literature. The combined influence of the women's movement and recent French linguistic and literary theory has generated speculation about the existence of a "dark continent" in literature, a repressed energy in human discourse: women's writing. For readers looking for continuity in women's writing, Colette refutes the notion that women were silent or absent from literary creation. And for those who look not to the past, but to the present struggle of women writers to speak in a mode specific to women, Colette inaugurates the search for a new literary discourse.

Colette has been called "the first woman in French literature to write as a woman."[1] She has been described as the link between the older writing about women, which tended to see women as objects of male desire, and the new feminist literature that has been produced by women in France since 1968, which glorifies the female principle.[2] Readers have long suspected that Colette's writing was intimately connected with her experience as a woman in a way that earlier writing, that of George Sand for example, was not. Traditional critics saw Colette's fiction as "typically feminine," but this femininity was viewed only negatively, as "non-male." Colette's writing was labeled instinctive, corporeal, sensual, pagan, anomalous, outside literary history. The authors in this volume reclaim these same traits — the presence of the body, a diffuse sensuality, an unrepressed female desire, the celebration

1

of marginality — for the female continent, recognizing them as the very elements which distinguish Colette from the male canon and draw her to her sisters. The authors focus on those narrative techniques which depart from patriarchal convention, leading toward the generation of the female text: the reversal of sexual stereotypes, the transcendence of genre, the alteration of image structure, and the discovery of new lexical codes. We suspect that something new in women's writing begins with Colette. The androcentric optic is displaced; a new subject appears: the woman who desires.

Colette not only writes about women; she writes through a woman's voice. Her narrator, the semi-fictional "Colette," speaks in the first person female, creating a bond of identity with her characters. All women are heroes in her fiction, from the adolescent androgynes who dwell in the earthly paradise of the matriarchal garden, to the "new" women forging careers and independence at mid-life, to the solitary aging women who return to the natural purity of their youth. As schoolgirls, actresses, dancers, courtesans, designers, businesswomen, or writers, Colette's women find their identities on the margins of male power, dominated not by men, but by work, by relationships with other women. Men are but peripheral stops in a woman's journey to self-definition. Even as they struggle with simultaneous desires toward freedom and submission, Colette's women refuse self-destruction. They do not fear silence or declining power, for they understand that their capacity for self-renewal is infinite, rooted in continuous erotic potential. Weakness and entropy are not female characteristics; on the contrary, women are defined by their activity. For Colette, women represent the life force.

The source of female renewal lies in the bond to the mother. From mother to daughter, an art of living, a respect for nurture is handed down. Colette and her characters retain the memory of a primary matriarchy where they reigned as queens of the earth, and where everything — nature, desire, language — belonged to them. Colette's own mother, Sido, assumes mythic proportions in her daughter's later works. As muse, mentor, and medium, she nourishes the writer's creative energy, bestowing the crucial gifts of language and of self. Sido called the youthful Colette "Bel Gazou" — "beautiful language" — imparting to the daughter the power to name, to appropriate, to create.

The purpose of this collection is to explore the source and practice of Colette's power. Colette's journey into creativity poses the central questions which preoccupy students of women's writing today: How does a woman come to writing? How does a woman inscribe her gender in her writing? How does the text of the woman writer relate to other texts? How is meaning produced in the woman's text?

The sections of this book reflect three major currents of contemporary feminist and formalist scholarship: biographical, contextual, and textual. The first section, "Genesis," introduces the paradox of the author's ambivalence toward her vocation. Colette insisted, "No, I never, never wished to write."

How did the woman "born *not* to write" become a writer? "Genesis" reexamines the biographical data to ask what particular elements of her experience and condition as a woman acted upon Colette's formation as a writer. How did the woman, who came to writing reluctantly, write so relentlessly? At the root of Colette's ambivalence toward her vocation lies her bizarre literary apprenticeship as unpaid ghostwriter for her husband Willy. Dominated by this conjunction of economic and sexual determinants, Colette nonetheless transformed the instrument of her oppression — forced writing — into her means of liberation. The opposing impulses, to be a "woman" and to be a writer, finally converge: the two vocations are both apprenticeships in survival.

For the woman writer, the creation of the self and the creation of the text merge: the woman literally must "write herself."[3] The second section, "Gender and Genre," explores the interrelationship between the life and the work, between the contexts and the texts. Colette's work was a lifetime dialogue, first with the self, then beyond to encompass the artistic and social movements of her day.

Colette's discovery is that women's writing is a dual creation: a generation of self, a living fiction, and a projection of the self in writing, an auto-fiction. Thus her forms are fully consonant with her fundamental theme, the exploration of female identity. Her dominant images are figures of self-reflection and illumination: mirrors, water, lamps, windows. Her favored narrative structures employ traditional female reflexive forms: letters, journals, self-portraits. Even narratives such as epistolary novels, which posit a correspondent, become instruments of *self*-discovery, inner dialogues. Similarly, the play-acting which infuses her novels is only superficially directed toward an outer audience; the real performance is for oneself. Colette welcomes all means, including the supernatural, to connect with past and present selves. In the mirror of the page, Colette discovers the exhilaration of continuity which triumphs over time and change.

The perpetual cycle of women's lives describes a movement away from and back to a psychic and sensual wholeness Colette calls "purity." Her characters are permitted a continuous desire which transcends the boundaries of age, gender, and even species. Colette admits women to the earthly paradise of pleasures "lightly called physical," and she dares to reveal that women possess a secret source of power, a superior libidinal economy based not on scarcity, but on abundance. Our authors attach new prestige to the erotic Colette, who appropriates for the female the full range of human desire, the freedom to partake of the plurality of pleasures, neither pure nor impure.

Colette placed herself on the boundaries of social and artistic respectability. As she identified with those who challenged conventional sexual mores, so too did she respond to the creative avant-garde of her day. She found her artistic community among those who dismantled prevailing patriarchal assumptions, to experiment with fluidity, whimsy, hermaphrodism, and the uncanny.

Colette's construction of the text is visual, musical. She possessed an artisan's respect for tools — lamp, pen, and paper — and for material — the words themselves. Words for Colette are simultaneously product and meaning, actors in their own right.

Colette anticipated the modern impulse of women writers to communicate in new forms, and her intuition led her to search for "a new alphabet." Feminist critics have speculated that if women have been excluded from power, from the social order and the order of language, if woman is *other*, then the unalienated woman will not write as a man; what she writes will be *other*. The final section, "Generation," explores the connections between women and language. Colette's apparent facility with words masks her struggle with an alien culture which strips language of its sensuality and its plasticity. Colette discovers that the woman writer has access to a basic, unmediated language filtered through knowledge of the primary female body, the mother. The dialogue of love between mother and daughter creates language, and, indeed, creates the text. As women rename the world, reappropriate matter through writing, they give birth to themselves. Colette literally had to name herself, choosing the single feminine patronym "Colette" to reconcile the woman "born *not* to write" with her ceaseless production of words. As Colette generated herself through her texts, she generated new, powerful figures: a recoding of women.

Notes

1. Louis Perche, *Colette* (Paris: Seghers, 1976), Introduction.

2. Claudine Chonez, "Hier, aujourd'hui, demain," *La Table ronde*, 99 (mars 1956), 61. Quoted in Germaine Brée, *Women Writers in France* (New Brunswick, N.J.: Rutgers University Press, 1973), p. 48. See also Eisinger and McCarty, eds., Special issue on Colette, *Women's Studies*, 8, No. 3 (1981). For a full discussion of women's writing in France, see Elaine Marks, "Women and Literature in France," *Signs*, 4, No. 4 (Summer 1978), 832–842; Carolyn Greenstein Burke, "Report from Paris: Women's Writing and the Women's Movement," *Signs*, 4, No. 4 (Summer 1978), 843–855; and Elaine Marks and Isabelle de Courtivron, eds., *French Feminisms* (Amherst, Mass.: University of Massachusetts Press, 1980).

3. Hélène Cixous, "Le Rire de la Méduse," *L'Arc*, 61 (1975), p. 40. Translated by Keith Cohen and Paula Cohen as "The Laugh of the Medusa," *Signs*, 1, No. 4 (Summer 1976), 875–893.

I. Genesis: The Coming to Writing

1 A Womanly Vocation

FRANÇOISE MALLET-JORIS
Translated by Eleanor Reid Gibbard[1]

In her book *Looking Backwards*, Colette once wrote: "When you can enter the enchanted kingdom of reading, why write? The distaste that the gesture of writing inspired in me — was it not a providential piece of advice? It is somewhat late for me to examine myself on this. What's done is done. But when I was young I never, never wanted to write. No, I did not get up secretly in the night and pencil poetry on the cover of a shoebox. No, I did not cast inspired words onto the west wind or into the light of the full moon! No, I did not get a perfect mark on a composition when I was twelve or fifteen years old! For I felt, more and more as each day passed, I felt that I was made, precisely, not to write. I never sent a well-known writer essays showing promise of a pretty talent. . . . So I was indeed the only one of my kind, the only girl sent into the world not to write. What a blessing that I could experience such an absence of literary vocation!"

This, in my view, is one of the most significant and singular quotations one could pick from any writer. It betrays, toward the phenomenon of writing, a sort of duality that was to follow Colette throughout her life, one that she pointed to more or less consciously in the account she gives of her first writing. And it is also a good point of departure from which to enter a body of work which is at once clear and complex.

When Colette recounts the birth of *Claudine at School*, her first piece of writing, she places considerable emphasis on the fortuitous nature of that sudden success. It's at the request, or rather the order, of her first husband that she writes these memories of her childhood. Quite readily she forgets these notebooks in a drawer. Only the greatest of chances causes Willy to

7

rediscover them there. She dwells on these three factors, all completely independent of her will: that she was ordered to write, that the result was consigned to oblivion, that chance alone brought it to light again. Willy was cleaning up his office when he found the notebooks; idly he leafed them through; then, suddenly, he saw how they could be turned to profit. "He gathered the notebooks all up in a jumble, seized his flat-brimmed hat, ran to a publisher — and that is how I became a writer."

This tone of resigned amiability, this alibi she gives herself, these excuses she keeps proffering for possessing an ever-flowering gift, all these she keeps repeating; before the Belgian Royal Academy she defined herself as having become a writer "without realizing what was happening," and declared herself still, at sixty, astonished. Such an astonishment has doubtless been experienced by everyone who has tried to create in any field, when inspiration strikes and then vanishes, to reappear only after persevering labor and near desperation. Rare, however, are those who thus deny even the first appearance of a hope, even the mirage of what we call a vocation.

Colette mentions briefly her father's literary ambitions. Captain Colette had gone so far as to prepare a dozen stiff-covered volumes bearing a variety of titles: *My Campaigns, The Lessons of '70, Marshal MacMahon Viewed by One of His Comrades in Arms, Songs of a Zouave,* etc. At his death his children discovered that these volumes held only blank paper. "Two hundred, three hundred, one hundred fifty pages to a volume," writes Colette, "fine creamy laid paper, or thick foolscap, carefully trimmed, hundreds and hundreds of blank pages. Imaginary works, mirage of a writer's career." And Sido wrote once to her daughter: "What a shame that he loved me so! His love for me is what annihilated, one by one, all his fine faculties that would have pushed him into literature and science. He preferred to think only of me, to worry for me, and that's what I find inexcusable. So great a love! What frivolity!"

Heir to her father's dream and to Sido's fierce energy, did Colette more or less consciously want to fulfill the destiny that the one dreamed and the other mourned the loss of? This would be a key to explaining the strange duality of the woman who devoted so much time, patience, and love to a kind of work she never quite laid claim to. When Colette declares there is no more merit in writing than there is, for example, in making shoes, she displays a taste for the concrete and an artist's modesty that many might envy her. But the repeated invocation of chance takes on another face, one of contradiction, when we also read from her pen, concerning her father: "It was he who was trying to come to the surface and live again when I began obscurely to write." And when she invokes at length the captain's powerlessness to write and his wish to write, we are led to compare that picturesque, erratic father with the writer's first husband, Willy, a curious and perhaps too much disparaged figure, who devoted so much ingenuity, energy, and talent to getting "ghosts" to write, men sometimes less gifted than he.

Colette herself invites this comparison: "He must frequently have thought, earlier, that he was on the verge of writing, that he was going to write, that he was writing. Pen in hand, he would be deprived of his illusion by a breaking of the tension, a failure of the will." The drama of these two men! Both aging, and both stricken with this inability to write, a difficulty Colette overcame in masterly fashion. While thinking she feels her father's vocation reaching fulfillment through her, she also portrays herself locked in her room by Willy; in both cases she is somehow being forced to write. Is she fulfilling, as a sort of instrument, the destiny of the two men? Is she but using them as her alibi? Who can say?

It is likely at the start — that loudly orchestrated start, the *Claudine* series — that she herself does not know. Willy's chronic need for money doubtless determines her, but is it pure chance that she has married a man who is a failure as a writer? Later on, when she is a woman alone, writing still while trying her hand at mime and theatre, she says she is irritated that she is always thought of not as an actress but as a woman writer gone wrong. Yet she continues to write, and she will go on writing, all the way to those last astonishing pages in which she at long last confesses her joy in writing, a joy in which she now feels excused by the habit of half a century.

Such insistence cannot be explained by modesty alone. Is it perhaps that Colette had a certain idea of the vocation of a woman? "To become just a woman! It's not very much, and yet I threw myself toward that common end," she says with a sort of nostalgia, evoking the difficult passage from childhood to adolescence. Elsewhere she recalls with melancholy a conversation with a man friend who is a great lover of women, a conversation that concludes: "'You, a woman? You'd like to be!'" "In my secret heart I'd have very much liked to be a woman," she adds, "but that man was not mistaken. He knew me to be masculine at some point I was incapable of defining, and he fled, although he was tempted." This feeling that she is not, at some particular point, wholly a woman, this nostalgia which touches almost on guilt — is it not precisely the act of writing, her writer's career, her man's career, which she takes so much care to present as fortuitous? All her life, and even in the honor of belonging to two Academies, the fact that she was a woman was emphasized, given importance, and invoked to explain her or criticize her. As she spoke of herself, however discreetly, Colette sometimes raised questions about her own womanliness, before assuming it and finally asserting its legitimacy.

An attitude of amusement too often accompanied the efforts women made as they took up literature and poetry in considerable numbers and with considerable success during the years in which Colette herself was making her beginnings. It explains in part Willy's behavior as an impresario, exploiting his wife as an income property, but in a context that could, to a certain extent, authorize him to do so. It also explains how, after a period in which she is both intoxicated by all the fuss being made over her and somewhat unconscious of the handicap it may represent, Colette feels the need to shelter her nascent vocation in Willy's voluminous shadow.

Claudine, Colette's first heroine, became famous. But what is Claudine? What does she have in common with Colette, with the idea Colette as a young married woman might have of woman, Colette still steeped in her provincial homeland and the first to characterize herself as a "country girl"? Claudine too is primarily a country girl, exiled to Paris, sighing for her native Montigny. A slightly affected unsociability, a waggish good nature too — cover for a shy sensitivity — these certainly are resemblances. In the little village of Montigny, a certain vivacity and a taste for books did make her stand out as remarkable. In Paris she is at first just slightly tomboyish. We find this type of adolescent girl in certain other characters of that period, from Gyp to Louisa May Alcott. Claudine's very real love of her home country is her most novel trait; otherwise, she is liberated only superficially. In Paris she will marry Renaud, a seductive "diplomat" quite lacking in substance.

Claudine, in fact, is afflicted with a childishness that was never Colette's. In the dialogue she wrote later to distinguish herself definitively from that burdensome character, Colette lays emphasis on this: "When you were little," this Claudine who is supposed to be her double is saying — and Colette answers her with new-found gravity, "I was never little." Claudine, when she stops being the cute little country lass, becomes a woman like any other, only a little more solemn, and a little better at observing nature and creatures. And as Renaud represents the love an as-yet-inexperienced young woman can dream of having, so may Claudine, perhaps, represent the woman Colette would have preferred to be at that time.

Claudine will become a widow, a faithful widow, solemn, but not sad. Her real originality at this point in her development is that she draws strength and consolation from the nature which surrounds her and from her inner life forces that keep her from despairing in her solitude.

Colette does not become a widow; she is divorced (and in that lies all the difference between a broken heart and a failure). Colette abandons her character Claudine at this time of inner turmoil, from which springs the one character we could in any sense call a feminist: Renée Néré, the wanderer, *The Vagabond*.

If Claudine represents the woman Colette would have liked to be when she was young and naïve, Renée represents the woman she might well have become, after the first disillusionments.

In her situation Renée is much closer to Colette than was Claudine. Ill-married, divorced, forced to earn her living, and even taking pleasure in writing, she is a more solemn Colette, a more austere one, less generous perhaps, and more of a rebel. More of an idealist too, we might say, if we disregarded everything Colette conceals behind an apparent hedonism.

Renée the Vagabond fears and refuses marriage and love. She fears not just the banal risk of suffering; she fears also that the love of a single being is at once a great gift and a confinement. "I refuse to have to view the most beautiful scenes in the world only in miniature, in the loving mirror of his eyes." Renée here joins Sido. "So great a love! what frivolity!" But the suggestion of pity we feel in Sido is nonexistent in Renée, who is edgy and taut in her struggle. Renée has come only to the refusal of love, whereas Sido, reaching a magnificent serenity, accepts but, within herself, goes beyond this love. The awkward, self-involved character Renée, while far from being the best drawn in Colette's work, is perhaps the least disguised, the truest. And in this first phase she is quite the opposite of a pagan, as Colette and her heroines have been very improperly called. She is a woman who *renounces* pleasure in the name of an idea — perhaps an erroneous idea, but a noble one — of her destiny as a woman. And when, in *The Shackle*, in a sudden reversal — one which Colette herself acknowledged is not very successfully brought off — the same Renée decides to give herself completely to love, this is also the result of a considered conviction, arrived at when desire itself is already waning and no longer obscures her reasoning power.

Here again we find a very obvious bond between the woman asserting her selfhood and the woman giving herself completely. A concern to be in control of her emotions, not to surrender to the "indiscreet poetizing" of the senses or even of superficial feelings. A concern for "dignity." How often this word dignity, this concern for *tenue* — good manners, proper behavior — recurs in Colette's writing.

When as a very young bride she discovers her husband is deceiving her, she is "pretty proud of having neither trembled nor threatened." She praises the "honorable silence" of a male friend who was in a position to watch this threatened conjugal life. Women who fight over a man are called "champions." And much later, when for a while she is in the beauty products business, she is struck by the "frivolous courage" of so many women, and writes: "Since I have been caring for my contemporaries and their makeup, I have not yet met a woman who was discouraged at fifty or one in a state of nervous exhaustion at sixty." Colette, who had long since observed and admired these qualities of courage and vitality in her mother, never considered weakness a virtue in a woman, or even something natural to a woman. The two Renées — for Renée is double, and more symbolic than any other of Colette's characters — show Colette's search for the *way* this vitality and courage are to be used. Do they not condemn the woman to solitude? Alone in her independence, Renée will remain alone even with her lover.

Thus there begins a period of solitude for Colette. She describes in various books her tours of the provinces, her activities as an actress and a journalist. From this hard-won independence she drew a new equilibrium, and it is this independence, specifically, that makes Colette a writer completely aloof from the women's movement. Renée Néré had uttered the only word of revolt in all Colette's work that could be considered a feminist statement: she, the ordinary little actress, had cried out with regard to her rich, idle suitor, "Of the two of us, *he*'s the courtesan." But that cry has no further echo, theoretically at least, in Colette's work. She contents herself with asserting peacefully, through her life, through her work, and through the quality of her attention, an independence which goes beyond the feminist claims. Colette tacitly claims for any person of singular attainments the right to hold to his or her own morality, conventions, and truth, while splendidly ignoring the prejudices of others. "I don't like to talk about myself," she would say — and yet she continually depicts herself in her writings. However, she does not explain herself. She shows herself, with neither complacency nor severity, as she shows others, and this is why her own character remains rather mysterious, and almost inhuman. Yet the attentive reader can observe the gradual modification of Colette's characters, to encompass a compassion for the disadvantaged, as well as a stoical optimism. These are the qualities found in the two great woman characters who will dominate Colette's work for some years to come: Sido and Léa.

On the surface, no two women could be more different. In the first place, Sido, Colette's mother, is a figure of flesh and blood, not a character. But she played so large a role in Colette's conception of life that we cannot tell which of the two, mother or daughter, influenced the other more. Sido is a country woman, a faithful wife, and an attentive mother. Léa is nothing of the sort. She is a rich courtesan, a celebrated Parisian. But certain common points emerge when we compare the two women: the wish for a certain harmony and perfection in daily life, an art of living which to Colette is far from frivolous; on the contrary, it is a discipline. What creates the ambiguity is that the discipline in question is based on the love of life. Sido, courageous as she faces old age and fatigue, who rises at dawn, then earlier, then earlier still, so that she may truly enjoy the "Birth of the Day," and Léa, who, prey to the pain of an inevitable separation, worries nonetheless over the condition of her silverware, her towels, or the quality of a wine or a dish — both understood, as Colette put it so magnificently, that "you don't have to believe in happiness to find life precious."

And so Colette defines more and more clearly the woman's vocation, the vocation of enduring, of giving daily life its symbolic and almost sacred meaning, of giving it that "precious" brilliance in its most humble manifestations. Colette evinces a secret admiration for any creature who struggles and clings to life, though it be for the wrong reasons. This is the merit, above all others, that she accords to woman. There are a few suicides in Colette's work, but they are all suicides of men: Chéri, certainly, disgusted with life; and *Duo*'s Michel, who kills himself because his wife has deceived him. And the faithless wife exclaims, with Colette's approval, "He's the one who's more to blame."

There is no greater fault than refusing life.

It is from this viewpoint that we must reread what is to my mind Colette's finest novel, her most significant in any case, *Break of Day* (*La Naissance du jour*). With all due deference to the author's touchy modesty, *Break of Day* must be called poetry. For it is poetry when the heroine, a false Colette, a Colette truer than life (since Colette, on the other hand, has just recovered her confidence in love) can exclaim, "How simple everything is now!" This simplicity regained is an expansion. With Captain Colette's aborted vocation brought to fulfillment, Colette will now magnify Sido, in pages that are marvels of simplicty and amplitude.

The portrait of Sido will help us toward a comprehension of what Colette considers to be the unfolding, the flowering, of the womanly vocation. It includes an idea of sympathy, of compassionate charity. "I am the daughter of a woman who, in a shameful, miserly, shut-in little backwater, opened her village home to lost cats, tramps, and pregnant servant girls." But she broadens this idea immediately by emphasizing Sido's independence of thought and judgment, which is neither revolt nor protest, nor even forbearance, but simply a sovereign animal contempt for conventions that are foreign to her. Here we have that privileged bond joining the Colette who admires work, constraint, physical and moral dignity, to the cosmic Colette, who embraces the mystery of animals and all natural phenomena. Giving the final touch to Sido's portrait, a portrait that is also a slightly inhuman symbol, Colette quotes the letter in which Sido refuses to visit the daughter she adores, who has just remarried, because her "pink cactus is probably going to flower." "That possible blossoming," writes Colette, "the wait for a tropical flower, placed everything else in suspense, and brought silence even to her heart made for love."

A capital statement. To believe in happiness, to believe in love in the narrow sense of the term, is still to restrict oneself, to refuse the wider dimensions of the love of life and of the marvels of creation, to set limits on the act of paying attention, an act so important for Colette that it takes on an almost mystical dimension. The silence in Sido's heart is a form of contemplation. And perhaps it is also a key to the fact that Colette so often denied having opted, of her own will, for the act of writing; it is after all an act that, however discreet, disturbs the silence.

Armand Lanoux has written, with great subtlety: "Colette lives with unassuming people, as does her mother, but as Michelet's *Sorcière* does also. She is a thousand years old, a direct descendant of the Great Mothers. Too much a woman to be a suffragette, she would smile at the excesses of Woman Power. She is *farther along* in unshakeable opposition to the *ordre adamique*, the male-dominated order of things; she is a loving rebel against Adam."

Here a fundamental contradiction is quite properly exposed. Colette, who was not a feminist, Colette for whom it was enough to be a woman, questioned whether the act of writing, whether action as such, would not somehow debase the womanly nature. Since attention and silence must be stronger and more meaningful than speech or writing, it seemed to Colette that woman fulfills herself better by being and enduring than by acting. She felt restricted within the compass of society, as within the compass of love. The heroine of *Break of Day*, who gives up trying to be a woman in the commonplace sense of the term, becomes one more fully after all by taking on the whole of creation.

Colette is not — cannot be — the novelist of the couple. For her, action and contemplation are irreconcilable. She cannot reconcile the two principles, and she cannot reconcile the couple, even the couple coexistent in her. This difficulty comes not from an idea that is weak and inferior, but from too strong, too beautiful an idea of the values that are called womanly. Colette's mother used to say, "Don't touch the butterfly's wing." When Colette declares herself "the impure continuation" of her mother, it is as if Colette harbors a fear: because she did, indeed, "touch the butterfly's wing," she wonders whether she has betrayed her childhood, or her womanliness, or her mother's example, or, more profoundly, the poetry that is not indiscreet lyricism but enters the sacred domain of pure attention.

Colette writes in *Bella-Vista*, "everything beloved strips you bare," showing us how essential to her is this feeling of duality, male-female, action-contemplation, entity-cosmos. Do we see melancholy in this, perhaps a form of despair? Colette promptly sets us straight. "Nothing is wasting away. It's simply that I'm moving away." In her last years, she finally confessed that she would never be through with writing. "With humility, I shall go on writing. There is no other fate for me." A last struggle proves vain. "To unlearn to write — surely that can't take long," but "I still don't know when I shall succeed in not writing. The obsession, the obligation — they are now half a century old." The word obligation is still there, but Colette no longer denies this pleasure of the mind's "continuing within her the gourmet's search, seeking a better word, and then a better than better word."

Suzanne Lilar says, speaking of Colette describing her pregnancy, "If there is virility in the critical resoluteness of this self-examination, the happiness encompassed in such a virile manner remains specifically womanly. In this robustly androgynous woman, the manly, far from extinguishing the womanly spontaneity, collaborates with it." We have here a rare originality that is too little recognized. "The paternal lyricism and humor, the maternal spontaneity," says Colette, "these I am now wise enough and proud enough to distinguish in myself." It is the constant tension between these two aspirations that gives to her joy its grave and almost mournful sound, and to her very sadness its tonicity and health.

"On a resonant highway the trotting of two horses in harness is in cadence and then out of cadence and again in cadence. Guided by the same hand, my pen and my needle, the habit of work and the wise desire to put an end to work, these two make friends, draw apart, make friends again. Slow chargers of mine, try to keep together. I can see the end of the road from here."

Note

1. This article originally appeared in French as "Une Vocation feminine?" in *Cahiers Colette*, No. 1 (Paris: Flammarion, Société des Amis de Colette, 1973), pp. 41–62. Ms. Gibbard's abridged translation is published here with the kind permission of Mme Mallet-Joris and Mme Colette de Jouvenel, Honorary President of the Société des Amis de Colette.

2 The First Steps in a Writer's Career
MICHÈLE BLIN SARDE

In point of fact, this paper could be titled, "How to renew feminist biographical criticism," for it deals with drawing theoretical lessons exclusively from concrete experience. I believe there is a close relationship between biographical analysis and sociological criticism, although I do not, however, grant preference to either to the exclusion of other critical methods. It seems to me that they provide a certain amount of necessary material without which other critical forms may seem artificial. In other words, in my view, sociological criticism, which I believe is linked with biographical analysis, is the foundation upon which a critical structure may be solidly based.

I began with a "recreational" reading of Colette, without having any particular hypothesis in mind but nevertheless aware that it was initially the psychoanalytic approach which most interested me. In spite of a certain indifference to biography attributable to formalist modes, be they structuralist or semiological, I read with interest material concerning Colette's life — and did so at the start probably more as a "woman" than as a "critic." I was struck by two things: first, the exceptional process by which she was brought to write (that is, her husband's coercion) and the time required before she achieved recognition as a writer, even though she produced a great deal at the beginning, and well-known books at that. Second, I was surprised by the indifference she constantly displayed toward her "writing" until the end of her life (and I cite but one example among many): "No, I don't know how to write. In my youth, I never, *never* wanted to write" (*Journal à rebours*).

In my view, these observations were very closely related to the absence of creativity so frequently used as a reproach of women. On the one hand, why are there so few women writers, since women did shed their illiteracy rather early and some of them had the leisure to engage in writing? And on the other hand, why did a woman such as Colette, endowed with true talent, have to encounter exceptional circumstances so that such talent might be realized and blossom? I tried to determine what had been the succession of restrictive socioeconomic circumstances — they were not merely psychological in nature — which permitted her potential to be realized while the talents of so many unknown women were probably stifled.

I began with *Claudine à l'école,* a work ordinarily scorned. Its somewhat scabrous characteristics had obviously been imposed by Willy, and Colette herself had always harshly criticized it. It seemed to me that it contained some very important documentary elements relating to the lay school for rural girls of the era. We have, and with good reason, few literary descriptions of this institution from the inside by the best possible witness, i.e., a former student. At that point the study of period documents and of the different histories of nineteeth-century education led me to a certain number of conclusions:[1]

1. Colette attended a school intended for poor girls — country girls as a general rule.

2. It offered very few opportunities for those who completed it. By way of example, the salary of Aimée, the teacher described by Colette, was 70 francs per month, of which she had to deduct 30 francs for her *pension* and 20 francs which she sent to her parents. The post of school teacher was the only possible outlet for the most brilliant students. According to E. Charles-Roux's survey on women and labor in the same period, "In 1896 a chambermaid earned 40–70 francs a month, a cook 50–75 francs."[2]

3. These schools had been established for the daughters of the common people (as opposed to the schools for the bourgeoisie, private boarding schools and religious schools) and sexual discrimination was practiced there without fail. "This education," writes Prost in his *Histoire de l'enseignement en France,* "was based upon a concept of femininity appropriate to the ruling classes."[3]

While comparing these different elements with the information we have on Colette, it occurred to me:

1. That at school, Colette did not suffer very strong discrimination and that she had been raised largely "like a boy," such being the model.

2. That being of bourgeois origin but of an impoverished family, in this school she found her social status extremely low.

3. That given the absence of real professional opportunities in this school and her situation as a déclassée bourgeoise, her only economic possibility was to marry. Now, to marry *without a dowry* was no mean feat, and Willy himself reacted to it with a measure of contempt. I quote from an unpublished letter to his brother written during the period of their engagement, "I am marrying the daughter of Captain Colette. She has no dowry, which does not thrill our parents. In their view, they have a right to show their disapproval. It's so rare, a marriage joining, like yours, the most exquisite tenderness and…how should I put it…real comfort. You have achieved the nearly impossible:

marriage for love grafted on marriage for money. It's almost unique."[4]

From that point forward, economic determinism explains much. If Colette had been a little country girl like her schoolmates, she would neither have met nor married Willy; but had her parents retained their fortune, she would perhaps not have married him either, for he had quite a bad reputation and it is evident that Sido was not pleased by this marriage. Above all, she would not have been at Willy's mercy if she had had a small personal fortune. For it was for financial reasons ("funds are low") that Willy obliged her to write, and it is because of his penury that she dared neither refuse him nor leave him, and found herself the victim of a horrible literary exploitation. This allows us to put an end to the errors of many commentaries, *some of them* indignant or surprised. Madeleine Raaphorst-Rousseau, one of the first biographers of Colette, was astonished that a woman with Colette's personality could have stayed so long with a man who thus deceived and exploited her. Others lead us to believe that it was for powerfully erotic reasons that Colette was attached to Willy. That there was between them a relatively complex sadomasochistic relationship is clear, but that does not preclude that relationship having been maintained unchanged for a long time for the simple reason that Colette had no economic means to extricate herself from it.

In this regard, the numbers speak eloquently: Willy constrained his wife to work by force, sequestering and blackmailing her emotionally. Unlike his other slaves, she was not paid. While Toulet received 1500 francs for his collaboration on *La Tournée du petit duc* and Curnonski found that "Willy was very proper, half the proceeds for him, half for the ghostwriter,"[5] Colette received nothing, a fact which does not prevent Alfred Draid from remarking perfidiously: "Madame Colette will permit me to recall that each Claudine, each Minne was paid for by a few pearls which lengthened her bridal necklace."[6] Outrageous!

After writing *Claudine en ménage* in 1901, Colette drew a monthly salary of 300 francs, summer months excluded. Considering that the Claudine novels were best-sellers and sold nearly as fast as they could be printed, her salary represented only about three times more than a cook's (and with no paid vacation!). Colette relates in *Mes apprentissages* that, after their separation, her former husband and employer had ordered for his next novel 20 pages of description, for which "he promised me 1000 francs. A thousand pre-war francs, a thousand post-separation francs, a thousand francs for twenty pages, when...for four volumes of Claudine...! I thought I was dreaming!"

When his worker escaped him, Willy hurriedly sold the publication rights to the Claudine series to publishers so that she could never profit from them. He sold the series in 1907, the first two and the fourth volumes to Albin Michel for 5000 francs, the third to the Mercure de France for 4000 francs.[7] "One would think," Colette wrote to Léon Hamel, "that he wanted not only to get very little money out of them, but also to make sure that *never*, even after his death, would I regain possession of those books which are mine."[8] When the couple separated in 1906, Colette was thirty-three years old and the actual author of seven works, four of which were extraordinarily famous: she gained neither personal recognition nor money for it. Willy, beyond the gift of several articles of furniture, seems not to have paid her even the slightest food allowance. She was therefore obliged to earn her living in the music hall, "the profession of those who have never learned one."[9]

It was not until the appearance of *Le Blé en herbe* in 1923 that Colette appeared to be economically independent and supporting herself with her pen, signing only her own name and freed of the infamous attachment of the pseudonym Willy. She was fifty years old.

Rapid analysis of these facts calls for some remarks concerning the potential of a new approach to biography. We have seen the importance that the addition of the economic variable can have when attached to the sexual variable. In the case of Colette, it is the mixture of the social component (bourgeoisie), the economic component (poverty), and the sexual component (woman) that has been determining; since the mixture was exceptional, there emerged this other exceptional occurrence, woman writer (had she met some man other than Willy, this would never have happened). It is, I believe, in such a perspective that it would be necessary to renew historical biographical analysis in the tradition of Taine.[10]

The appearance of true literary pandering assumed by Willy's exploitation of her literary talent could be perfectly studied from a feminist perspective. I see no better point of reference than that of pandering: instead of prostituting his wife's body, Willy prostituted her literary talent, drew from it the financial and moral profit (for it was he who was famous and recognized) and, in exchange, ensured conjugality (that is, a type of vague protection and even vaguer emotional security). He offered therefore the material, emotional, and social means of production in exchange for work whose material, social, and emotional profit accrued to him and permitted him to conceal and justify a husband's exploitation in addition to the exploitation of the slave driver. Colette is therefore doubly alienated by her position, *both* as writer-proletarian in her husband's workshops *and* as unpaid writer-wife. The relationship of economic domination (duplicated by other, psychological aspects) is at the heart of male-female relationships in the works of Colette. It always coincides with the same structural components, which are linked together according to complex displacement mechanisms. The most classic example is the pure and simple "keeping" of the man by the woman as in *Chéri*, or the operation of financial dispossession imposed on Julie de Carneilhan by her former husband. Here it seems to me that the instruments of Marxist analysis, in particular the theory of value, can account for this double alienation as well as for the process of reification, which tends to reduce women to the state of fetishes. Stripped of their authentic value, of their importance as "humans," women are then reduced to their exchange value, i.e., their capacity to finance in one way or another the men they love.

Colette's ambiguous position, that of bourgeoise of degraded social status both at school and in the music hall, poor in a world of money, provincial in the Parisian milieu, famous but unrecognized writer, woman in a world of men, masculinized by writing, in short the eternal outsider, seemed to me to be expressed in the world she describes, the world of marginality, in sum what is called "the demi-monde." Lukács' concept of "world vision," repeated by the critic Lucien Goldmann, could account for this representation of marginality in Colette's work: the world vision is understood as the sum of the aspirations of a group defined in relation to another group (most often but not exclusively a social class), in such a way that these aspirations are more or less consciously given vehicles by a literary work. In this case, the world vision unconsciously expressed throughout Colette's work would be that of a marginal group, devoid of political identity, that violates, without the slightest pangs of conscience, a certain number of social or moral conventions. But perhaps there is more, and in a world dominated by phallocratic power, does not every woman's work provide the vehicle for a certain marginality? Does it not always appear as an attempt to translate from a foreign language into the language of power?

When it is a question of reflecting on the way a woman has successfully taken up writing (somewhat as I would say taking up sailing or taking up an opportunity to speak), socioeconomic determinants seem essential to me, as do psychological determinants as well. There remains the role of choice, the individual's choice. In his preface to his study of Jean Genet, Sartre says: "Genius is not a gift but the product of desperate necessity. To regain the choice which an individual makes for himself for his life, and for the universe, even to the formal character of his style and composition, even to the structures of his images and the particularities of his tastes, to retrace in detail the history of a liberation, that is what I wanted to do."

If we work successfully in this perspective, in other words, if we make histories of liberation out of the biographies of women who have succeeded in becoming writers, we will I believe have contributed to the development of the newborn feminist criticism. It seems to me that from this point of view, existentialist criticism, which seems partially buried these days, may also add some wind to feminist sails.

Notes

1. For more detailed information see Michèle Blin, "Une pédagogie pour jeunes filles pauvres," *Romantisme*, vol.13–14 (1976), pp. 215–227.

2. E. Charles-Roux, *Les Femmes et le travail du Moyen Age à nos jours* (Paris: Editions de la Courtelle, 1975), p. 132.

3. Antoine Prost, *Histoire de l'enseignement en France* (Paris: Armand Colin, 1968), p. 261.

4. Quoted by Paul de'Hollander in his thesis "Colette à l'heure de Willy," Université de Paris III, Sorbonne, Paris, 1976.

5. Hollander, pp. 84–85.

6. Ibid.

7. Hollander, p. 472.

8. *Lettres de la vagabonde*, November 21, 1908.

9. Ibid.

10. Margot Peters, in a paper presented to the Annual Meeting of the MMCA in November 1976, perfectly theorized the perspective in which feminist biographical criticism could renew Taine's thought.

3 Colette and the Enterprise of Writing: A Reappraisal

ANNE DUHAMEL KETCHUM

Colette made no attempt ever to present a conceptual system of thought. However, she set priorities for any would-be writer, including herself: that first of all, words should fortify, "warm-up," regenerate; that they are to push towards life, not away from it; that language has its own organic life and it is important to preserve it. Indeed Colette should be recognized as one of the first French writers to understand that it is through de-intellectualizing writing that it has a chance to be restored to life, that the body, sensual enjoyment, sensuality itself will awaken from inertia and indifference. "I try to reach beyond the perfidious zone of logic," she exclaims in *Paysages et Portraits*.[1]

The lack of an organized system of thought or dominant ideology has been a major objection to Colette's work, to the point of denying her reflection of social reality. To require that an entire thought process be reduced to a conceptual, "philosophical" system would seem to bring on atrophy on all sides; one may even doubt its feasibility. It would not seem possible today to envisage a work of art simply as an illustration of a given system of ideas, and the content of a text as proof only of the existence of a mode of thought, well-known in advance. Colette mentions the remark of a famous politician who wished to "enlarge (I would say *limit*) my life to some great idea which would have served me in lieu of religion, dignity (sic), and inspiration" (*Le Fanal bleu*, XIV, p. 184). She shudders at the idea of "an existence devastated by one unique thought," and, should we add, one truth and one sex. I touch here an important aspect of Colette: she is never where you expect her to be; she is on this side, and beyond, never fixed, rigid, or condemning; she is not like so many famous writers, her contemporaries, who, judging, ruling, and forbidding, measured life according to its degree of violence and its degree of conformity to their preset ideas. Facing such rigidity, Colette chose pleasure, the instant, all that which is condemned as frivolous. She also chose to be *mobile*, to move between the archaic and the future, between Sido and the Vagabond, and, among so many fixed-sexed beings, between man and woman.

Deemed void of any concern for major social issues, Colette's writing was never apprehended as a product of, or a possible reaction to, a social context. Today, even after Lucien Goldmann's theory of genetic structuralism, preoccupation with the social — particularly sociology of creation and sociology of reading — is still often "rejected as impure, inessential ... [The] investment of the social in the literary object ... is generally acknowledged in a mode of concession."[2] I agree with the authors of this article, however, that "the social is tied to relations of production. It is not *reflected* in the text, but it is actively reproduced there."[3]

Frédéric Jameson has brilliantly demonstrated the existence of a "political unconscious" with "political fantasms" born, like all fantasms, from *desire*.[4] No one can avoid the social, nor be unaffected by the dominant ideology, and there is no reason to deprive Colette of her political unconscious on the basis of her reluctance to express it in a systematized way.

I propose, therefore, a new *reading* of Colette, from her arrival in Paris in 1893 through the writing of some of her most striking yet often mysterious and least understood works: *La Vagabonde*, *L'Entrave*, *Chéri* and *La Fin de Chéri*, *La Chatte*, *La Seconde*, and *Duo* and its sequel *Le Toutounier*. Inasmuch as a rich text holds the principle of its own transformation, reading *is* rewriting. The process of creation of these works reflects Colette's experience of the complex and changing world she lived in, as it interacts with her particular concerns, to which she remained very faithful through many themes and variations. The narratives of Colette constitute in themselves ideological acts, attempts to express fantasms, and at times to solve oppressive contradictions, at least in the imaginary. However, no matter how deeply such fantasies seem to be rooted in the imagination of their author, their existence depends on preexisting conditions in the outside world: in this case the sociopolitical and economical structures in France at the turn of the century, including the relative positions of the sexes in terms of social mores, civil and labor laws, and power. Colette's work should be read for what it is: an expression, through the mediation of writing, of an experience of the social order.

Paris in 1893: the luxury of the first auto-show, the glow of the Franco-Prussian alliance, do not quite hide from young Colette the deep underlying unrest. It is a year when the workday is "limited" to twelve hours for men and eleven for women, who still receive only half the salary of men for the same work, and cannot freely dispose of it. Women's labor is so cheap that it is in great demand. Paris is full of working women: servants, "midinettes," typists, dancers and singers, actresses — country girls, most of them, dazzled and bewildered in the streets of Paris. From the outset, we can assume that life in Paris was a shock for Sido's child, for she mysteriously grew weaker and weaker and found herself fighting for her very life for months. In her memoirs (*Mes apprentissages*) Colette mentions poverty, seclusion in dark, ugly quarters, the poisonous coal-stove, the exploitation of her young talent as a writer by her husband, Willy, his "stable" of other ghostwriters, his double standards, and ultimately his numerous infidelities. In short, all the abuses by a powerful conjugal "master" of his "slave."

Small-scale representations such as the details from Colette's memoirs of her personal life upon her arrival in Paris may be interpreted as the signs of another untold and repressed reality, far too frightening for a twenty-year-old girl, helpless and overcome. The depravity of the Paris of the boulevards masks a society where work and desire, failing to contribute harmoniously to the happiness of its members, enter in contradiction: Paris was divided between those who lived according to their slightest whims, ignoring work and restraints, and those who knew nothing but the hardest work and the total repression of their desires. This violent contradiction, which could ultimately give Europe over to totalitarian regimes and their total destruction of desire (see below), is in fact the central issue in Colette's work, although almost entirely unrecognized.

Is it not possible, then, to assume that the mysterious sickness of Colette shortly after arriving in Paris may well have been some Sartrean nausea, a brutal awakening of consciousness at finding in Paris, institutionalized on a large scale, the relations of power, of master and slave, the exploitation from which she suffered so much in her private life? And we would agree to see with David Cooper, in this first experience by a woman of her own oppression, a true political act.[5]

The very insouciance of the upper classes in the face of the serious social problems of the time must have been in itself particularly frightening. In brilliant salons, such as that of her friend Mme Arman de Caillavet, Colette met with a rather puzzling array of people. There were young dandies such as Proust, who found themselves at a young age in control of a fortune and forever leading a life of idleness. Accompanying them were brilliant actresses and courtesans whose success and beauty, Colette discovered, were the result of incessant effort. Between the two, Colette's judgment is made: the person living off the work of others but giving little of himself, "he is the courtesan."[6] In the courtesans, actresses, music-hall dancers, little seamstresses, Colette will salute the victims of society, who embody all the suffering which human beings endure as a result of oppression and social injustice. In them, she discovers the mythical dimension of women who experience the essential absurdity of life.

In 1894, the Dreyfus affair unleashes all over Europe a wind of fanaticism and rage. The bourgeoisie feels threatened by the creation, the same year, of the first major union, the General Confederation of Labor (C.G.T.). This is a time when the split between the classes deepens in France, when traditional relationships will no longer do and a new world is about to set in.

Where is this better expressed than in *La Vagabonde*? How did one not see it? What better representation of the decadence of the ruling classes than the "Big Noodle," heir to a fortune made in lumber? Where is marriage better presented as false security in exchange for the freedom of a woman? When he announces triumphantly that she will no longer be able to roam the roads of France but will be grounded permanently at his side, the heroine recognizes in him the "master" who "wants me no good, just wants me." His letters which she awaits so longingly bring nothing but a "sound of banknotes." Eager to elope with her, he pushes her to forfeit her professional obligations, offering to pay whatever the cost may be. He is astounded at her reluctance, for professional pride for him has no meaning. In the Paris of 1910, a divorced woman had the choice between quick remarriage or gallantry, both socially acceptable. To choose to work instead, and particularly as a music-hall dancer, was the shocking thing to do, enough to become forever outcast socially; to feel pride in such work was simply inconceivable.

The novel was indeed received as a woman's appeal for freedom and, consequently, often criticized for "poor taste." What was less seen is the important denunciation it holds of patriarchal values. The novel can be understood as the painful discovery by a sincere woman that her only worth is an *exchange* one and is linked to the question of the power of the male, in a society where men are the only *exchangers*. Colette is also telling us in *La Vagabonde* that, in their scornful rejection of the working class, the bourgeoisie of the turn of the century were using intimidation in an attempt to shift the focus away from their own shameful idleness and lack of values.

Almost a Marxist pamphlet on the struggle of classes, *La Vagabonde* may well have scared Colette herself, given her dislike for any systematization. Besides, she was particularly sensitive to the reproach that the Vagabond was "aping men" and totally unfeminine. This accusation of lack of femininity, along with that of "bad taste" already mentioned, is devised to induce guilt in women.[7] From childhood, Colette was deemed, by her own mother, a "tomboy." Her narratives and correspondence abound with subsequent expressions of feelings of inadequacy as a woman and fears of being masculine. Her constant interest in homosexuals of both sexes and the bittersweet acceptance of her bisexual nature can be linked to such feelings. At the time, the social image of the "good woman" — always a wife and a mother, the model of whom Colette had found in her mother Sido — was so strong that Colette felt nostalgia, if not guilt, whenever she wandered away from her model.

The radicalism of *La Vagabonde* subsided somewhat with Colette's second marriage and the birth, late in life, of her child. The year is 1913, a period of great international unrest. Feelings of apprehension and helplessness prevail in Europe in the face of the threatening cataclysm of World War I. *L'Entrave*, a strange novel received as a failure, follows. In it, a petrified Colette renounces all the ideals of the Vagabond and gamely accepts the chains of enslavement. Shocking as the change may seem, it may be that Colette felt some of the Vagabond's intellectualizations to be arbitrary; obscurely, at a time when life was gravely threatened, Colette has her heroine choose its very support: the senses, the body, both that of her lover Jean and her own. Thus, the troubled period of pre-war Europe found an echo in Colette's sensitivity; in both, we see apprehension for the conflict between the violent forces of power and the elemental forces of life. Interpreted as an attempt at reconciliation with men, *L'Entrave* should be more appropriately recognized as a rare example in Colette's work of submission to the established order, prompted by an overwhelming fear.

The inner conflict between masculinity and femininity should not therefore be considered as solved by the panicky surrender in *L'Entrave*; this conflict, which Colette could not satisfactorily resolve alone, will be given other dimensions through the brutal intrusion of social forces. World War I shapes *Chéri* and *La Fin de Chéri*, which should be considered as the two sides of a "before" and "after" diptych. The violence institutionalized by the war is the omnipresent theme of both novels, which can be summarized as the struggle between the desire for life and the forces of destruction, the timeless struggle between Eros and Thanatos. Appropriately, Eros here is represented by the only human being who is professionally dedicated to making life pleasurable, a courtesan.

The sad destiny of Chéri has often been attributed to his being fatherless. Perhaps the importance of this condition has not been fully appreciated: if Chéri had had a father, he would have learned how to "become a man," definitely a socially acquired status; he would have practiced sports, learned how to thrive on challenge, to compete, command, forbid, crush. Because he did not learn the patriarchal law, Chéri cannot survive in a male world; but because of this, he *is* Chéri. He has never learned that power constitutes the distinction and thus the definition of man in relation to woman, who is denied power; he cannot participate therefore in the collective delirium of men to master the real, to circumscribe it, to lock it up.

Paradoxically, Colette repeatedly refers to Chéri's "bad education," while she clearly offers him as the only possible answer to a self-destructive male-centered society, as a model of the truly "natural" man who has nothing more essential to do but to experience all the joys life can bring. Universally received as "effeminate," a "sensual coward," a "gigolo" — the latter inappropriate, as Chéri owns a personal fortune — he joins the long list of Colette's male characters whom critics have always considered "weak," either because, like Phil or Alain, they refuse to play the male game, or, like Farou, Michel, or d'Espivant, they play it too well and abuse their power.

The war acts as a brutal catalyst: what was until then Chéri's natural inclination will become, in the second volume, his deliberate choice. Sent to the front line, Chéri soon becomes overcome by the criminal absurdity of war and later on by his distaste for male pursuits such as business machinations, speculations, and the male notion of success. Condemned in a male world founded on competition and destruction, he discovers through Léa an alternative, an economy of abundance dear to Colette, where Nature produces without exhaustion, is exchanged without work, gives itself for free; Léa represents gratuitous pleasures, well-being without pain, enjoyment without possession. Published in the year of the First International and the imposition of the treaty of Versailles on Germany, both seedbeds of totalitarianism, *Chéri* reopens for us the Garden of Eden, tells us that the flesh is redemptive, for it becomes Spirit. In death, Chéri recovers the purity of Léa's abundance.

Time is the accomplice of evil in both books. Léa's renunciation, no matter how graciously accomplished, is an admission of defeat by time. But its effects are felt far beyond Léa's boudoir, as the inexorable march of History, through the war, precipitates the end of an era which Colette loved and marks the advent of a ruthless, joyless world where desire has been all but killed.

In 1929, Colette produces *La Seconde*, which is a violent commentary against the dominant law of the Father. It is the epic of the "paterfamilias," the all-powerful master who rules, unquestioned, over his family of slaves: his wife, his adolescent son, his secretary-mistress. A rich bourgeois and a writer *à succès*, he fully plays the game of a society which grants him unrestricted recognition and, at least at home, power. He is therefore the exact opposite of Chéri. Colette does not spare any details to describe his shallowness, his self-satisifed cowardice, his wily selfishness.

Faced with the same predicament, both his wife and his mistress discover that, far from being enemies as convention would have it, they have much in common, including their feelings for Farou and reactions to his infidelities. Their life depends entirely on him in a society which sees to it that wives are kept without marketable skills and secretaries are so poorly paid that they cannot survive on their own. Colette not only denounces an all-too-common situation, but also studies the means devised by women for survival. "Two are not too many" to face Farou, they conclude, and they slowly discover "feminine solidarity" and mutual dependence. In 1941 *Julie de Carneilhan*, although in a different situation, will again oppose masculine baseness — this time the dangerous machinations of d'Espivant — to the courage of two women.

Man remains "the beloved enemy," and from then on Colette engages in a systematic analysis of the ways devised by women to survive in a man's world. She finds that, out of necessity, they often lead a life of "duplicity, resignation, vile and delicate diplomacy."[8] She also finds out that such abnormal conditions breed all sorts of distortions, in women as well as in men. She devotes to the question a book of short pieces on sexual ambiguity, *Le Pur et l'impur* (1932). At a time when the rigidity of pre-determined sex roles was already painful if not crippling, Colette is attempting in *Chéri* and *Le Pur et l'impur* the unusual: to bridge the gap between the sexes.

Danger lurks, however, in those relationships where the desire for life takes violently opposing forms. In 1933, in a France divided by the Stavisky scandal and stunned by the accession of Hitler to power, Colette gives us *La Chatte*.

Blond Alain, born of a "good family" of rich silk-makers, and overprotected by a loving mother, is a vulnerable brother of Chéri. Still attached to his childhood, its dreams and "infantile" ways, his crime is to wish to retain the feeling of happy plenitude derived from the celebration of such innocent daily rituals as breakfast in the garden in the company of his delicate and beautiful Siamese cat. But in a society where life is no longer meant to be enjoyed, the destruction of desire, and consequently of the individuals who still dare to experience it, is the major theme of the book, as it already was a major theme of *Chéri*. In 1933, though, things are different; desire for life and its joys is met here with outright violence and brutality.

Alain's fiancée — dark, dazzling Camille — drives her sports car too fast, smokes too much, speaks and laughs too loudly, displays without modesty her naked body and her desire for Alain. A "realist," she is typical of modern "efficiency" and takes her due without hesitation or scruple. Like her *nouveau riche* parents, she is a product of the war and represents, on this side of the abyss of World War I, the distorted counterpart of Léa. In the mercilessly white "modern" apartment — all in sharp angles and glass — where the young couple moves, Alain and the cat, desperately looking for a shelter, "a shaded corner where to cultivate their dreams," slowly waste away. Feeling that she is losing Alain to Saha, "her rival in purity," Camille raises a criminal hand on the cat, who escapes miraculously. Outraged, Alain leaves with the cat for the shade of his childhood willow tree; deliberately he "regresses" to the animal world, clearly the only one left where can be found the "human" feelings of love and respect for the desire and dreams of individuals.

The work was interpreted as a book on jealousy and bestiality. But *La Chatte* is a parable and a warning and should be interpreted as such. As the powerless witness of the systematic degradation of humans through the "rat race," its abusive demands, the abuses of power and the violence and crimes they lead to, Colette feels the need to return to the primal innocence, the unrepressed world of Nature.

Duo (1934) is a case study of a "happily married" couple confronted with the destructive forces of the power relationship. In this book, Colette completely isolates a young couple in their summer country house. With almost no outside interferences and very few secondary characters, the focus is entirely on the interior life of the couple. A scant one hundred pages, this small masterpiece records the terse counterpoint of the male and female voices.

Michel is a young stage manager, very much in love with his wife of ten years, Alice. Not too successful in his job, he had to mortgage the family estate, but his pride kept him from mentioning the fact to his wife. This initial concealed act implies a breach of trust, and a first betrayal.

As a young Parisian girl, Alice and her sisters earned a meager living as members of a small orchestra, learning very young the necessity of competition. Significantly, Alice exchanges the family "orchestra" for the "duo" of marriage, where the wife depends entirely — emotionally and materially — on the husband. Alice then designs costumes for her husband's shows, a work for which, in the best bourgeois tradition, she accepts not being recompensed. Bright and active, she spares no effort for the success of the couple. Unlike Sido, Léa, or Fanny, therefore, Alice found neither protection nor security after her marriage. But she is a *natural* being unashamed of the ferocious desires Nature provided to her. She fits the definition she herself gives of a bee, attracted by the food on their table, which Michel was chasing away: "Let her be! She is hungry, and she is working!"

When her husband discovers an old love letter from a desultory affair, she never feels that she has betrayed him in the least. Bracing herself, she fights bravely for the salvation of the couple, her only care.

But such is not the concern of Michel. He soon becomes caught in the role of husband he believes he ought to play. Nothing natural remains in him; instead, with a new pomposity, he moralizes endlessly. Even his speech, Alice notices, becomes unnatural and stereotyped: "Subordinate clause and cliché, cliché and subordinate clause. . . ." Thus, he "preaches":

> "A sensual brutality is almost always, in a woman's life — I mean a balanced woman — an exceptional crisis, a morbid change. You understand, Alice?" " — Very Well."

> "And I keep a straight face! [she comments] but why is it that a man can never speak of feminine sensuality without saying enormous stupidities?"

Michel paces the room, "opening his arms to express that he was going to achieve calm, to reach mansuetude. But at the end of the room, between the two bookcases, he swung around on one heel with a violence which, each time, belied his laborious good-naturedness." He is no longer the man who loves Alice; he is the Master, with his anger, his desire to dominate and punish. Thus he demonstrates that he belongs more to the established patriarchal order than to his wife; in so doing, he is the one who deeply betrays their union.

He nevertheless expects tears, remorse, self-humiliation from the "sinner," and her "begging" his forgiveness. In the absence of that, he becomes more and more insecure and upset, while she remains in control. "Why should you feel good, you who do not deserve it?" he asks. "Because I feel like it" is her answer. Again we are here in the presence of Eros and Thanatos and their somber "duel." Faced with a wife who makes clear her will to work at making life together pleasurable, Michel, taken at his own game and having killed his desire for life, has nothing left but to let himself drown, thus accomplishing the ultimate betrayal.

Taking place in the daily life of a middle-class couple, this drama is closer to a representation of current reality than any other of Colette's; in it the destructive forces of repression are represented by the man, against the woman's efforts for the preservation of life and desire.

In the following volume, *Le Toutounier,* a widowed Alice left with nothing but debts rejoins her sisters, also the victims in various ways of the aberrations of a male-dominated society. Rejecting all bitterness, Alice then works at securing a refuge, the "toutounier," where the girls could feel relatively secure and free to be themselves. Colette sadly implies that such merely defensive measures are the only recourse women have in a society which leaves them powerless. The battle between the sexes in Colette's works, "le drame du couple," reflects fundamental economic and political struggles.

Without developing a systematic approach to the conflict around her, Colette's writings clearly denounce the implantation of totalitarianism whereby the joy of individuals, caught in the gears of the State, must forever become mute and dead. To the power of men and the delirium it awakens in them, Colette opposes what Annie Leclerc so beautifully calls "the springing-forth of life, where power falters,"[9] a faculty of joy she found only in women.

Notes

1. Colette, *Paysages et Portraits* (Paris: Flammarion, 1949), p. 168. All references within this article are to the *Fleuron* edition of the *Oeuvres complètes* of Colette, 15 vols. (Paris: Flammarion, 1948–50).

2. Claude Duchet and Françoise Gaillard, "Introduction," *Sub-stance,* No. 15 (1976), 2–5.

3. Ibid.

4. Frédéric Jameson, "L'Inconscient Politique," in *La Lecture Sociocritique du Texte Romanesque,* Graham Falconer and H. Mitterand, eds. (Toronto: S.S. Hakkert & Co., Publisher, 1975).

5. David Cooper, *The Death of the Family* (New York: Pantheon Books, 1970), p. 93 ff.

6. Colette, *La Vagabonde,* p. 144.

7. The perversion of social attitudes is such that whenever a woman expresses herself, her own desire, her thought, she ceases to be a woman. A number of women writers — Nathalie Sarraute, Simone de Beauvoir among others — have thus been judged at times "virile," or excessively masculine.

8. Colette, *La Main*, p. 392.

9. "le jaillissement du vivre, où le pouvoir défaille."

4 Colette and the Art of Survival
JANET WHATLEY

Colette has said that her most certain art is not that of writing, but "the domestic art of knowing how to wait, dissimulate, pick up the pieces, reconstruct, stick back together ... to lose and regain in the same instant the frivolous taste for life" (p. 418).[1] These words are taken from *Mes apprentissages*, a memoir of her first marriage, written when she was in her early sixties. By the time Colette was writing this memoir (in fact long before), she had achieved something of the identity of a sage: she is conscious of her life as exemplary — not exactly in virtue, but in richness and significance. And, like Montaigne, with whom she has certain affinities, she assumes that any frank self-portrait, consciously edifying or not, is of general use. She is part of the French classical tradition in her assumption that one can generalize about human experience: there are maxims, there are communicable rules about living and about what one can expect from life. *Mes apprentissages* treats of a triple apprenticeship: as a woman, as a writer, and as a survivor. (However, these three categories contain a redundancy: to be a woman and to have a gift for survival — for duration — are virtually synonymous in Colette's view of things.)

Just what was it that demanded of the young Colette this talent for survival? Her marriage plunged her into a set of circumstances so special that one can wonder what communicable lessons of apprenticeship they promise. Henri Gauthier-Villars, known as Willy, was thirteen years older than she (and seemed older than that). He was a publicist, a producer — but not writer — of titillating novels. His household was a fantasy mill, where the manic master pieced together potboilers out of the efforts of impecunious hacks. This unpromising setting was to be Colette's *atelier*, her "school" of realism and discipline.[2]

The older Colette remembers her younger self without much pity: she does not believe in victims, except willing ones. The young Colette was eager for some of the "guilty" knowledge that Willy had to offer in abundance: "I had begun by intoxication, a culpable intoxication, a dreadful and impure adolescent impulse. There are a lot of them, those scarcely nubile girls who dream of being the spectacle, the plaything, the libertine masterpiece of a mature man. It's an ugly desire that goes along with the neuroses of puberty, the habit of nibbling chalk and coal, drinking mouthwash, reading dirty books, and sticking pins in the palms of your hands" (p. 392). The delicacy, the fragility of virginal young girls is, for Colette, a myth that it is time to dispel: "In a few hours, an unscrupulous man can make of an ignorant girl a prodigy of libertinage, who reckons with no disgust. Disgust has never been an obstacle. It comes later, like honesty. . . . The eager prey fears nothing — to begin with. She is often even amazed: 'And what else do we do? Is that all? Can we at least start all over again?'" (pp. 409–410).

For her brash bid for initiation, the young Colette pays dearly. However, she pays nothing like the price that is conventionally supposed to have been exacted. (The French tradition provides a model treatment of this motif in *Les Liaisons dangereuses*, a great and influential eighteenth-century novel of libertinage, in which, axiomatically, the ingenue who becomes the libertine masterpiece is destroyed). For Colette, there is no knowledge, sexual or other, which is in itself catastrophic. A first rule of survival is the realization that human beings — and particularly women — are exceedingly resilient.

Nevertheless, the young Colette suffers. She is separated from her beloved mother, Sido, who represents all the beneficent forces that nurture living things, and from her native village, which came more and more to represent a lost Eden; cloistered with Willy, that "rotund incubus,"[3] whom she calls "worse than mature"; surrounded by a strange group of obscurely damaged young men who, through caprices of luck or temperament, have become Willy's slaves. She is learning the difference between "the presence — or at least the illusion — of happiness and its absence, between love and the laborious, exhausting sensual pastime" (p. 397). Hoping for a miracle, a "death and resurrection," to undo an error that seems irremediable, she has, rather, to free herself by a day-to-day self-mastery of which she is often hardly aware.

Colette has a distinctive vocabulary and a particular sense of process in recounting how she regained her self-respect and discovered her own resilience. At the first encounter with one of her husband's mistresses (the first of many such encounters), the "taste for survival" manifests itself, and the qualities of the *jeune fille* in her — "intransigent, beautiful, absurd" — die, to be replaced by the impure, unvirginal, but infinitely useful qualities of "tolerance and dissimulation, consent to pacts with the enemy . . . diligence, humility" (p. 136). She will not escape her circumstances until she has immersed herself in them, learned everything they have to teach, and transcended them.

The circumstances of her literary apprenticeship are well known: Willy, feeling perpetually broke, compels her to join his stable of hacks by locking her in a room and telling her to write some memoirs of her schooldays — spicing them up, of course, for his particular public. Colette is unaware that she is about to undertake her own salvation. She is chiefly conscious of a return of the old homework itch, the passivity of accomplishing a commissioned work: "I wrote with diligence and indifference" (p. 389). She wrote, in fact, the Claudine books. They are not yet the great Colette, but they are considerably better than they needed to be for Willy's purposes. *Mes apprentissages* does not tell us how those books came to be as good as they were; it speaks of a pattern of activity, of a temperament in relation to a task, that made those books possible at all. *Mes apprentissages* reveals how closely integrated were the "goût de durer" and the ability to work.

Certain recurring rhythms, phrases, metaphors tell us something about how her apprenticeship was accomplished and what it means. The word *apprentissage* itself, of course, implies a long, slow process of learning, in a position of inferiority; it also implies learning a métier, a craft.[4] She speaks of a "slow and bureaucratic courage" which has never left her since; she speaks of a time when she was becoming "punctual as if I had already known that *la règle* cures everything" (p. 425). "What a workshop a jail makes!" Willy's bizarre atelier produced in Colette, she says, along with the habit of working, "the character of a porcelain-repairer." That *raccommodeur de porcelaines* image joins up with the quotation with which I began: "Peace, then, to that hand . . . [Willy's hand] which never hesitated to turn the key in the lock. To it I owe my most certain art, which is not that of writing, but the domestic art of knowing how to wait, of dissimulating, of picking up the pieces, reconstructing, sticking back together, regilding, changing the last resort into something better, losing and regaining in the same instant the frivolous taste for life" (p. 418).

A stylistic habit of Colette's is the multiplicity of verbs or phrases in apposition, standing for the many small but essential elements which compose a given reality. In this apprenticeship of art and survival, there are many chances, many throws of the dice. The domestic art is a fight against entropy, in which women, in Colette's view, are the specialists. (I might add, as an American, that it is a European specialty.) One is piecing together something that is always falling apart; saving rather than throwing away; conserving what you have rather than getting something new: because there *isn't* anything new (nor is that really cause for regret). The diminutive and the ornamental predominate: "ramasser les miettes," pick up either the pieces or the crumbs. The porcelain-repairer knows how to "regild" as well as to stick back together. One loses and immediately regains "le goût frivole de vivre." Survival in Colette is bound up with a sense of ornament and play. The frivolous and the essential are not two distinct categories. (The pictures of the old Colette, her eyes still outlined in blue kohl, tell us something about the ornamentation of the person which was part of her pact with life.) The very strangeness, the quasi-perverseness of her marital milieu, full of bizarre fauna, interacts with her own dogged courage and permanently enriches her imagination. Her new acquaintances include eccentrics such as Paul Masson, who forges entries for the card catalogue of the Bibliothèque Nationale, and who drowns, ether-intoxicated, in a foot of water: his relentless frivolity masks a loyal affection; his peculiar choice of the practical joker's identity enlarges Colette's sense of the immense variety of means by which human beings seek to realize themselves.

The art of knowing how to wait, of dissimulation: Colette dissimulates her unhappiness, her humiliation, and an unspecified fear — "my faithful old fear" — and waits out the thirteen years of apprenticeship dictated by some inner clock. How does one know when it is time to make the dash for freedom? While she waits, too frightened to leave, she is learning about her own courage as she watches Willy, utterly dependent on his stable, who prefers writing twenty pages of feverish correspondence about a twenty-line article to writing that same article himself. What he lacks is what she has: the "grave constancy one needs to sit down without nausea in front of the immaculate field, the irresponsible, raw, blinding, famished and thankless" white page (p. 422).

In the last years of her waiting, as she approaches thirty, her body is more supple and her soul is tougher. With the same semi-absentmindedness with which she began to write, she now begins, casually and almost lazily, to stretch and pull and dangle from the gymnastic equipment in her apartment. In retrospect, "it seemed to me that I was exercising my body like prisoners who do not clearly meditate escape but who cut and braid a sheet . . ." (p. 446). The slow and barely conscious process of training is preparing her body for the second métier, that of music hall mime, which will double her independence as a writer.

Age thirty: "the age when the forces collect which assure survival, the age of resisting disease, the age of no longer dying for anyone, nor of anyone. Already this toughening which I compare to the effect of petrifying springs...A warm drop-by-drop glides from the forehead to the feet, and one is frightened: ah! it's blood, it's my blood...No, it's this fluid which leaves as it dries a fine and dusty ash, thickened little by little... [. . .] About thirty, and the taste, the habit of living thanks to the callus that is forming, the daily challenges I was imposing on myself..." (p. 437).

Let us examine a moment these images of survival for what they do *not* represent. The porcelain-repairer, the picker-up of pieces, does not get new materials to work with, but must repair what is there. The possessor of that slow and *bureaucratic* courage which gets her to the desk at the same time every day, does not wait for inspiration — does not even think in terms of inspiration. The amateur gymnast, casually doing her stretches on the bar, is moving without urgency or design. And the spirit, slowly developing its callus, does not lament any lost sensitivity. What counts, for the woman and the artist, is robustness: the real, the necessary sensitivity will take care of itself. The will, as Colette implicitly presents it, does not operate as a conscious push for "creativity," or greatness, or the cultivation of a sensitive soul. The will attaches itself to a multiplicity of small tasks, to the preservation of order in the humblest chronological and physical senses. Survival and the ability to create do not depend on the conscious awareness of a vocation or even a direction.

"I was learning to live. One learns to live? Yes, if it is without happiness. Bliss teaches you nothing. To live without happiness and not wither away, that's an occupation, almost a profession" (p. 426). When Colette is spoken of as a *grand classique*, I think of this passage. She belongs to the tradition of Montaigne, or Voltaire, or her contemporary Proust — who regard "happiness" as all well and good, but not man's real state. (Candide's experience would say nothing about the common lot of humanity if he had found a radiant and loving Cunégonde at the end of his journey.) Happiness, particularly in the sense of happy love, is such an exceptional or transitory state that one can base no habits or expectations — or morality — on it. Colette writes better than most on the pleasures and pains of love — but she has much to say everywhere in her work on what else is there when happy love is not: animals, gardens, friends, food. ... And in this period of learning to live without happiness, she is learning to write something other than the Claudine books: for instance, *Les Dialogues des bêtes*, "sweated out drop by drop," "where I gave myself the pleasure, not keen but honorable, of not speaking of love. ... I did not go back to putting love in my books and enjoying it until I had recovered my esteem for it — and for myself" (p. 426).

She waits; she stalls. A fortune-teller tells her: get out of wherever you are; you have already delayed. "I agreed with her at the time," says Colette, "and then, looking back I realized that we were both wrong; I had not waited too long. It is good not to look too closely at ten years of one's life ... provided that those ten years be taken off one's first youth. After that it is appropriate to be stingy" (p. 448). The presages, the messages begin to come in: it is almost time. Someone offers her a music-hall routine involving thirteen greyhounds — a terrible and wonderful temptation; but she turns them down, and alas, thirteen greyhounds are not offered twice in one's lifetime.

Finally, one day, Willy casually suggests for her a music-hall job, a chance to get rid of the apartment: "While I was dreaming of escape, next to me someone was meditating putting me conveniently out the door — my own door" (p. 453). She has lost her chance for romantic flight, the noble farewell letter, the scarf blowing in the wind. But it doesn't matter, any more than those extra years of humiliated waiting matter, or even her faithful old fear, which is not about to leave her soon. Although Colette is not explicit on this point, she has been showing us throughout *Mes apprentissages* how her decisive acts had been those small daily fidelities to her life-saving routines, which add up to the artist's "grave constancy." Given that porcelain-repairer's patience, there is *time*: there is no need to panic or regret the years passed, and no need to have the last word. Colette reveals a deep retrospective confidence in her own unconscious workings, her own hidden timing mechanisms. Momentarily disconcerted by her sudden, if longed-for, exile from marriage, she begins to realize that "my life was changing its taste, as the bouquet of a wine changes according to the slope that bears the vine." If she were to write of that other slope, she says, the groan of effort would yield a sound of celebration, "and I could only complain with a happy face" (p. 454).

Mes apprentissages is a relatively late work. If one looks back at Colette's novels and stories after an immersion in this autobiography, one realizes how important these dominant metaphors and associations have been all along, divided up among various feminine characters. There are heroines who closely resemble Colette — Renée of *La Vagabonde*, for instance — and heroines who do not. Survival in Colette's fiction is sometimes joyous, occasionally terrible, and frequently ambiguous. But the tough elasticity is a shared feminine trait, and in her elaboration of that strength, we cannot help noticing that she loads the deck against male characters. There is no question that Colette has created a mythology of the sexes with which one can seriously quarrel, in which it is the men, such as Chéri, or Alain of *La Chatte*, who are enamored of purity, who cannot tolerate change, who shudder at the traces of age on a face or body, who are vulnerable to sexual disgust. In *La Chatte* a sterile, nostalgic purity (male) and a fertile, vigorous impurity (female) are locked in combat. Alain prefers the silent love of his exquisite cat Saha to the demands of his brash, bouncy young wife Camille. There is inevitable warfare between wife and cat; Camille almost succeeds in killing Saha; an estrangement between husband and wife ensues. At the inconclusive ending, Alain, appalled and admiring, contemplates his wife's gift for repair and survival, using the metaphor of a craft analagous to that of the porcelain-repairer: "Already she is organizing, already she is casting yarns, footbridges; already she is picking up, resewing, re-weaving...It's terrible. Is that what my mother values in her?" (II, p. 543)[5]

In a strange short story called "La Main," the feminine gift for tolerance and dissimulation appears in a nightmarish context. A complacent young bride looks closely at the hand of her sleeping husband and suddenly sees it as hideous: "Then she hid her fear, controlled herself courageously, and, beginning her life of duplicity, resignation, of base and delicate diplomacy, she leaned over and kissed the monstrous hand" (p. 88). The feminine capacity for survival is sometimes the ability, whether admirable or not, to inure oneself to disgust. Rarely, but occasionally, at the dark end of her spectrum, Colette describes an abyss that can open up without warning in human relationships.

She who would survive must disguise and surmount her panic.

A theme more central to Colette's work than the domination of horror is the métier of living without happiness. Most of Colette's heroines place a certain value on unhappiness. They do not wallow in it: they use it as a source of energy. To be unhappy is to make one's own acquaintance. The very young Vinca, of *Le Blé en herbe*, already has "the mission of survival, handed down to all the female species, and the august instinct of installing oneself in unhappiness and mining it like a lode of precious ore" (II, 294). Renée, of *La Vagabonde*, reflecting on a past much like that of Colette, thinks of her suffering as a period of exercise, "as in a daily gymnastics full of risks." Free, alone, testing her hard-won strength and suppleness, she is not sure that the amorous happiness offered her by a new lover is enough from now on. "It isn't only happiness that gives value to life. In front of you, I would not have the right to be sad" (I, p. 836). The middle-aged Marco, of *Le Képi*, gives herself too unguardedly to a sudden amorous happiness; she forgets to distrust it, and she also — fatally — forgets about the sexual delicacy of the male. One day, in bed with her young lover, she dons his officer's cap (*képi*) in a nonchalant, tomboyish gesture that she can no longer afford. And then, unfortunately, there is nothing left for her *except* a bureaucratic courage; the affair ends brusquely, and a diminished Marco, whose survival is minimal, returns to the Bibliothèque Nationale and her métier of writing pot-boilers at ten sous a line.

An undiminished survivor of middle age is Léa of the *Chéri* books: the generous courtesan, who has combined the mores of the demi-mondaine with those of a *bonne bourgeoise*, survives the transition into old age with an equanimity born of her love of order and of the proper timing of things — aspects of Colette's most communicable wisdom.

It would take a much longer study than this brief essay to do justice to the relations between the autobiography and fiction in Colette, but this assemblage of images and associations may offer a point of departure. It is clear that the terms of Colette's survival were most fortunate ones. The capacity to endure, to pick up the pieces, to return to the desk, can be spoken of as an aspect of the will. For Colette, to be born female is already to have inherited this capacity. But for it to be fruitful, there must come into play innate and acquired qualities, mysteries of temperament, happy chances of upbringing, peculiar treasures of early impressions that no rules of procedure can quite account for or replace. It helps — immensely — to be Sido's daughter. While all of Colette's heroines have in some measure the gift for survival, in none of them is that survival as complete and as enviable as it was for Colette herself.

Notes

1. *Mes apprentissages*, in *Oeuvres de Colette* (Paris: Flammarion, 1960), III. All page citations in the text refer to this edition, and, unless otherwise noted, to Vol. III. The translations are my own.

2. Among the works that deal with the period of Colette's *apprentissages* are the following general studies: Robert Cottrell, *Colette* (New York: Frederick Ungar, 1974); Margaret Crosland, *Colette: The Difficulty of Loving* (Indianapolis: Bobbs-Merrill, 1973), Chaps. 2–5; Anne Ketchum, *Colette, ou la Naissance du jour* (Paris: Minard, 1968), Chap. 3; Elaine Marks, *Colette* (New Brunswick: Rutgers University Press, 1960), Chap. 4; Yvonne Mitchell, *Colette: A Taste for Life* (New York: Harcourt Brace Jovanovich, 1975), Chaps. 2 and 3. William Gass offers a particularly powerful evocation of the apprenticeship years in "Three Photos of Colette," *The New York Review of Books*, 24, No. 6 (April 14, 1977), 11–19. The photographs which serve as points of reference in his essay are to be found in Yvonne Mitchell's book.

3. Cottrell, p. 41.

4. In *Colette par elle-même* (Paris: Editions du Seuil, 1973), Germaine Beaumont speaks of Colette the artisan: "Ce n'est pas sans raison que Colette place dans sa bibliothèque, à côté de Balzac, à côté du théâtre de Labiche, les substantiels petits manuels Roret consacrés aux métiers. Colette eût été un ébéniste, un verrier, un potier, un tisserand parfaits. Et de même qu'elle sait choisir ses mots, elle eût su choisir ses outils, que dis-je, les créer, les amener peu à peu jusqu'à l'ultime dépouillement de l'efficacité" (p. 9).

5. Among others, Robert Cottrell (p. 92) speaks of the "limitless capacity to adapt and adjust" possessed by Colette's women, but not her men.

II. Gender and Genre: Texts and Contexts

5 Colette and the Epistolary Novel
JOAN HINDE STEWART

The Vagabond (1911) and *Mitsou* (1919) are anachronistic in two senses. In the first place, by virtue of certain feminist preoccupations and attitudes, they anticipate the most modern novels. And in a contrary sense, by their use of letters, they recall the fiction of a much earlier period. These novels look backward, therefore, as well as forward, but the contradiction is only apparent, for the recourse to the outmoded epistolary form is in fact coherent with the attempt to express, thematically, female identity.

In the early years of its history, when the novel could perhaps aptly be described — as one critic put it half a century ago — as "woman's fief,"[1] a favored vehicle of expression for literary women was the epistolary novel. On both sides of the Channel, the female practitioners of the form during its heyday, the mid- and late eighteenth century, were many; their talents, like their output, considerable. Mme de Grafigny, Mme Riccoboni, Mme de Charrière, Mme Cottin, Eliza Haywood, Clara Reeve, to name only a handful, produced letter-writing heroines whose amorous adventures and intimate epistles fired the imagination of the public. Various hypotheses have been advanced as to why women writers particularly affected the letter-novel, but none is entirely satisfactory, any more than literary critics have fully explained why it is that, even in letter-novels written by men, the lone or at least the major fictional writer tends to be female — think of Guilleragues' Portuguese Nun, of Richardson's Pamela and Clarissa, of Rousseau's Julie. While examples of the epistolary form occur after the turn of the nineteenth century — for example, Balzac's *Mémoires de deux jeunes mariées* (1841–42) — few notable illustrations postdate Laclos's *Liaisons dangereuses* (1787), the masterpiece of the genre.

Colette's adoption of a modified letter-form, therefore, is an experiment which places her squarely in a certain feminine tradition of fiction, that of women novelists creating analytical and articulate letter-writing women. Both novels are concerned, like their ancestors in the corpuses of sundry eighteenth-century women writers (Mme de Grafigny's *Lettres d'une Péruvienne* [1747], for example, or Mme Riccoboni's *Lettres de Mistriss Fanni Butlerd* [1757]), with a young woman whose letters to a lover are, on the one hand, the expression of her passion, and on the other, the means of coming to terms with an event of import and, frequently, of finding her own truth in the process. The Colette works, in which the letters are addressed directly *to* the loved one — as distinct from novels where the lover is the *subject* of the letters, the addressee being a third party — are examples of the kind of epistolary novel which is most dramatic (even literally, for its relation to theatre is intimate). Since the addressee is a protagonist, writing is itself an event of moment, and letters are the means of creating emotions and reaching decisions, not merely instruments for conveying them.

The use of an archaic device closely associated with women is significant because the two novels in question are precisely concerned with women's affirmation and discovery of themselves. *La Vagabonde* is the story of a renunciation: pursued by a wealthy suitor, divorcée Renée Néré — as introverted and reflexive as her name itself — eventually opts to remain single and continue to exercise her profession of dancer and mime. The second novel recounts a brief and poignant affair between another dancer, Mitsou, and a young soldier, the Blue Lieutenant. Self-knowledge is attained by each of the two women through letter-writing and the parallel use of mirrors.

Both novels are set in a theatrical milieu: the opening scene of each is a music-hall dressing room, a closed, close space where the actress (almost friendless, by choice solitary) is surrounded by her own reflection. Her very profession obliges her endlessly to contemplate this duplicate of herself: typically, Mitsou "studies her lovely flowerlike reflection in the mirror."[2] These initial reflections are as inauthentic as they are exact, because in this setting Renée and Mitsou are costumed, made-up, masked. Into this world comes an outsider who threatens its tranquility — and one who is in each case yet another mirror image of the heroine. Robert, the Blue Lieutenant, is exactly Mitsou's age (twenty-four), while Max is even more exactly Renée's (thirty-three and a half). For the women, these resemblances are beguiling and significant; Robert hooks the back of Mitsou's costume, and Mitsou says thank you to his reflection in the mirror:

> Their two dark young heads, large eyed, resemble each other as though they belonged to brother and sister. Mitsou smiles, the lieutenant in blue smiles, and they look more than ever alike. (p. 23)

In one of her letters to him, she will compare herself and Robert to "two friends" or "two twins" (p. 76). From the narcissistic setting of the theatre, with its possibilities for spatial identification, the heroines return to apartments which also reflect them: Mitsou's is heteroclite, its furnishings as anomalous, as devoid of sophistication as she. Renée Néré's manifests her own ambiguity: to her suitor it appears a charming nest, while she maintains, on the contrary, that it "gives an impression of indifference, neglect, hopelessness, almost of imminent departure."[3]

Eventually there develop the correspondences which provide the most revealing image of the heroines: a verbal likeness. In the first place, their very handwriting reflects them: as Robert comments on Mitsou's "schoolgirl's writing," so Renée speaks of her "rapid, uneven writing which he [Max] says is like my mobile face, exhausted from expressing too much" (p. 199). Moreover, Renée's complexity, ambiguity, and fears are reflected in her writing, as Mitsou's simplicity and eagerness are mirrored in hers. These traits are more or less apprehended by the recipients of the letters, but the more crucial function of the correspondences is to provide for the heroines themselves another reflection, an orthographic counterpart to the specular image. (The journal kept by Renée gives, of course, an additional reflection of her, but one which in a sense is less revealing, since it does not manifest the curiously telling distortions which letters contain by their very nature: written, ostensibly, for the other, they are speech acts, not merely descriptions.) Writing is intimately associated with discovery — so much so that it even supplies the metaphors where seeing and knowing are evoked: when her internal formulation of an idea strikes her as powerful, illuminating, Renée exclaims: "This time the formula is clear. I saw it written in my mind and I see it there still, printed like a judgment in small, bold capitals" (pp. 202–203).

A dichotomy between writing and speech informs Mitsou's experience just as it does Renée's, for both are normally taciturn: Renée acknowledges that her real vocation is one of "silence and dissimulation," while Mitsou's easygoing friend Petite-Chose admonishes the Blue Lieutenant at his first meeting with Mitsou: "Don't count too much on her for keeping up the conversation" (pp. 21–22). And she herself writes him that "I'm counting a lot on my power of keeping still, when you are here, near me" (p. 89). Yet she composes long and vibrant letters, so captivating and compelling that they elicit equally long answers. Writing is posited equally in the two works as an unexpectedly welcome alternative to speech, even when the composition of a letter is inherently difficult, as in Mitsou's case. But while Renée, in the last analysis, writes chiefly for herself and communicates principally with her looking-glass, Mitsou communicates with her Blue Lieutenant. While Renée is "almost sincere," as she assures herself, and ready to "write — briefly, for time is short — and lie to him" (p. 195), Mitsou proclaims herself to be perfectly sincere and convincingly assures her correspondent that "I write you without lying." And while Renée's engaging words are only the shadow of her thoughts, the Blue

Lieutenant can remark: "Mitsou without any pretense at style; Mitsou, with the schoolgirl's handwriting, has never failed in her letters to tell me exactly what she wished, no more and no less" (p. 78). Renée draws back from a tentative engagement and confirms her solipsism, whereas Mitsou from indifference accedes to commitment, eager to give what she has never before offered.

The form of the novels reflects these differences. *The Vagabond* contains Renée's letters to Max, but only fragments — or reflections in her own — of his to her; *Mitsou*, on the other hand, presents a veritable exchange of letters: seven by the heroine as well as the five complete responses they elicit. Nor are the letters worked into the text as in the earlier novel: the first eleven letters of *Mitsou* appear one directly upon the other, without commentary; the twelfth closes the volume. *The Vagabond*, then, is essentially a monologue; Max's very words are subordinated to Renée's, filtered through her consciousness. Its form is linear, there being no real exchange. *Mitsou*, however, is a duo, the two voices speaking out with equal strength.

An epistolary exchange requires, first and foremost, a separation between the correspondents, and this necessary absence — which, according to Roland Barthes, constitutes one of the chief figures of amorous discourse — also functions differently in the two Colette novels. Barthes notes that in general it is the man who leaves, while the woman remains — waiting, sedentary, faithful. It is therefore she who experiences absence.[4] *Mitsou* presents the classic situation of which he speaks: the woman temporarily abandoned. In *The Vagabond*, on the other hand, it is Renée who leaves, Max who idly awaits her return. In Barthes' sense, then, Renée cannot be said to suffer from absence, and the letter is not for her the means of filling a void, but rather the desired substitute for an intolerable presence.

The use of letters, objects, and even characters as reflections of the protagonists is reinforced in both novels by the theme of spectatorship. The four central characters continually engage in acts of contemplating, watching, observing, spying on themselves and each other. Even from afar, with the mind's eye, they watch: "I see you so clearly, now that I'm far away" (p. 191), writes Renée to Maxime. The Blue Lieutenant gets his first chance to study Mitsou when he hides in her closet and watches her as she makes up before her mirror, and Maxime in fact falls in love with Renée while watching her — assiduously, evening after evening — perform on stage. In her apartment, Maxime stares at a sleeping Renée. Mitsou watches Robert asleep in her bed; when she eventually dozes off, he awakens and, in turn, watches Mitsou. Renée Néré's lucidity leads her to realize that her first concession to Max is a surrender to her desire to keep "not an admirer, not a friend, but an eager spectator of my life and my person" (p. 111). A capital moment is the one where Renée chances to find herself in the wings, invisible, observing the observers — among them her suitor: "By a curious transposition, it is he who becomes the spectacle for me" (p. 95). The oscillation of the "spectacle" between the stage and the house attenuates Renée's experience of her own alterity: for once, she is not herself the exhibition. She assimilates the moment to sleep:

> I think in fact that I must have fallen asleep, or else I am just emerging from one of those moments when one's mind goes blank before some painful idea is set in motion, moments which are the prelude to a slight loss of morale. (p. 95)

It is the start of a revolution in her relation to Max because the temporary dislocation — like sleep, with its function of restoration, of reintegration of body and soul — permits Renée to begin a reappropriation of herself.

There are, of course, other works by Colette in which letters figure importantly,[5] but in none other do they occupy so much space and play so extensive a role as in these two. Commentators on Colette's recourse to the epistolary form normally cite only *Mitsou* and make no mention of *The Vagabond*.[6] *Mitsou* does in fact put letters to a striking — and indeed traditional — use, for its heroine affirms her priorities and her very identity by means of her correspondence. She meets the Blue Lieutenant, as Renée does Max, the "Big Noodle," early in the novel when he barges into her dressing room, and the intruder is initially as unwelcome as Maxime Dufferein-Chautel. At her first writing to him, Mitsou is all the same intrigued, at most infatuated; by the time she sends him her sixth letter, she is in love. Yet no meeting has intervened between the first and the sixth letters, nor has the soldier — far more sophisticated than she — seduced her through his responses: Mitsou, for the most part, does not even fully grasp their meaning. It is rather her own epistolary efforts — unprecedented, exceedingly demanding: "I'm trying to make you understand that to write a letter is an event in my life" (p. 75) — which are the cause of her falling in love. Writing to the Blue Lieutenant demonstrates to Mitsou that she whose long relationship with her present lover, the "Man of Means," has been as unproblematic as unexciting, she who has never truly loved, never much desired, never even quarrelled, is ready to do all of these.

Initially less self-aware than Renée, Mitsou undergoes an evolution through letters which is in some ways therefore all the more stunning. Yet it is nonetheless the earlier novel which most rewards inquiry into the homologies between the epistolary form and woman's search for identity; it is *The Vagabond* which best illustrates both the form's complexity and its unique suitability for the development of questions of self-image. This is not to say that *The Vagabond* is a letter-novel in a strict sense; it is rather, like *Mitsou*, a mixed form. *The Vagabond* is essentially a journal, but one which evolves in the third and final part into a letter-novel of sorts.

Language is characteristically a central preoccupation in epistolary novels, where protagonists deal not with each other but with pen and paper, where lovers communicate not by sound and touch but through graphemes, and where articulating an emotion is therefore at least as crucial as experiencing it — if indeed emotions are not actually born of the attempt to evoke them in writing. *The Vagabond* — whose heroine is a sometime novelist, a diarist, and a letter-writer as well as a professional mime — written in the first person and the present tense, poses the problem of language as central. Renée's dilemma, with regard to the man who burst into her life (through the door of her dressing room) and tried to lay the world at her feet, is precisely linguistic. Her inability to come to terms with her would-be lover is revealed, symbolically, by her inability to find terms in which to speak to him; in her journal she writes:

> I don't know how to talk to you, poor Dufferein-Chautel. I hesitate between my own *personal* language, which is rather brusque, does not always condescend to finish its sentences, but sets great store on getting its technical terms exact — the language of a one-time blue-stocking — and the slovenly, lively idiom, coarse and picturesque, which one learns in the music-hall, sprinkled with expressions like: "You bet!" "Shut up!" "I'm clearing out!" "Not my line!"
> Unable to decide, I choose silence. (p. 83)

When Renée evokes the language of the music hall and contrasts it with the language of the ex-bluestocking, she is hesitating between two forms of expression, both of which would in effect trap her in a closed universe of discourse at the very moment when she is trying to find herself and a new means of expression. The temporary choice of silence, in the absence of an appropriate idiolect, is the recognition of the inherent unsuitability of both these forms.

How indeed is she even to address Max? Her ambivalence toward him is translated by her refusal to accord him a Christian name; she affects instead to call him by his absurd, multi-syllabic, hyphenated family name:

> "Well, then what d'you want me to call you? Dufferein or Chautel? Or Duduffe? Or...just Maxime, or Max?" (p. 106)

> I called him Dufferein-Chautel as usual, as though he had no Christian name. I always call him "You" or "Dufferein-Chautel." (pp. 121–122)

The definition of his relationship to her is equally an area of linguistic difficulty, for she must settle not only on a second-person appellation, but also on a manner in which to refer to him in the third person: "For I have an admirer. Only this old-fashioned name seems to suit him: he is neither my lover, nor my flame, nor my gigolo; he is my admirer" (p. 75). The outdated "admirer" ("amoureux") comes closest to Renée's sense, as the old-fashioned letter form best suits her story; literary history thus parallels psychological analysis.

The naming of Max is not, of course, the most vital issue in the novel. It represents rather the projection onto the lover of an internal dilemma; it is an appendage of Renée's difficulty in naming herself. The novel is literally Renée's search for an identity, coupled with an attempt to verbalize that identity, to arrive at a definition of herself. Settling the question of her suitor involves coming to terms with herself. Society, Renée's friends, her former friends, her admirer, all endeavor to classify her, to label her, to sum her up in a single expression: for her concierge, she is "a lady on her own," "an artiste," while for her bluestocking acquaintances she is "a woman of letters who has turned out badly." Renée collects these definitions, pores over them, implicitly rejects them. Max himself proposes a definition, and this turns out to be a grave error: sure of her love, he writes Renée that soon "you will no longer be Renée Néré, but My Lady Wife" (p. 191). Max's avowed project of replacing a proper noun — "Renée Néré" — with another substantive can only represent a threat of alienation to her whose name would be thus suppressed. This is the letter, and this ostensibly the expression, which triggers her defense mechanism and results in her ultimate decision to refuse Max. A name is a word invoking a certain code, and as much as Max himself, it is the code to which he refers and the limitations it implies which Renée rejects. The definition to which she finally acquiesces is part of an entirely different code, confining her less than any of the others. It is the very definition proposed by the title: she is and will remain a "vagabond." This term recurs throughout the journal, considered, appraised, nuanced —

> A gipsy henceforth I certainly am, and one whom tours have led from town to town, but an orderly gipsy. ... A vagabond, maybe, but one who is resigned to revolving on the same spot like my companions and brethren. (pp. 73–74)

— before being at last accepted in her own personal sense of the word as synonomous with free, in the concluding paragraphs: "A vagabond, and free."

The working-out of her own definition for herself — an articulation involving a decision, a stance, a gesture: renunciation and flight — depends considerably on the letters addressed to Max which are incorporated into the journal fabric of part III. The correspondence is motivated by Renée's departure on a forty-day tour of music halls throughout France; she has promised Max that, on her return, she will be his. Unlike speech, where Renée is prey to reservations and hesitations, constantly tempted by the alternative of silence, writing — or at least familiar letter-writing — presents little difficulty for this former novelist: "Heavens, how I write to you! I could spend my whole time writing to you, I believe I find it easier to write than to talk to you" (p. 182). Writing appears less imperative, more esthetic, pleasantly nugatory, and, most important, admitting of endless ambiguity: "No, I should say nothing to him. But to write is so easy. To write, to write" (p. 199). Letters may be viewed as creating events, but since they are based on an absence, the events created are such that the writer is excluded as a present participant in them. Hence their attraction for Renée, who prefers silence to speech, dissimulation to frankness, and absence to presence.

Her letters are the agents of the resolution of her relationship with Max; yet far from being a veritable means of communication with him, they are in fact a way of gaining time, of keeping him at bay through concealment of the essential truth: her growing consciousness of her own ambivalence and fears about love, passion, marriage. "To speak the truth is one thing, but the whole truth, that cannot, must not, be said" (p. 201). Rich, subtle, lyrical, her letters are as equivocal and complex as Renée herself. In fact, she comments that her lover's responses so little take into account the implications, the shades of meaning of her words, her *arrière-pensées*, that she might have written the opposite of what she actually did. On occasion, nonetheless, an unsigned one-line note from an unexpectedly perspicacious Max — "My Renée, do you no longer love me?" — stuns her: "I had not foreseen that gentleness and the simplicity of that question, which confound all my literature" (p. 216).

Thus does Renée evoke the essential literary nature of her enterprise: what she composes is literature in the sense of *écriture* as opposed to expression — an exercise in writing. It is literature too in the sense of game, literature finally because she never does find her idiolect; her continuing search for an alternative to music-hall discourse and the discourse of the bluestocking bears no fruit. She never in fact truly communicates with Max.

The epistolary dialogue, then, is a false dialogue (even formally, since the letters of Max do not appear) and Renée's gesture is essentially solipsistic: her epistolary "literature," like her journal, is composed as much for herself as for Max. So little are the letters intended for his consumption that Renée admits on occasion to the "strange impression" that a letter she has just written "was on its way to a man who ought not to have read it" (p. 187). In the letters she writes — and of course rereads — Renée is searching for her own image, her truth, an accurate reflection of her mind and heart. Thus it is Renée, ultimately, who is her own interlocutor, while her words are an effort to reconstitute herself. To these letters might be applied the curiously narcissistic comment that she makes regarding her last novel, poorly received and little understood by the public: "Even now, whenever I open it, I love it and wholeheartedly admire myself in it" (p. 28).

The letter's function is duplicated, its role extended, by another item of structural importance: the mirror. The juxtaposition of the two may be said to effect a "mise en abîme" — an internal reflection or repetition rendering salient the formal structure of the work.[7] If in her journal and letters she is trying out various definitions and poses, she is literally interrogating her mirror at every step of the way; mirrors provide her another kind of reflection of herself and lead her, as do the letters, to self-awareness. The first mirror allusion in the novel occurs as early as the fourth paragraph: "I'll find myself all alone, face to face with that painted mentor who gazes at me from the other side of the looking-glass" (p. 5). Each of the following three sentences evokes the fear and the fascination exerted by this other, this stranger, this indefatigable observer. Renée is as menaced and as mesmerized by her mirror image as she is by the various perceived attempts to define and categorize her: an "artiste," "My Lady Wife," etc. She catches, accidentally or intentionally, and studies her reflection every few pages throughout the novel. She looks involuntarily into the mirror of her dressing room; at home, the long mirror in her bedroom reflects her "just as I am!" (p. 11); in the street, she quickens her pace "every time I see my reflection in a shop window" (p. 118); and after embracing Max, she fumbles, almost frenetically, for the small pocket mirror in her handbag. Occasionally, the physical image converges with a verbal definition of Renée: "Facing me from the other side of the looking-glass, in that mysterious reflected room, is the image of 'a woman of letters who has turned out badly'" (p. 13). Renée gives form here to the discourse of the other, inevitably recalling Lacan's discussion of the mirror stage: discovery of the self — "identification" — through the otherness of the image.[8] The reflection is the paradoxical self/other, alienated at the moment of inception. In Renée's case, moreover, the implicit linking of mirror and letter — culminating perhaps in the last pages of the text when an "ephemeral arrangement" of her writing table results in her composing a letter as she sits beside a cheval-mirror — suggests a restitution of the primordial relationship between self and language: according to Lacan, it is language which restores to the *I* its function as subject.[9]

Dressing-room mirror, bedroom mirror, hand mirror, store window, even her reflection in Max's eyes — Renée is never far from her duplicate, who not merely returns her gaze but proffers advice as well. This function of the mirror as advisor is underscored on three occasions when Renée alludes to the "mentor," painted, pitiless, staring, spying, and speaking "from the other side" (pp. 5, 6, 129). It is her unconscious confrontation of the lesson Renée draws from the mirror and what she learns from her epistolary experience that compels her to conclude against returning to Max. In the mirror she observes change, rapid and fatal; still lovely, but less beautiful than she once was, she sees herself growing even less so. "How quickly everything changes!... Especially women," she exclaims, and again:

> He [Max] thinks that I am young too, and he does not see the *end* — my end. In his blindness he will not admit that I must change and grow old, although every second, added to the second that is fleeting,

is already snatching me away from him. (p. 193)

Renée herself "sees" clearly the "end" of which she speaks, for the mirror seems to have the terrifying potential for actualizing her own inevitable decline and disappearance:

> There's no getting away from it, it really is me there behind that mask of purplish rouge, my eyes ringed with a halo of blue grease-paint beginning to melt. Can the rest of my face be going to melt also? What if nothing were to remain of my whole reflection but a streak of dyed colour stuck to the glass like a long, muddy tear? (p. 7)

On the other hand, the awesome stability which she senses in herself becomes clearer to her through her letters to Max; as she meditates on their future together, she ineluctably assimilates him to her first husband and views their love in terms of that disastrous first marriage:

> After we have risen from a short embrace, or even from a long night, we shall have to begin to live at close quarters to each other, and in dependence on each other. He will bravely hide the first disappointments that I shall cause him, and I shall keep silent about mine, out of pride and shame and pity, and above all because I shall have expected them, *because I shall recognise them.* (p. 194–195)

She is afraid of passion, of another marriage; she is too old to change her ways. In the third paragraph of the novel, she implicitly classified change as alien to her: "After three years of music-hall and theatre I'm still the same" (p. 5); and so her letters confirm it to be. She grows daily older, *visibly* changes, but is at heart incapable of change: the divorce between these two truths leads her to reject Max. Renée eventually becomes what she has always been, the person she has occasionally caught sight of in the mirror, beneath the make-up and the masks: a vagabond, herself. She chooses solitude over engagement and turns in on herself — "have I not become again *what I was*, that is to say free, horribly alone and free?" (p. 214) — just as her name, containing its own echo, turns in on itself: "Néré" is a nearly perfect reverse mirror image of "Renée." As the title of the novel foreshadows the decision which concludes it, so the repetitions in Renée Néré's very name effect a closure, suggesting from the start the choice which she makes in the end.

Mitsou's name, on the other hand, intimates that her trajectory will be the opposite. The invention of her first lover (the Man of Means), "Mitsou" is the acronym of the titles of the two corporations with which he is associated: Minoteries Italo-Tarbaises and Scieries Orléanaises Unifiées. While Renée Néré's name suggests narcissism and self-sufficiency, Mitsou's implies a link, a bond; it is given her and freely accepted by her, apparently without an afterthought.

By a historical accident, the letter as literary form is peculiarly female, and it is no accident that Colette aligned herself early in her career as a writer with a host of women authors by reverting twice to the outmoded epistolary novel. The works in question are thus not merely anachronistic in the sense in which we usually understand the term (i.e., prochronistic: they anticipate the concern in fiction of the last few years with female identity); they are para-chronistic (for they go backwards in time) as well. In these complex texts — at once therefore remarkably experimental and highly traditional — form, theme, symbol, and autobiography (*The Vagabond* is a strongly autobio-graphical work and Colette was herself a prolific, talented letter-writer) are interwoven and function as mirrors of each other. The thematic use of theatre, for example, parallels the formal use of letters: the epistolary novel is a near relative of drama, for both theatre and letter place protagonists in a privileged position, allowing for an exchange unmediated by a narrator. The texture of these two works is thus rich, varied, and deep, displaying constant plays of light and images, which illuminate and give relief to the central experience: a woman's achieving self-knowledge.

Notes

1. Jean Larnac, *Histoire de la littérature féminine en France* (Paris: Krâ, 1929), p. 251.

2. Colette, *Mitsou*, trans. Jane Terry (New York: Albert and Charles Boni, 1930), p. 33. Henceforth, page references will appear in the text.

3. Colette, *The Vagabond*, trans. Enid McLeod (New York: Farrar, Straus and Giroux, 1955), p. 76. Henceforth, page references will appear in the text.

4. Roland Barthes, *Fragments d'un discours amoureux* (Paris: Seuil, 1977), pp. 17–24.

5. The celebrated rose-cactus letter, for example, is placed at the start of *La Naissance du jour*, and, in *Duo*, the letters from Ambrogio to Alice — although cited for the most part only indirectly — are nonetheless crucial.

6. For example, François Jost lists *Mitsou* in his extensive inventory of letter-novels through 1966 (*Essais de Littérature comparée*, Vol. II: *Europaeana* [Urbana: University of Illinois Press, 1968]); similarly, Jean Rousset, in an appendix to "Le Roman par Lettres" in *Forme et Signification* (Paris: Corti, 1962), cites only two examples for the twentieth century: *Mitsou* and Montherlant's *Les Jeunes Filles*.

7. See Lucien Dällenbach, *Le récit spéculaire: Essai sur la mise en abyme* (Paris: Seuil, 1977). Dällenbach presents the *mise en abîme* as a "modalité de la réflexion," whose "propriété essentielle consiste à faire saillir l'intelligibilité et la structure formelle de l'oeuvre" (p. 16).

8. Jacques Lacan, *Ecrits: A Selection*, trans. Alan Sheridan (New York: Norton, 1977), Chap. 1: "The Mirror Stage."

9. *Ecrits: A Selection*, p. 2.

6 The Relationship between Meaning and Structure in Colette's *Rain-moon*

DONNA NORELL

It has been generally accepted that Colette's famous imperative "Look...look..." is a call to readers to look more objectively at the world about them, to shed their prejudices and their preconceived ideas in an effort to see that world as it really is. Colette's own considerable descriptive powers were so firmly rooted in long-standing habits of observation that Thierry Maulnier wrote: "Colette never supposes, she sees, she hears and she notices, implacably."[1] His is a judgment almost universally shared by critics, who agree that she was, in fact, a writer who took no detail for granted.

Many of Colette's readers discover with surprise, therefore, that she dabbled in the occult. Her fascination with the material world and her insistence on the importance of the senses in evaluating terrestrial phenomena might seem to preclude the idea that she could be seriously interested in such activity. That is not the case. Colette gives the senses the chief role to play in interpreting the world only because most of the time she is dealing with material phenomena, which must be sensually perceived. But her basic canon of objectivity holds true for every kind of experience. In the twenty or so volumes of fiction, essays, and correspondence that she left to posterity, references to the occult reveal that Colette had direct contact with certain occult practices and that, although she was far from being credulous, she at no time dismissed occult phenomena as nonsense.

Her ventures into this domain were, however, both haphazard and intermittent. Her first important encounter with it took place early in the century, when she accompanied a friend to visit a Russian psychic "Saphira." The friend, a lesbian, was told that she would soon run off with a young man. This event, which none but the psychic foresaw, proved to be true. Over the years, Colette visited other psychics, of various kinds. Two women, "the sleeping woman of Caulaincourt Street" and Elise, "the woman with the candle," demonstrated, she says, a "not very believable (but verified) infallibility" (*L'Etoile vesper*, XIII: 271)[2] to read the past and the future of their clients; while a third, whom she calls simply "Mme B..." and who "saw" the spirits of Colette's father and brother (*Sido*, VII: 216–219), gave her pause to reflect by mentioning certain facts known only to Colette herself. These visits were few in number, but Colette mentions them time and again in her essays.[3] She finds them fascinating, because they are incomprehensible. Looking back, some thirty years later, on her initial experiences, she writes:

> Who will give me the key to Saphira? How does one distinguish, among all that hodge-podge of tinsel, banality, Slavic origins, kabbalistic names, make-up, huge rings and fitted frock coats, the extent to which he possessed real lucidity and powers of sorcery, to use the word that satisfies me the most? (*L'Etoile vesper*, XIII: 269–270)

That showmanship, and even quackery, often play a role in such practices, she readily admits, but her observations left her persuaded that there is sometimes an authentic gift involved. As essay of 1922 sets out her position on the whole subject:

> Do I believe, then, in this candle that burns and drips tears of stearin, in the images of the future and the past its disagreeable-smelling fumes form and dissipate? Not exactly. Yes and no... Let's get this clear. Pierre Faget and his colleagues in magic... they only make me shrug my shoulders. Reading coffee grounds is childish. Playing with yarrow sticks is gross superstition. But the woman with the candle...(*Prisons et paradis*, VII: 396)[4]

Colette's view remained unchanged until her death. She held that, although one must not be blindly superstitious, anything may be possible in this world: personal experience is the only real test.

This is precisely the position taken by the narrator of *La Lune de pluie* when confronted with the enigma of Délia Essendier, sister of Rosita Barberet. In this *nouvelle*, published in 1940 and the only one of Colette's fictional works in which the occult is a major theme, the narrator is presented with a whole series of riddles. Why is Rosita so secretive about Délia? Why has she been crying? How can "thinking" make Délia so tired? What does Délia do with the scissors? Though the narrator is reluctant to abandon her original idea that Délia is pining for her estranged husband, these and other considerations lead her to say: "Since I had come to know Délia Essendier, it . . . seemed to me that more than ever I needed to know [things] by myself, and without consulting anybody else" (p. 385). None of the explanations she can think of seems to stand. Yet she is completely unprepared for Rosita's disclosure that Délia is practicing black magic, that the young woman is attempting to "convoke" Eugène Essendier and thereby weaken and destroy him.

To believe or not to believe in black magic? That is the question posed to the reader of *La Lune de pluie*. It is never openly presented as such. Colette has long had the reputation of a writer who weds prose style to matter. In *La Lune de pluie* she goes farther than that. The entire work is built upon a network of structural elements — narrative movement, digressions, symbols and leit-motifs, symmetrical characterization and relationship of characters — so carefully arranged that all serve to decoy the reader into a position where he is obliged to pose this ultimate question to himself, and even to answer it in a certain way.

The tale (for such it may be called) gives the impression of being constructed upon very informal lines. The narrative seems rambling. Passages on what is ostensibly the subject — "the Barberet story" (p. 374) — are interrupted by reminiscences and discussions of apparently irrelevant topics. Close examination reveals, however, that there is not one narrative movement but two, and that the digressions have important functions of their own.

The narrator begins by relating how, on her first visit to her new typist Rosita Barberet, she discovered that Rosita was living in an apartment in which she herself had once spent many unhappy hours brooding on the unfaithfulness of her (now ex-)husband. As she recognizes one familiar object after another — the window catch, a panel of old wallpaper, the ceiling rosette, the floor plan, the sound of a door, the slope of the front steps — she is left in no doubt but that the house was previously her own. What renders the situation even more strange is that it is because of a man from B..., whose accent recalls that of her former husband, "that other man from B..." (p. 367), that she has visited the house once more. At her next visit, she learns that the apartment is shared by Rosita's sister Délia, who, estranged from her husband, spends most of her time in the room the narrator calls *"my* room." The coincidence becomes too much to resist. She penetrates into the room, sees the young woman on the divan, and believes she has found in her what she later calls "my young self that I would never be again, that I never stopped disowning yet regretting" (p. 378). Thus is born the narrator's fascination for Délia Essendier.

The double narrative movement arises out of the narrator's decision to keep secret her discovery of the "coincidence." Colette establishes the duality in the opening scene. There, she presents, in carefully alternated passages, the banal conversation and gestures of Rosita and the narrator, as well as the secret small discoveries that the latter is simultaneously making. For example:

I lifted the muslin curtain with my forehead and placed my hand on the window catch. Immediately, I experienced the slight, rather pleasant giddiness that accompanies dreams of falling and flying . . . For I was holding in my hand that singular window catch, that little cast-iron mermaid whose form my palm had not forgotten, after so many years. [. . .]

Not having put her glasses on, Mlle Barberet noticed nothing... [. . .] a few square inches of wallpaper remained bare: I could distinguish its roses whose color had nearly vanished, its purple convulvus fading to grey and . . . I could see again all that I had once left behind. [. . .]

"This view is pretty..."

"Most of all, it's bright for an upstairs storey. Let me arrange your papers, Madame [. . .]." (p. 361)

And during all the rest of the *nouvelle* the narrator continues, through an alternating inner-outer movement of past description and monologue, to relate what is, in effect, two separate series of events: one, external, centering on the activities of Délia and Rosita; another, internal, centering on the narrator's own reactions and thoughts. Each furnishes the reader with a series of mysteries, strange events, and questions, which are one by one cleared up or answered in the course of the story, but only as they give way in turn to new mysteries, events, and questions.

Actually, the story has begun with an emphasis on strangeness, for the narrator's interest in Délia has been engendered by her discovery of the coincidence of the lodging. It is nourished, however, by concerns that are narcissistic (and not altruistic, as her readiness to accede to Rosita's request that she "talk to" Délia, might suggest). This explains why she is so slow to understand that there is something sinister about Délia's behavior. She is given a whole series of clues, dating even from before the discovery that she has once lived in the apartment. Rosita seems to lie about the length of time she has lived there (p. 360); she does not want to discuss her sister at all (p. 368); she is vague about the nature of Délia's "sickness" (p. 371); she says that Délia has an *idée fixe* (p. 377). As for Délia herself, she claims that her "work" is extremely fatiguing, though she seems to do nothing but lie about all day; she says also that it is good for her to touch pointed objects (p. 392); "I'm looking after him," she says, ironically, of her "boyfriend" standing in the street (p. 394). But so caught up is the narrator by the coincidence of the lodging, that for a long time she fails to realize that the picture she has painted of Délia's psychology has its counterpart only in her own memory.

The reader soon ceases to marvel at the "coincidence." Instead, one's attention is drawn first to the clues, that is, to the many small mysteries in the behavior of the two sisters, and secondly to the narrator's changing attitudes.

More than once the latter is tempted to wash her hands of the sisters, but each time something occurs to change her mind. Early in the story, she experiences a moment of aversion on learning that Délia is unhappily married, for, she says, she does not care for "other people's conjugal difficulties" (p. 372); then, her first sight of the "rain-moon" — a halo of refracted light on the wall — and the news that Délia is actually living in her old room reawaken her interest (pp. 372–373). A similar movement takes place when she first suspects Rosita of jealousy, because, she admits, she does not like jealousy either; but again the movement is checked, this time by another mystery — when, reluctantly, she knocks once more at the sister's door, Délia's prostrate form bars her way (pp. 380–382).

It is only after this visit, about halfway through the story, that the narrator herself analyzes the situation. Her awareness of her own emotional attachment to Délia, an attachment in which, however, affection plays no part, now becomes equal to the reader's understanding of it. She says: "Yet I did not like Délia Essendier, and the cherished companion whom I sought, was it not my former self, its pathetic form stuck between the walls of this wretched lodging like a petal between two pages?" (p. 388). She understands that she has *wanted* the coincidence to be significant. Now she sees, as well, that the sisters present a mystery far more challenging than the strangeness of the original event. And so, as has always been her habit, she seeks enlightenment in her own experience. But no amount of reflection sheds light on the enigma of Délia's behavior. Nor, indeed, does further investigation, for Délia's bizarre replies to her questions furnish more mystery than explanation, and the only conclusion supplied by her observations is that the resemblance she has believed to exist between Delia's situation and her own former one has no basis in fact:

> "It's fatigue." But what kind of fatigue? That caused by an unhealthy life? No unhealthier than mine, and just as healthy as that of other women and girls of Paris. A few days earlier, Délia had touched her forehead and clutched at her temples, saying: "That's what makes me tired... And that..." The fixed idea, yes, the absent, the unfaithful Essendier... In vain I contemplated that perfect beauty — and, studied feature by feature, Délia's face was flawless — in vain I sought there signs of suffering, signs, that is, of suffering from love. (p. 394)

The narrator has finally joined the reader in remarking the oddity of the two sisters' conduct. But the reader's interest in her psychology will continue, for her reaction to Rosita's revelations will be every bit as intriguing as was her reaction to the coincidence of the lodging.

With Rosita's disclosure, the narrator comes into possession of all the facts. The disclosure takes place in two stages — the initial one at the sisters' apartment, and its continuation the next evening at the home of the narrator. The latter remarks that Rosita herself has changed. "In less than two weeks," she says, "my 'old young girl' had become a real old maid" (p. 397). And, even though for her visit to the narrator's she has redonned her usual correct costume, Rosita "seemed to have repudiated forever the two little ringlets on her shoulder. The brim of her hat came down over the mournful snail-shaped bun, symbol of all renouncements" (p. 406). This change is significant: Rosita has given up the struggle to save Eugène, believing him doomed.

The tale is remarkable for the abruptness with which it ends. The day after Rosita's visit, the narrator renounces the two sisters, even though she is still enough attracted to Délia to arrange to meet her "by chance" three more times. Then, one final time, she happens to see Délia from afar. Délia is wearing widow's weeds. All the events preceding this last one are reported with commentary, but the last incident is described briefly, cryptically. The abruptness of the ending strikes the reader, for it is extremely effective dramatically. In the course of the narrative, mystery after mystery has been dispelled or cleared up, but not the final mystery of Eugène's death. And, at intervals during her rambling recital, the narrator has informed the reader of her views on a good many subjects, but on the last and most important subject she is silent. The result is that the reader finishes the story with two questions uppermost in his mind. Has Délia's magic actually been successful? And what is the narrator's opinion on the matter?

On the surface, it appears that the reader is free to judge of these questions for himself. But there is evidence that Colette actually wishes to influence the reader, that she wishes, in fact, to oblige him to abandon a good part of any skepticism to which he may be prone.

The first corroboration of this idea can be found in the inner narrative movement, which suggests that the narrator is secretly willing to admit of the efficacy of Délia's activities. Very early in the story, she has shown herself to be secretive, by concealing from the sisters — for no very clear reason — her discovery of the "coincidence." Later, she conceals something else from them, something more important: a familiarity with the occult. Immediately after her first visit, long before she suspects that any untoward activities are taking place in her former abode, she reminisces on her own visits to psychics. "Among fortune-tellers," she says, "those to whom a fleeting gift of second sight is given on our behalf, are rare" (p. 366). It is a statement of faith. Further passages mention similar experiences (pp. 374, 402–403). And, indeed, the narrator confesses that even on the subject of black magic she is not uninformed. "Certainly," she says, "on the subject of simple and popular magic, I was not so unknowledgeable as I had wished to appear in Mlle Barberet's eyes" (p. 403). The inner narrative and the digressive passages are thus useful. They serve, in part, as a portrait of the narrator, leading the reader into her mind so that he may be influenced by her attitude whether he wants to be or not. And they also show that she is not the complete skeptic she pretends to be in front of Rosita Barberet.

They do more. They reveal that, despite the impression she gives the reader of confiding everything about herself, it is completely within the narrator's character to withhold important information. And if she does that with Rosita, why not with the reader as well?

The reader at whom this particular deceit is aimed is, of course, the die-hard skeptic, whose attitude is such that he has decided *a priori* that any so-called experience of the occult is so much nonsense. Ordinarily, such a reader might be expected to dismiss the story from his mind once he gets to the end of it, even assuming that he does get to the end. But the narrator has laid down a special trap for him. Throughout the story, she has continually emphasized the fact that all her judgments are based on observation of empirical data; she has given numerous examples of this type of reasoning.[5] She therefore appeals to the skeptical reader on his own ground of rationality, so that if he accepts the idea that the data she presents on "the Barberet story" is accurate, then he must also accept the conclusion implied. But why does she not state what that conclusion is? Because the conclusion to which the narrator is obliged to come is one at which the rational mind balks. The skeptical reader who identifies with the rational viewpoint repeatedly expressed by the narrator becomes, then, at the end of the story, a skeptic at bay.

Other influences are at work on the more pliable reader. The subject matter of the digressive passages themselves is significant here, for they fall into two main groups. One group deals with what the narrator's past can conjure up of strangeness, that is, with coincidences and contacts with the occult. More than once, in these passages, she concludes that nowhere has she encountered anything quite like the two sisters. For instance:

> Thus, I reckoned up everything inexplicable that had more or less become part of my experience thanks to dull-witted intermediaries, vacant creatures whose emptiness reflects fragments of destinies, modest liars and vehement visionaries. None had done me harm, none had frightened me. But those two dissimilar sisters...(p. 404)

The second group deals with her current activities — writing, bicycling, dining out, going to the flea market, and entertaining her mother, whose presence, she says, "recalled my life to dignity and to kindness" (p. 396). These two types of passages seem to have little in common; but, in fact, the harmlessness of the *voyantes* and the eminent sanity of the narrator's own activities serve to set the present situation in relief and to point up the reason for her uneasiness: "the Barberet story" is singular because it is of evil.

What disturbs the narrator, then, is not Délia's practice of the occult, but her evil intent. After the renouncement, the latter's attraction lingers on, but the narrator is prudent. Recalling the three "chance" meetings, she says of Délia: "Something unnamable, deep within me, stirred and spoke in her favor. But I did not respond" (p. 415). The truth is that Rosita's disclosure has pushed her to the limits of her credulity, for Rosita has insisted that the practice of black magic is far from rare. "She [Délia] isn't the only one who does it. It's quite common," she says (p. 401). "In our neighborhood there are lots who repeat the name. [. . .] It's well known" (p. 412). The narrator muses on this idea: "Whispers, an ignorant faith, even the habits of a whole neighbor- hood, were *those* the forces, the magic philters that procure love, decide questions of life and death, and move that haughty mountain: an indifferent heart?" (p. 412). She offers no answer, and the reader is left with the question still open three pages later, when the narrative ends.

The double narrative movement and the digressive passages both support, therefore, the idea that, however much the narrator may *wish* not to take the idea of black magic seriously, her rational mind is tempted to accept it, because even in her own broad experience the case is exceptional. Rosita has believed in it all along, and, since events suggest finally that the latter's opinion on this one case has been well-founded, the implication is that perhaps her remarks on society as a whole repose on something more solid than superstition as well. The idea that, under the apparently humdrum stream of everyday life, there flows a darker, persistent current which many people cannot or do not choose to recognize is suggested many times by Rosita. "And the confectioner from downstairs, what has she done, then, with her husband?" she asks. "And the dairy-man from number 57, it's a bit strange that he's a widower for the second time, isn't it?" (p. 408). "It's very well- known" (p. 412). Rosita reproaches the narrator for her ignorance: "A person as well-educated as you..." (p. 407). And, indeed, in the lives of the two sisters themselves the narrator has seen evidence that people, and events, are not always what they seem.

This idea is central to the deeper significance of *La Lune de pluie*: the notion that individuals and society as a whole have often a hidden side which we are sometimes reluctant even to know. Certainly, Délia Essendier is not what she seems when the narrator first meets her; nor, according to Rosita, is the little society of the *quartier*, which the narrator had always considered so innocent and picturesque. And Délia and her fellow-practitioners of magic are not even exceptional in this way. Colette suggests, by her portrayal of the other two major characters, that the situation may be universal. The narrator has shown herself to be garrulous or secretive according to the moment. And in Rosita's eyes, her image is that of a "woman alone" (p. 395), that is, of the separated or divorced woman obliged to live, in that first decade of the century, outside respectable society; yet we know, through what the narrator says about herself, that her conduct gives rise to no scandal and that her activities are, in fact, thoroughly wholesome.

As for Rosita, she is, oddly enough, the key personage of the three. Colette has distributed the weight of the narrative interest more or less equally on the three women. The plot, or dramatic interest, weighs most heavily on Délia, since both the narrator and Rosita are interested primarily in her. The psychological interest is, of course, borne by the narrator, in her reactions to events both inner and outer. But the import of the tale is concentrated in Rosita. She is quite unlike Délia. As she says, "First of all, there is a certain difference of age between us, and she is dark. Besides, as far as our characters are concerned, we're not at all alike" (p. 373). She is also different from the narrator, in that she is considered respectable where the narrator is not, and in that she harbors ideas completely at variance with those sanctioned by the respectable society of which she is a part, while the narrator displays no such leanings. And, whereas Délia and the narrator have "hidden" sides, Rosita reveals considerable paradox within herself. This "old young girl," whose correctness of dress and manner is the first thing one notices about her, invites the narrator to watch her step, saying "My sister is lying on the floor" as if she were saying "My sister has gone to the post-office" (p. 382). Even her beliefs are unsoundable. "And what about the devil, Rosita?" asks the narrator, attempting to comprehend the other's ideas. And Rosita replies, surprised: "But, Madame, what do you mean? The devil is for imbeciles. The devil, just imagine..." (p. 413). In a flash of intuition, the narrator guesses that "it's in Rosita, so colorless and prim, that one must seek the solution to this little puzzle" (p. 395). And, indeed, it is Rosita's character which most accurately reflects the central meaning of the tale: that paradox and strangeness are but the obverse of the commonplace.

The characteral significance is supported, in part, by symbolic names. Actually, the narrator herself is never named. To all appearances, she is one of the many Madame Colettes whose lives resemble their creator's own. But Rosita calls her simply "Madame," so that that assumption is never completely valid and the ambiguity of her identity merely adds to the general atmosphere of secrecy surrounding her. On the other hand, "Rosita" signifies "little rose," and is coupled here with the surname Barberet, a play on the French word *barbare* (Latin *barbarus*; Greek *barbaros*), meaning, in its first sense, an outsider, a foreigner, a stranger, and in its second sense, an uncivilized person. Together the two names are perfectly descriptive of Rosita, who in many respects is an innocent young girl but who places faith in practices banned by the civilization to which she presumably belongs.

Her enigmatic sister is "this Délia who did not want to be called Adèle" (p. 415). Adèle is a saint's name,[6] but Délia is an epithet of the goddess Artemis, derived from the name of her birthplace, Delos. The adoption of the name Délia is therefore symbolic of her intention. Less innocent than Rosita, she has abandoned altogether the Christian religion into which she has been born, in order to participate in rites that seek their origin in pagan antiquity. The name

Délia is well chosen, for Artemis is goddess of the hunt and of the moon. It is therefore apt that she should assign to herself that identity while she "hunts" Eugène Essendier under the auspices of the "rain-moon."

These names form part of a network of minor symbolic elements designed to support the main idea and to add to the accumulated impression of strangeness. The central symbol is the one designated by the title, the "rain-moon." In the story, the term refers to a halo of refracted light, by which the sunlight separates into its component colors as it passes through thick glass and is projected on the wall. It seems at first to be merely one more of the many things the narrator recognizes as she confirms the fact that the apartment was once her own. But, unlike the other objects, it is mentioned again and again, and takes on additional importance with every repetition. Although the narrator has once considered it to be a symbol of hope, Rosita says that her sister is afraid of it, that Délia calls it "an omen" (p. 372). Later, the narrator asks: "A blind alley haunted by evil plans, was that what had become of the little apartment where once I had suffered so innocently, under the guardianship of my rain-moon?" (pp. 403–404). In folklore, the term used in its original sense signifies something else: a moon with a diffused halo around it, and the belief is that the "rain-moon" betokens rain for the morrow.[7] So Délia is right. Just such an announcement, just such an "omen" it turns out to be, not of love requited but of death.

A system of number and color symbolism is related to the central symbol and to the central meaning of the tale. The number three, which has mystical overtones because of its association with the Trinity as well as with various unholy mythical trios, recurs often. There are three women, of whom now one and now another becomes prominent, depending upon which aspect of the tale is being considered. Three segments of society are also presented: the wholesome one in which the narrator moves, the strange but harmless milieu to which the *voyantes* belong, and the sinister world of the two sisters. Three times the narrator speaks of her experiences of the occult and three times she arranges to meet a weakened Délia in the street. Symbolically, three represents the synthesis of duality and unity, so that its use here evokes the idea that room must be made in our concept of reality for the hidden side, for the incomprehensible, because it, too, is part of the whole.

Seven is equally important. "The three is after the seven," observes Rosita, as she rearranges the narrator's pages (p. 362). She offers to retype the last page, since "it will only take seven minutes" (p. 362). As she arrives to confide in the narrator for the last time, the clock strikes seven, and her revelations are delayed only long enough for her to drink "a glass of Lunel wine" (p. 406), which is, she says, "a magic drink" (p. 406). In the language of the occult, the number seven signifies completion, termination, and so in despair Rosita tells the narrator that Eugène is doomed, that "six moons have already passed, the seventh is here, it is the fatal moon, the poor man knows that he has been summoned" (p. 407).[8]

Significantly, the number of colors in the spectrum and so of the "rain-moon" itself is seven, with the seventh color being violet. Mention of this color runs like a refrain throughout the tale, as Rosita asks what color of typed copies she should make: "In violet or in black?" (p. 362). But at the last visit she does not ask. "Like a stranger, Rosita listened and said, 'Very well...Fine...In black and in violet...It will be finished Wednesday'" (p. 398). And events do prove finally that the two colors signify the same thing, for when the seventh and fatal moon is past Délia wears "a dress whose black turns to violet in the sunlight" (p. 415). The seventh color, like the seventh moon, is death.[9]

La Lune de pluie is not a particularly profound work, although Colette is a far more profound writer than she is currently given credit for. But in any case, this tale certainly provides ample evidence that she is a superb craftsman. What seems to be a rambling but simple narrative is actually a tightly constructed maze of significant detail, ordered in such a way as to lead the reader down one or more paths of the author's choosing. Even in her use of digression Colette achieves considerable economy, for she ensures that at one and the same time these apparently superfluous passages dramatize the exterior action, offer the reader insight into the narrator's psychology, and provide the skeptic with food for thought.

Many of these passages also add to the immense accumulation of suggestive matter that Colette amasses to back up the main idea. References to coincidences, mysteries, presentiments, experiences with the occult, symbolic names, numbers and colors, and, of course, the ever-recurring "rain-moon": the sheer weight of these is impressive. Events, we are shown, are not necessarily what they seem, nor are people. Every phenomenon has two aspects, the seen and the unseen, and, in that, it resembles the room wherein Délia weaves her spell, "dark on one side, bright on the other" (p. 363). What we consider to be true depends, like the color of Délia's dress, on our perspective.

So suggests Colette in *La Lune de pluie*, where the narrator consciously chooses to rely on her rational mind, on her experience, on *herself,* but in the end can only suspect.

Is Colette, finally, asking the readers of *La Lune de pluie* to believe in the occult? Not necessarily, for her intention is always to tell a good tale. But many times in her works, she expresses the thought that man is afraid of anything which upsets his serenity, his sense of being in control. Any occult phenomenon will disturb him in that way. Of her own contacts with the occult, Colette wrote: "I believe that during my lifetime I have not consulted more than four or five persons gifted with second sight. But it gives me pleasure to recognize that their various gifts had the potential to upset our human view of events" (*L'Etoile vesper,* XIII: 268). The structure of *La Lune de pluie* is designed to do the same thing.

Notes

1. *Introduction à Colette* (Paris: La Palme, 1954), p. 58.

2. Unless otherwise stated, all references to Colette's works are to the fifteen-volume *Oeuvres complètes* (Paris: Flammarion, 1948–1950). References to works other than *La Lune de pluie*, which is in Volume XI, will give both volume and page numbers. Translations are mine.

3. The most important passages dealing with the occult are, in addition to *La Lune de pluie*, the following: *Aventures quotidiennes*, VI: 428–431; *Sido*, VII: 216–219; *Prisons et paradis*, VIII: 394–396; *L'Etoile vesper*, XIII: 264–273; *Journal intermittent*, XIV: 260–261.

4. Pierre Faget was a country sorcerer whose arrest and trial caused a minor sensation in France during the winter of 1921–22.

5. See, for example, p. 359, where the narrator discusses the differences in the wear of cuffs and sleeves between scribes and typists; and pp. 384–385, where she remarks on how the movements of certain animals betray their species, and how certain gestures and tics reveal the innermost thoughts of people.

6. The Benedictine abbess, Saint Adela, daughter of Dagobert II, c.675–c.734.

7. In a letter to Lucie Saglio, tentatively dated by researchers as mid-September 1940, Colette wrote: "You know, it's the moon that has a rainbow halo around it and that announces bad weather" (*Lettres à ses pairs* [Paris: Flammarion, 1973], p. 135).

8. According to J. E. Cirlot's *A Dictionary of Symbols* (trans. Jack Sage [New York: Philosophical Library, 1962], p. 223), seven is "symbolic of perfect order, a complete period or cycle." *The Encyclopedia Americana* (Canadian ed., 1950, Vol. 24) gives this explanation: "Various reasons have been given for the peculiar regard had for this number, such as that seven is a symbol of completeness, being compounded of three and four, perfect numbers, they being representable in space by the triangle and the square."

9. Color symbolism is more variable than number symbolism. However, Cirlot says that a superficial classification will have the "cold, 'retreating' colors" ("blue, indigo, violet and, by extension, black") corresponding to "processes of dissimulation, passivity and debilitation" (p. 50). The novel suggests a movement from violet to black in the progressive debilitation of Eugène that will end in his death. This idea is consistent with the more obvious symbolism of violet in the tale, for there violet derives most of its symbolism from its relationship to the number seven, being the seventh and last color of the spectrum. Beyond it lies (in non-scientific terms) the void (i.e., blackness). As an echo of seven, therefore, violet acquires the meaning of something ended or completed, and in *La Lune de pluie* that something is Eugène's life. In this way, black — a universal symbol of death — is but the extension of violet, or, in other terms, Eugène's potential death realized.

7 A Typology of Women in Colette's Novels

SYLVIE ROMANOWSKI

This study takes the novels of Colette as constituting a totality, and assumes that each character can be properly understood only if she is situated within a typology, in a structure of the types of women in the novels.[1] The scope of the study is limited in two important ways: it will deal only with women, and it will not attempt a description at the level of each individual work. Furthermore, it will not attempt to discuss all the women in all the novels, but will focus rather on the ones that have been found to be more complex and richer illustrations of the types. The reader is free to take this study as a hypothesis and test it in relation to the other women in Colette's works. A complete exposition of Colette's woman population will not be attempted, but only suggested by means of some of her outstanding creations.

One critic, Elaine Marks, notes that "Colette's female characters may be divided into two family groups: the 'Colette-Claudine' branch and the 'Colette-Sido' branch."[2] But she goes on to link these characters with the author, as her choice of labels clearly indicates, a practice which will be avoided in this essay. I would propose, in basic agreement with E. Marks' analysis, that there are indeed two major types of women in Colette's writings, which can be called, very simply, the adolescent and the mature woman. Each of these types can in turn be subdivided into two variants, which can be called the positive and the negative variant. It should be stated here first that these are relative terms indicating a position that the characters occupy in a structure. Second, these types and subtypes are not realized absolutely in any one novel; in addition, there are nuances and shadings. After analyzing Colette's women in terms of these types, certain questions can be asked concerning her understanding of woman in general.

The young adolescent woman is the type that is the most clearly divided into the two subtypes. The best, least ambiguous examples are Vinca (*The Ripening Seed*) for the positive variant and Camille (*The Cat*) for the negative one, and this analysis will concentrate on these two characters. Colette delineates and suggests the values of each character through the accumulation of numerous details of description and associated imagery as well as through the contrast within the novel between characters belonging to another type or subtype.[3]

Thus descriptions of Camille are punctuated with reference to her nouveau-riche background, her slight vulgarity, her obvious make-up, and her lack of both finesse and modesty. In the very first paragraphs the colors of her face appear too clear-cut to be natural: "she would . . . look pale again, her chin white, tired little lines under her ochre-tinted powder." The portrait continues in the chapter with mention of her "white fingers and lacquered nails" and her "wiping with her pointed nail two little clots of red saliva from the corners of her mouth." The impression, almost that of a collage of flat painted surfaces, is enhanced by a reference to her solid black hair, "brilliantined, and the color of a new piano" (*The Cat*, 473– 475).

Moreover, references to her habits of driving a bit too fast, her swearing at cab drivers, and the unevenness of her temperament continue to give a somewhat pejorative coloring to her, which is not compensated for by Alain's reflections on her beauty. And surely her family's recent wealth, acquired in the modern business of washing machines, contrasts with the old, slightly declining but still aristocratic making of silk, a cloth of time-honored noble and distinguished connotations.

In this novel, the most obvious and persistent contrast is drawn between Camille and Saha, the Chartreuse cat who seems to be everything that Camille is not. The contrast between the loves of Alain, particularly well-explained by Mieke Bal,[4] is clarified by an examination of the positive subtype of the adolescent woman, Vinca.

Vinca also moves from girlhood to womanhood in the *The Ripening Seed*, though not in an official manner through marriage, and with a slower, more reluctant pace than Camille. Just as the opening portrait of Camille inclined the reader toward a somewhat pejorative judgment, so the opening portrait of Vinca sets the tone for the remainder of the book. Her tomboyish dress and attitude is mixed with young-girlish clothes and grace. No make-up or artifice here: her eyes are "the color of Spring rain," her legs are deeply tanned by the sun to a "color of terra-cotta," her hair is "golden like straw," her neck "milk-white" (*Ripening Seed*, 3– 4). Though she too seems a collage of colors, unlike Camille she derives her colors only from nature and not from self-consciously applied make-up. The association with nature of both positive subtypes, the adolescent and the mature woman, is opposed to the negative subtypes' association with civilized, manufactured articles, artificial beauty, and urban life. Camille likes to go to casinos and drive fast cars, whereas Vinca likes to go fishing and walking in sand dunes.

Saha the cat is also a creature of nature, not merely because she is a cat, but because she lives by nature's rules, by instinct, and in nature's place, the garden, her favorite location. While Camille remains on the porch, Alain "sought safer refuge in the lawn" where Saha hides; "a silvery flash leapt out from the hedge and glided around Alain's legs like a fish" (*The Cat*, 476). This sentence describes Saha only in nature images, ending a poetic evocation of the garden illuminated by moonlight. Her aristocratic, delicate manner of being contrasts with the nouveau-riche and less-than-subtle Camille. This clash is one of the principal themes of the novel, as the two females vie for one man's attention and devotion.

The method of contrast between the two female characters in *The Cat* is also used in *The Ripening Seed*, with the brief apparition of the somewhat mysterious and elusive Madame Dalleray. Always dressed in white and visibly (though rather discreetly) made up, she lives in a house closed off from the outside world by a high wall, isolated from the sun's light and heat by heavy curtains of red, white, black, and gold. She lacks all of Vinca's natural colors, and Vinca's openness and sincerity as well. For when Madame Dalleray seduces Phil, she does so out of calculated selfishness and acquisitiveness, "entirely for her own pleasure and with little thought for him" (*Ripening Seed*, 112).

Vinca gives herself, hesitatingly and awkwardly, in an outdoor setting of recently beaten buckwheat. Significantly, Colette does describe fairly directly the first sexual encounter of Phil and Vinca, which, though clumsy, might be "perfectible," while the encounter of Phil with Madame Dalleray is not described, but only indicated in terms of symbolic images of falling.

The positive subtype of the young woman is delineated in terms of union not only with nature, but also with the loved partner. Both Vinca and Saha, at the end of the novels, find the most intimate kind of rapport with their men. Vinca is able to make love to Phil, and the union of Saha and Alain is represented in the vision of the final paragraph by an exchange of human and feline characteristics: Saha "was following Camille's departure with the expression of a human being," while Alain "played deftly, making the palm of his hand hollow like a paw, with the rough green chestnuts of early August" (*The Cat*, 563). The negatively valued women (such as Madame Dalleray, who leaves abruptly and has a little boy say good-bye to Phil in her stead), on the other hand, experience loss of love, deprivation, and separation not only from nature, which they never truly appreciated, but from human companionship as well.

Many of the same associations and nuances can be found in the depictions of the older woman, although the positive and negative subtypes might be slightly less differentiated at times; or, more precisely, while there is clearly a positive subtype, the negative variants are not so clearly set off and often possess some positive connotations and attributes.

Apart from the obviously antipathetic and ridiculous old women that abound as minor background figures, the clearest example of a relatively negative variant of the older woman is Léa in *Chéri*.

The initial impression the reader has of Léa is of "two magnificient thin-wristed arms, lifting on high two lovely lazy hands." The voice is "soft, deep," and her common sense, her gentle and tolerant attitude toward the boy-man Chéri complete a rather sympathetic picture of the forty-nine-year-old Léa. Yet, immediately, mention is also made that her "throat had thickened and was not nearly so white, with the muscles under its skin growing slack" (*Chéri*, 3). And she acknowledges the subtle aging process by noting that she takes off the necklace so as not to attract Chéri's attention to her aging neck, which presumably she did not do at the beginning of her six-year liaison with him ("she put it away at night now" [*Chéri*, 7]). The delusion of Chéri becomes self-delusion in the next chapter, as she blames the heat for her swollen legs, an excuse that does not even fool the servant.

During the course of the novel, the aging process seems to accelerate. After an absence of only six months during Chéri's marriage, Léa has acquired a "nervous twitch of the jaw" and the beauty of her tanned complexion is offset by the fact that her neck "had shrunk and was encircled with wrinkles that had been inaccessible to sunburn" (*Chéri*, 104). The subtle, beneath-the-skin sagging has become an all-too-evident degradation. Like Camille, she too has harsh colors: "careless henna-shampooing had left too orange a glint in her hair" (*Chéri*, 171). The dreaded adjective is finally said aloud, "'What lovely handles for so old a vase!'" (*Chéri*, 126), as she contemplates her raised arms in the ever-present and truthful mirror.

Aging, itself a natural phenomenon, is nevertheless given a pejorative connotation in the description of Léa; there is a further factor that contributes to the negativity of Léa, the disproportion of age between her and her young lover. She becomes aware of this, as her growing older moves her ever further away from Chéri's youthfulness and beauty: "'It serves me right. At my age, one can't afford to keep a lover six years. Six years! he has ruined all that was left of me'" (*Chéri*, p. 124). The aging process seems to reach a climax by the end of the novel, when Colette uses the strongest possible terms: "An old woman, out of breath, repeated her movements in the long pier-glass, and Léa wondered what she could have in common with that crazy creature" (*Chéri*, 154).

The jolt of seeing her unflattering image in the mirror might be, however, a crucial experience that will lead her to a new understanding of herself, just as the mirror stage ("le stade du miroir") is crucial to the child's development of his identity in Jacques Lacan's analysis.[5] The child's experience is one of recognition, accompanied by jubilation and playfulness, whereas Léa's experience is one of bewilderment and shock. Both the child's and the adult woman's experience have a positive, founding aspect that can propel them into a new self-understanding and identity, but for Léa the text remains silent on the outcome, in the interrogative mode ("she wondered . . .").

Léa's life, though filled with so many men that she herself loses count, ends in solitude; Chéri, she remarks in the novel's final sentence, seems to be happy to be leaving her: she sees him, from inside her room, "fill his lungs with the fresh air, like a man escaping from prison" (Chéri, 154). Society seems to have no place for the woman who had lived in defiance of many of its norms. Solitude, separation, resignation — such is the lot of Léa, and of others in her category.

The acknowledgment of separation underlies the stories of Chéri and Break of Day. Both novels describe an older woman who has a relationship with a considerably younger man. Both men are loved by younger women but do not return that love in equal measure. In the end, both older women decide to give up their young admirers. Though the plots resemble each other, the similarities end there. The feelings and attitudes of the older women, on whom the novels concentrate their attention, are so different that, though both experience the same kind of loss, the results are quite dissimilar. Colette takes the same plot, the same problem, and seems to be saying that the same experience can be lived in two very different ways, one resulting in emptiness, solitude, and sorrow, as with Léa, the other resulting in a much more positive outcome, as with the narrator of Break of Day.

Like the positive variant of the younger women, the positive type of the mature woman such as the narrator of Break of Day lives a simple life close to nature, surrounded by the sea, her garden, her animals, in a non-urban setting. Her friends are not ridiculous, catty old women as in Chéri, but healthy young men and women who tan on the beach and eat the simple foods grown in the country. Though she realizes that she is much older than they, that does not prevent her from enjoying their company, and she is much less self-conscious about her age than they are. Unlike Léa, she is not obsessed with growing older, and she accepts the signs of age with good grace: "He [her young friend, Vial] looked at my hand, which proclaims my age — in fact it looks several years older — . . . It is a good little hand, burnt dark brown, and the skin is getting rather loose round the joints and on the back." (Break of Day, 37).[6] Aging is seen as the natural process that it is, and accepted with ease and cheerfulness.

Neither does aging seem to be the threat to love and passion that it was for Léa — perhaps because the nature of the sensuality and sexuality in Break of Day is quite different from that in Chéri. In the latter novel, Léa's relationship with Chéri is unambiguous from the very beginning where Léa is shown in her bed, with Chéri nearby in his pyjamas. The focus of Léa's and Chéri's relationship is narrowly sexual, as had indeed been most of Léa's previous encounters with men. In *Break of Day* the relationship is never clearly defined, only hinted at; it is not so much sexual as sensual, consisting of a diffused sensuality that does not exclude friendship with the total person and is not completely dependent on physical attractiveness.

Moreover, unlike Léa, the narrator of *Break of Day* does not live by love alone: she has much to fill her day, such as other friends, gardening, and, chiefly, her writing. When she realizes that she would "incur ridicule" by continuing her attachment to Vial, especially since a young woman is in love with him, she accepts that, before Vial leaves her, she must leave him: ". . . it's a question of beginning something I have never done. So understand, Vial, that this is the first time since I was sixteen that I'm going to have to live — or even die — without my life or death depending on love. It's so extraordinary. You can't know. You have time." (*Break of Day*, 112)

She shares with Léa some feelings of regret and even anguish at the coming separation, not only from Vial, but from being in love. Her life style and her acceptance of herself mitigate powerfully the grief and possible loneliness, so that the novel is able to end on a very positive note of openness to the whole universe. There is another factor, however, in the narrator's generally positive experience of aging and loss of love, and that is the ever-present figure of her mother. Together with the other semi-autobiographical books *Sido* and *My Mother's House*, *Break of Day* portrays the most unambiguously positive subtype of the older woman. That Sido, the mother, represents "an ideal, a woman living in harmony with nature, and who has given, as she says, only a limited place to love" is unquestionable and has long been recognized by Colette and critics alike. In *Break of Day* Colette calls her "my model,"[7] with the difficulty that the word implies of ever being her equal.

As would be expected, Sido shares all of the characteristics that make up Colette's positive women, in particular the older women. Sido does not care for life in the big city which she visits very infrequently, preferring to stay in the provinces, close to her animals and plants which she understands better than anyone else in her family. Like the narrator of *Break of Day*, she accepts growing older, though the harsh limitations caused by her last illnesses and extreme old age are hard for her to bear because of her strong and independent nature. She does not suffer from loneliness. For a long time she had a devoted, passionate husband still as in love with her as when they were newly wed. Her life is full in many ways: full of love of children, spouse, neighbors, animals, because she is full of love for them, generously giving and sustaining life in all its forms.

Sido's superior knowledge and wisdom give her an added dimension compared to Colette's other women. This knowledge is rooted in her understanding of nature, but goes far beyond that. When she wanted to know the time, "she consulted, not her watch, but the height of the sun above the horizon, the tobacco flowers or the datura that drowse all day until the evening wakes them" (*Sido*, 170). This is only a small symbolic example of her insight into plants, animals, and people that reaches deep below the surface, as she gazes with "those deeply divining and completely undeceived grey eyes" (*My Mother's House*, 61). Not only does she seem to be gifted with "infallibility" with regard to understanding plants or forecasting the severity of the coming winter, but she also seems to possess some kind of special power: "I am sure she still is, with her head thrown back and her inspired look, summoning and gathering to her the sounds and whispers and omens that speed faithfully toward her down the eight paths of the Mariner's Chart" (*Sido*, 174).

It is noteworthy that it is only with respect to Sido that Colette brings any metaphysical or religious dimensions into her writings, a dimension which is hinted at by the use of such words as "divining" and "omens." Although Sido follows the rituals and precepts of her church quite exactly, at least in outward appearance, she does treat them somewhat lightly, seeing no objection to taking her dog to the service or to reading Corneille's plays hidden in her prayer book. This attitude cannot be explained only by her strong individualism; it stems from a deeper conviction that the divine is not to be found only, or primarily, in churches. When her daughter brings back from church a flower bouquet that has been blessed by lying on the altar, her mother "laughed her irreverent laugh, and looking at my bunch of flowers, which was bringing the may-bugs into the sitting-room right under the lamp, she said, 'Don't you think that it was already blessed before?'" (*Sido*, 165) Irreverent perhaps, but only with regard to religious observances. Relating another incident, Colette says significantly that "I found my mother beneath the tree ... her head turned towards the heavens in which she would allow human religions no place" (*Sido*, 165). Her superior understanding of nature and people does not come from some mysterious or magical power, but from her instincts, her intuitive participation in nature, her reverent respect towards the holiness of all life.

Sido is in fact portrayed as being so superior to all other human beings that even the narrator of *Break of Day*, herself a much more positive character than Léa, sometimes takes on a negative connotation. An excellent example of this ambiguity caused by Sido's presence is the letter that is quoted at length in *Break of Day* concerning Sido's discovery that a wool-seller, an "ugly little fat man .. plays a subtle game of chess." She continues: "We play and I think of what is imprisoned in that fat little man." The narrator reflects: "Flair, instinct for hidden treasure. Like a diviner she went straight to what shines only in secret" and she contrasts this with her own unsubtle behavior: "She would never have asked brutally: 'So, Vial, you've become attached to me?' Such words wither everything" (*Break of Day*, 131).

That Sido is idealized from childhood perceptions that persist into adult memory is quite possible; yet in the novels she appears not to be overly idealized or made into a totally unreal person. She remains a woman of flesh and blood with her own shortcomings and idiosyncrasies that make her a very concrete person on a par with other women in Colette's writings. Both an ideal figure and real person, Sido is the least ambiguous woman among the four types: her presence leads to some questions that can be raised about the constellation of women outlined in this essay.

The principal types of women that Colette focuses on are the young adolescent and the mature older woman: the inexperienced girl turning into a woman through love, and the older woman who is at the threshold of giving up youthful passion. One kind of woman is opening up to new experiences of adulthood, the other is leaving them behind. It seems that Colette is focusing of moments of passage, of change from childhood innocence into adult awareness and responsibility, or from the adult fullness of life into the renunciation of old age. Colette does not often dwell on the woman between the beginning and the end of life.

In short, with the possible and partial exception of Sido, the position of the principal kinds of women in Colette's writings is that of desire, of change, of wanting something that is not fully known, or of leaving something that is no longer rightfully possessed. It seems that the writer, then, is best able to portray womanhood in moments of lack, of movement toward or away from the essence of woman. Sido, as suggested earlier, is only a partial exception: although she enjoys plenitude of being, in harmony with herself and with the universe, she is so much an ideal that she too creates a desire, a lack in others who can never measure up to her. In the void of desire is born the work of the writer: truth, says Gérard Genette, "inhabits the work, as it inhabits every word, not by showing itself, but only in hiding."[8] Or, in the words of Paul de Man, the writer discovers "desire as a fundamental pattern of being that discards any possibility of satisfaction."[9] The essence of woman is unsayable, and constantly calls forth words to bespeak its ever-absent reality.

Notes

The works of Colette are quoted in the following translations. *Chéri* and *the Last of Chéri*, trans. M. Bentinck (New York: Farrar, Straus & Giroux, 1951). *The Cat*, trans. M. Bentinck, in *Short Novels of Colette* (New York: Dial Press, 1951). *The Ripening Seed*, trans. R. Senhouse (New York: Farrar, Straus & Giroux, 1955). *Break of Day*, trans. E. McLeod (New York: Noonday Press, 1966). *My Mother's House* and *Sido*, trans. U. V. Troubridge and E. McLeod (New York: Farrar, Straus & Giroux, 1953).

The French edition used is: *Oeuvres complètes* (Genève: Editions de Crémille [various dates]).

1. Some important works of criticism that deal with the concept of character and have been consulted for this study are: Roland Barthes, "Introduction à l'analyse structurale des récits," *Communications*, No. 8 (1966), 1–27; R. Barthes, *Sur Racine* (Paris: Seuil, 1963); W. Booth, *The Rhetoric of Fiction* (Chicago: University of Chicago Press, 1961, rpt. 1967); Jean Ricardou, *Pour une théorie du nouveau roman* (Paris: Seuil, 1971); W. K. Wimsatt and C. Brooks, *Literary Criticism: A Short History* (New York: Vintage, 1957).

2. Elaine Marks, *Colette* (New Brunswick, N.J.: Rutgers University Press, 1960), p. 58.

3. Yannick Resch points out in her *Corps féminin, corps textuel* (Paris: Klincksieck, 1973), p. 200: "Characterization in Colette is always indirect, ambiguous." I find it difficult to agree with another statement that she makes at the beginning of her excellent study, that there is *one* feminine archetype in Colette (pp. 16, 18).

4. Mieke Bal, *Complexité d'un roman populaire (ambiguïté dans La Chatte)* (Paris: La Pensée Universelle, 1974), pp. 60–67.

5. Jacques Lacan, "Le stade du miroir comme formateur de la fonction du Je," in *Ecrits* (Paris: Seuil, 1966), pp. 93–100; summarized in "The Mirror Phase," in *The Language of Psychoanalysis*, eds. J. Laplanche and J. B. Pontalis, trans. D. Nicholson-Smith (London: Hogarth Press, 1973), pp. 250–252.

6. I would like to emphasize at the outset of the discussion of *Break of Day* that I am studying it primarily as a literary text, and not as an autobiography, although it does have some autobiographical elements. As the writer of the introduction to the English translation says, "Thus we may conclude that *Break of Day* was a hypothesis which did not come true. . . What Colette had to say farewell to was just a part of herself, and just one aspect of love" (pp. viii–ix).

7. Madeleine Raaphorst-Rousseau, *Colette: sa vie et son art* (Paris: Nizet, 1964), p. 190. My translation.

8. G. Genette, *Figures II* (Paris: Seuil, 1969), p. 292. My translation.

9. P. de Man, *Blindness and Insight* (New York: Oxford University Press, 1971), p. 17.

8 The Test of Love and Nature: Colette and Lesbians

JACOB STOCKINGER

Colette received many honors in her lifetime, but it is only recently that she has at last taken her rightful place among the greatest writers of this century. In *Le XXe Siècle: 1895–1920* (Paris: Arthaud, 1975), P. O. Walzer is the first critic to treat Colette as one of the "grands maîtres" of early modern French literature, officially placing her in the company of Proust and Gide.

This revision of literary history is long overdue and can probably be best appreciated in the wake of two major contemporary events: the postwar development of new critical methods and the renewal of the women's movement. Together, these two currents of thought have shifted the emphasis from Colette the author to Colette the writer, bringing us a new awareness of the activity of her art and new perceptions of her themes and forms. Feminism and formalism have transformed a body of work that seemed marked by personality and spontaneity into a corpus that remains a virtuoso performance in narrative voicing and structure, characterizations, discourse and sign systems, and the portrayal of sex roles and sexual politics. What has emerged is nothing short of a new Colette.

There is an additional aspect of Colette's contemporaneity which, though less frequently commented on, is also illuminated by the legacy of recent times and events. The matter in question is the homosexual liberation movement that emerged in America, England, and Europe in the late 1960's and has continued for the past decade. Specifically, we are now in a position to have our understanding of Colette's achievement benefit from the current lesbian-feminist coalition. No longer must the lesbian Colette remain problematical, a minor idiosyncrasy that in the past proved embarrassing to even her finest critics. Minority sexuality, now openly discussed and analyzed, need no longer be regarded as an obstacle to her art but as one of its sources. The lesbian Colette must be viewed as further reason for securing her status as one of the early pioneers of modernity in the conjoining traditions of French literature and women's writing. More than previous criticism would have us believe, lesbianism constitutes a significant and integral strand of Colette's work. It is an especially vital part of Colette's legacy today and without it, any consideration of her writings remains incomplete, perhaps even distorted.

Historical and Biographical Contexts

Colette did not of course introduce the lesbian into French literature.[1] Stretching behind her were centuries of preparation evolving toward greater visibility and more nuanced treatment of lesbians. The eighteenth century was a particularly rich formative period for minority ethics which also saw the appearance of a lesbian organization with chapters throughout France.[2] Nineteenth-century literature abounds in lesbian figures and themes, most prominently in Balzac's *La Fille aux yeux d'or* (1835), Gautier's *Mademoiselle de Maupin* (1835), Baudelaire's *Les Fleurs du mal* (1857), Zola's *Nana* (1880) and *Pot-Bouille* (1883), De Maupassant's "La Femme de Paul" (1881), Verlaine's *Parallèlement* (1894), and Pierre Loüys' *Chansons de Bilitis* (1894) and *Aphrodite* (1896). But it was Colette who, even more than such secondary writers as Renée Vivien and Natalie Clifford-Barney, successfully wrested the lesbian tradition from male authors, gave it the female perspective it had lacked for so long, and pointed the way to the modern lesbian tradition as marked out by the works of Simone de Beauvoir, Christiane Rochefort, Violette Leduc, and Monique Wittig. Through a variety of works and over a period of forty years, Colette returned to lesbianism with a persistence and refinement that is too deliberate and consistent not to make her the indisputable pioneer in the literary legitimization of the lesbian.

Proust, Gide, and Colette all granted a major place in their work to homosexuality. If we are to believe the argument advanced by George Steiner,[3] this common trait is not just a coincidence of personal life entering into an author's work. It stems instead from the problem of finding a productive artistic marginality in the modern age, of satisfying the need for an ethical extraterritoriality that generates esthetic originality. Yet the homosexual linkage of the three authors occurs only on a general level. In many more ways Colette stood apart from her contemporaries, not only the host of second-rate popular authors[4] but also Proust and Gide. However implicitly or undidactically, her own work dissents from the distortion of the lesbian experience in Proust's *À la recherche du temps perdu* and posits a response to the misogyny of Gide in his apology, *Corydon*. The lesbian Colette represents, then, a break with both the past and the present.

The background for her own achievement was not only literary, however.

Although Colette officially eschewed the feminist movement that occured in France at the end of the nineteenth and beginning of the twentieth century, there can be little doubt today that such an atmosphere was conducive, however indirectly, to her ongoing project.[5] Though too frequently received as piecemeal, Colette's work, once completed, recalls the great holistic designs of Balzac's human comedy and Zola's social panorama, for it set down in near entirety the woman's condition. From its very inception, her work provided room for lesbian explorations. Historically, one can also discern an infleunce exerted on Colette by the sexual ambiguities and freedom of *fin-de-siècle* decadence and the "Paris-Lesbos" community in the early years of the century. Though only infrequently acknowledged by Colette, it is difficult in retrospect not to see as central the role that social realities played in the genesis of her work.

Colette's personal life is also not without relevance to her accomplishment as a lesbian writer. There is no need in this study to delve deeply into biographical details, for nearly all the standard critical works about Colette admit some degree of candor when it comes to her personal relationships. We do know that she had a long and close relationship with the Marquise de Belboeuf, known as Missy, after the breakup of her marriage to Willy; that she was close to a large number of homosexual men during her early years in Paris; and that she moved easily in lesbian circles, where she became friends with Renée Vivien and Natalie Clifford-Barney. Despite speculation by some critics, it seems unlikely that she ever had consummated affairs with Polaire or Marguerite Moreno. But neither is there reason to assume that she did not have lesbian relationships which remain undocumented, for she was surely at ease with the possibility.

The details of Colette's lesbian life remain clouded for the large part. Still, enough emerges to be of some use in considering her writings. A proper reading of Colette's life, for example, tends to discourage rather than provoke any sense of scandal. Sexuality was always integrated in her personal life, forming a continuum in which she moved freely from male to female lovers and back again. Though she realized and expressed the various lines of demarcation between male and female experiences, she never behaved as a separatist or imposed categorical restrictions on herself or others. Perhaps it is possible, then, to see in the acts and attitudes that mark her own life the reason why she never wrote an exclusively lesbian work but why she also consistently incorporated lesbianism into her writings.

To look at Colette's life is also to realize that its lesbian episodes remained unexceptional for her, never sparking a crisis or causing her to elaborate some system of justification. Her approach to her life and the people who figured in it was a relaxed denial of stereotypes and preconceptions coupled with the lack of a sociopolitical framework. As her works make clear, Colette had definite ideas about the meaning of the lesbian experience for the individual involved and for society. But in her research and her expression, she was not a systems builder. The realities of personal situations, either her own or others', sufficed, given the keenness of her own observing eye, as a source of information. Reality was always its own morality, whether in heterosexual or homosexual love. Again, this ease of personal viewpoint can be seen as a telling prelude to a body of works which avoids both the esthetic obliqueness of the Albertine transpositions in Proust and the defensive polemics of Gide. Colette's lesbian works ring with a casual verisimilitude and an informal forthrightness that was new in the literary treatment of homosexuality.

This is not to suggest that Colette accepted all that she experienced or observed. Her viewpoint is frequently ambivalent, at times even disapproving. But one of the lasting appeals of the lesbian Colette is that she exhibits neither compensatory pride nor condemnatory guilt. Without borrowing concepts and terminology from the social sciences, Colette is nonetheless one of the makers of the modern age by forging a new path for the entry of lesbians into literature. Even more than in her life, of course, it is in her works where lesbian knowledge and drama reside. It is there where, narratively rather than argumentatively, Colette quietly but progressively advanced our understanding of lesbianism by violating and reworking history, and by bringing her consummate artistry to bear on revealing love between women openly and truthfully not as deviance but variance.

The Claudine Novels

Colette's first works, the series of Claudine novels that were written between 1900 and 1907, have been the source of two commonplaces of Colette criticism with which the present study takes issue. The first is that the novels are largely immature apprenticeships served by Colette under the oppressive guidance of Willy, that it is only after the Claudine novels that we begin to see Colette writing as her own person. From a number of important perspectives — description and dialogue, sex roles, theatricality of characterizations, the issues of female identity and independence — the Claudine novels increasingly demonstrate the very qualities that would mark Colette's maturity. For this reason, the novels merit closer readings than they have generally received.

The second commonplace, closely tied to the first, concerns the lesbian moments in the Claudine series. Virtually every major study of Colette asserts that lesbianism was inserted by Colette at the behest of Willy in order to assure their scandalousness and, therefore, their commercial success. To some degree and for several reasons, this is no doubt true. Willy was surely a masterful opportunist who could manipulate and exploit public relations. And history encouraged him, for female eroticism has traditionally been more voyeuristically exploited for profit than male sexuality. Yet to examine the Claudine series is to come away with the impression that it was precisely through the lesbian aspects of the novels that Colette began to annex her work from Willy and to stamp both their themes and their formal features as her own. To penetrate behind whatever melodrama and immaturity can be found in the works is to glimpse the later Colette clearly in the making.

From her first work, *Claudine à l'école* (1900), Colette proved herself to be the century's first great demystifier of female eroticism. Her demystification was, moveover, doubly transgressive insofar as it involved adolescence and lesbianism, an even more volatile combination than the adolescent male-female relations that would generate enough scandal to cause the serialization of *Le Blé en herbe* (1926) to be suspended. Yet an appreciation of the achievement represented by the first Claudine novel is somewhat deflected by the work's appearances.

There is much that is traditional in the surface of the work. To the degree that adolescent sexuality had previously been treated in French literature, it was often within a pedagogical setting, as is the case in Diderot's *La Religieuse* and Rousseau's *Confessions*. Certainly the lesbian attraction between Claudine and others, first the schoolmistress Aimée and then the student-peer Luce, seems to fall squarely within that tradition.

But Colette reworks the traditional components of her tale in two ways. First, there is no guilt attached to the young Claudine's sexual desires, whether for men or women. Long before Freud's concept of polymorphous perversity gained currency, Colette shows her fifteen-year-old narrator-protagonist with no shame but only a clearheaded sense of the awkwardness of attaining what she wants. In short, she makes Claudine a self-conscious adolescent, a forerunner of her older women who also never cease to question both the source and the consummation of their desires from a purely behavioral and personal, rather than moral and social, point of view.

Coupled with this adolescent consciousness of lesbian eroticism is a role inversion which represents an even more radical departure from the traditional treatment of teenage homosexuality. Often cast as victims of adult mentors who use their influence to coerce their young disciples into sexual initiation, young people and especially girls have generally been portrayed as the misgiving recipients rather than initiators of sexual attentions. In the social mythology, young women had to come of age and desire with a certain purity intact and protected. Colette inverts this model, however. In *Claudine à l'école*, the would-be seducer is the student, not the teacher. It is the older woman Aimée, not the younger Claudine, who is marked by "a need for affection" and "repressed gestures."[6] Claudine's attraction to Aimée remains admiring and unconsummated, but it is very far from being latent in the usual meaning of the term:

> Little Mademoiselle Lanthenay, your supple body seeks and
> demands an unknown satisfaction. If you were not an assistant mis-

> tress at Montigny you might be . . . I'd rather not say what. But how I
> like listening to you and looking at you — you who are four years older
> than I am and yet make me feel every single moment like your elder
> sister! (p. 7)

Though its original purpose might well have been to shock readers, the erotic
consciousness that Colette instills in Claudine survives beyond its intent to
stand as a landmark in the literary portrait of young women, one not to be
rivaled or surpassed until fifty years later with Violette Leduc's portrayal of
adolescent girls in *La Bâtarde* (1964) and *Thérèse et Isabelle* (written in 1955
but not published until 1966).

Other lesbian moments in the same work run along more traditional lines,
with peer relationships developing between Mlle Aimée and Mlle Sergent
and between Claudine and Luce. Still, it is in keeping with the lines of
development of the later Colette that the young Claudine, like the more adult
reader, knows that such affairs are dictated by circumstances, by age and
power relations. Whether it is a question of consummating or refusing desire,
the consciousness of Claudine anticipates Colette's later women, such as
Renée in *La Vagabonde* and the "Colette" of *La Naissance du jour*, who are at
odds with love.

With *Claudine à Paris* (1901), the narrative focus shifts from individual
lesbian relationships to male homosexuality, specifically to the schoolboy
relationship between Marcel, Claudine's cousin and future stepson, and
Charlie Gonzalez. Once again, Colette returns to the school-bound world of
young people to violate society's normative view of adolescence. This time she
uses the two couples, Claudine-Luce and Marcel-Charlie, to establish an
alliance. It is a coalition that grows out of curiosity, not political commitment,
an affiliation of young people who accept each other's deviance and enthusias-
tically want to learn its lessons, even when their own families and society do
not. It is revealing that the only condemnation Claudine can make of her
cousin's relationship, aside from the obstacle it represents to her own attraction to Marcel, concerns the exaggerated feelings and pretentiousness of
Charlie's letter to Marcel. Her criticism is thoroughly in keeping with
Claudine's distate for Parisian cosmopolitanism and suggests early on that
"unnatural" love can be both natural and unnatural, depending not on moral
conventions but on the authenticity of the emotions involved and the measured genuineness of expression that such emotions find. On both these
counts, the shared interests of homosexual women and men and the critique of
artificiality, the novel foreshadows Colette's later work. It is especially in *Le
Pur et l'impur* that she will again take up and expand the themes of the
similarities and contrasts between homosexual men and lesbians and of the
perverted and natural forms of sexual variance.

It seems both ironic and appropriate that Claudine's lesbianism finds its most overt expression in *Claudine en ménage* (1902) where she enters adulthood as a married woman. Attracted to the stunningly beautiful Rézi, Claudine manages to consummate the affair with the help of her husband Renaud, who procures a private apartment for the two women so that a disastrous confrontation with Rézi's husband can be avoided. It is an event that anticipates other works by Colette and later writers in several ways.

The desperate sides of Claudine's and especially Rézi's situation as dependent wives posit an implicit sociopolitical critique of the powerlessness and lack of sovereignty — spatial, temporal, emotional, and financial — of women. The affair looks forward to Beauvoir's comments about the importance of lesbian attachments as a possible resolution to the sex-role inequality and alterity that marks the woman's situation in a patriarchal social order. Even in the details of the Claudine-Rézi match, the novel seems an early version of the lesbian alliance of bourgeois housewives in Christiane Rochefort's *Les Stances à Sophie*. The question of female independence, whether couched in heterosexual or lesbian terms, haunts Colette's complete works.

It is also indicative of what is to come in the later Colette that she chooses to emphasize not any compensatory or separatist aspect of the affair, but its complementarity: "Renaud, Rézi, they are both necessary to me, and there is no question of choosing between them" (p. 478). Later, of course, Claudine does choose in favor of Renaud, not out of moral renunciation of lesbian love but out of a sense of personal honor and ethics in her dealing with her husband. The unhappiness of being trapped in the intricacies of two relationships will be picked up in the last Claudine novels and will enter time and again in Colette's later works. Here, as later, there seems too often to be little choice between either a multiplicity of loves which work at cross-purposes or a total abstention from romantic entanglements. Early in her work, and through lesbian relationships, Colette demonstrates how difficult it is to limit or discipline our sensual interaction with the human world, just as it is with the natural world.

The Rézi episode represents an evolution in Colette's lesbianism in another way. No small part of its seriousness is conveyed, beyond events, characters, and narrative asides, by the style in which it is cast. Just as a certain innocence of romance has disappeared, most traces of girlish flippancy have gone. And it is this stylistic shift which, along with the success and visibility of the lesbian subject matter, announces that the novel now belongs more to Colette's purposes than to Willy's. Although actual sex acts would never become explicit in the hard-core sense in Colette, the sensuality of descriptions and narrative language becomes, together with the introduction of details which border on explicitness, the logical outcome of the erotic consciousness that has marked Claudine from the start:

> I roused myself to life again by straining close to the warm body that adapted itself to mine and flexed when I flexed; the beloved body, so fleshy in its tapering slimness that nowhere could I feel the resisting skeleton beneath. ... In the bright bedroom, where Rézi's Iris and Claudine's harsh sweet Chypre mingle in the air, in the great bed that is fragrant with our two bodies, I avenge myself for many a hidden, bleeding wound. ... Afterwards, curled up against me in an attitude blessedly familiar now, Rézi talks and questions me. She is irritated by the brevity and simplicity of my answers, avid to know more, incredulous when I assure her of my former virtue and the novelty of this madness of mine. (pp. 471, 476)

These passages, along with many others, are serious, not teasing, in their sensuousness of act and word. There can be little doubt that Colette has, even at this early stage, launched her work on the path of serious investigation of love in which lesbian relations are an integral part, that she has left behind Willy's exploitative designs for her own intense explorations of love between women.

Although the climax of overt lesbianism in the Claudine series occurs in the third volume, all of its lessons and characteristics pass into the sequel, *Claudine s'en va* (1903). One of the major differences is that this volume is narrated by Annie, Claudine's friend who must come to terms with being abandoned by her husband. The attraction between the two women is mutual, though each has a reason for refraining from her impulses. Annie, torn by what she has experienced heterosexually, is mistrustful of the novelty and perhaps manipulations of a lesbian affair. Claudine, for her part, has sworn loyalty to her husband in the wake of her betrayal at the hands of Rézi, who had an affair with Renaud.

Yet the denials of lesbianism are circumstantial. It is paramount to realize that it is only individual actions which appear threatening and are therefore called into question. The lesbian sensibility itself survives intact, bearing all the potential for satisfaction and fulfillment that it first carried in the previous work before Rézi's treachery. In her farewell letter to Annie, for example, Claudine feels called upon to admit her desires and their potential course:

> You are going away, and your flight and your letter are like a reproach to me. How much I regret you, Annie, who smells like a rose! You mustn't be angry with me for that. I am only a poor brute who loves beauty and weakness and trust and when a little spirit like yours leans on mine, when a mouth yearns, like yours, towards mine, I find it very hard to understand why I must not embellish both the one and the other with a kiss. I tell you I still don't properly understand the reason, although it has been explained to me. ... I kiss, from

the eyelashes to the chin, your whole face that has the tapering shape and almost the exact colour of a ripe filbert. From so far away, kisses lose their poison and, for a minute, I can pursue our dream in the Margravine's garden — without remorse. (pp. 616–617)

The dream in the garden, of consummated affection between Claudine and Annie, remains subsumed by other women's issues — marriage, freedom, identity, and other problematics that will recur throughout the later Colette — or else is deflected, especially in the final *Claudine* volume, *La Retraite sentimentale* (1907), by the complicated intrigue with Marcel and Annie or by Claudine's complete withdrawal from human affairs. For all its suggestive possibilities, the dream stands unfulfilled.

Jeannette Foster is largely correct when she asserts that "Taken together, the five *Claudine* novels present a complete sexual philosophy."[7] That philosophy is marked by a tolerance of all varieties of love, with personal preference given to a resolute heterosexual monogamy that is arrived at only through a range of other experiences. And if there were no other works after the *Claudine* novels, Foster would also be correct in her remark that "Lesbian attractions are legitimate but they belong to youth."[8] For that is indeed the lesson to which Claudine's progress in love seems to point. But the rest of Colette's work reverses that judgment by taking the lesbian points of departure of these first novels and developing them into integral parts of a mature art of loving.

Reprises

Far from abandoning the theme of lesbianism with the end of the *Claudine* series and her breaking away from Willy's influence, Colette continued to pursue and extend her examination of the issue through a variety of later works.

One critic finds *Les Vrilles de la vigne* (1908) to constitute the work of passage by which Colette crossed over into an art of her own.[9] The associative short pieces, a blend of prose and poetry in which a seemingly autobiographical coincidence takes place among narrator, observer, and character, seem clearly to lead to the mature Colette. Thematically, they are also vintage writings by Colette, returning again and again to the themes of maternity, childhood, nature, and love. It is, then, significant that this formative work also discards the immaturity that seemed to enshroud lesbian love in the *Claudine* novels in order to situate minority sexuality within not only the given interests of Colette but also the adult love between women.

In "Jour gris," "Le Dernier Feu," and "Nuit blanche," the recollecting narrator, her own female identity firmly established, addresses her monologues to an anonymous but undeniably female lover. The first distinction of the lesbianism in the work is the seriousness of its treatment. That is, all trace of gratuitous scandalousness has vanished, as has any suggestion of immaturity. The narrator situates her lesbian love squarely within the realm of the adult woman, bringing it into an informative harmony rather than contrast with the other themes such as maternity, childhood, and the melancholy that accompanies the end of love's innocence. Perhaps for this reason, it is difficult not to see the narrator's apostrophes as words written by Colette and addressed to Missy, the woman with whom Colette lived after the separation from Willy and during the composition of *Les Vrilles de la vigne*. Yet it would be a mistaken reading to interpret the work only on the biographical plane. The very impersonality bespeaks the importance of lesbianism outside of purely personal referents, for it is, to use the controlling metaphor of the work itself, just another of the entrapping tendrils of love's vine that impels the nightingale-narrator to song.

Through her techniques for bringing the reader to feel a personal contact in an essentially impersonal narration, Colette demonstrates surprising subtlety even in this beginning work. She avoids, for example, the usual gender signifiers of names in favor of more nuanced markers such as descriptive details and especially adjectives with the feminine ending to convey the persons involved. The work shows, then, not just a thematic evolution in Colette's treatment of lesbianism but also a stylistic one. For the sexuality in question is largely discursive, established through the qualifiers of the "*je*" and "*tu*" between which the poetic meditations are generated. Yet these techniques of indirection are not camouflage designed to conceal and transform the homosexual reality. Their purpose, in keeping with the overall scheme of the work, is to poeticize, to find a textual ambiguity that corresponds to the androgyny and "mental hermaphrodism" of which Colette is so fond. Colette was not protective or fearful when it came to lesbianism, as her other less poetic or dreamy prose narratives make clear.

La Vagabonde (1911) is primarily a story of Renée Néré's coping with the past failures of love and marriage and with the need to choose between solitude or male companionship, both of which promise certain difficulties. The story is cast within a set of heterosexual relationships between Renée, Max, Brague, Taillandy, and Hamond. Renée herself is a vagabond or wanderer, a music-hall artist who lives within concentric exiles as a divorced woman, a working woman, a professional *déclassée*, and a writer. The mythical dimension of the tale taken as an example of the woman's situation centers understandably on her, with few references to other women. Yet there are two brief moments in the latter part of the work where the theme of relations between women, especially lesbian relationships, is convincingly inserted as another measure of the marginality of women within a patriarchal social order and of their estrangement from even the most intimate of male companions.

While on tour, Renée writes to Max about her reunion with Amalia Barrally, a fellow vagabond and music-hall wanderer. Her remarks are casual, expressing a fondness of Amalia and the values she represents:

> What I appreciate in her, in addition to her gaiety which is proof
> against poverty, is her protective nature, that skill in looking after
> people, a delicate motherliness in her gestures which you find in
> women who have sincerely and passionately loved women; it confers
> on them an indefinable attraction which you men will never per-
> ceive.[10]

Renée's remarks are not stridently separatist, just a recognition of where
female reality leaves male reality behind. Again the theme of the mother
appears — Sido is never far in the background — this time as another tie which
creates the alliance between women that men, threatened by female collectivity, would thwart.

At no time does Renée suggest that she herself has experienced this kind of
love. But just her sympathetic, perhaps even admiring approval, is sufficient
to upset her would-be lover Max, who berates Amalia in his return letter:

> Unluckily he recalls from it that my comrade Amalia Barally was not a
> lover of men and, like the "normal" and "well-balanced" being that he
> is, he has not failed to cast a bit of a slur on my old friend, by poking
> fun at her, and to vilify something that he does not understand. What
> would be the good of explaining to him? Two women enlaced will
> never be for him anything but a depraved couple, he will never see in
> them the melancholy and touching image of two weak creatures who
> have perhaps sought shelter in each other's arms, there to sleep and
> weep, safe from man who is so often cruel, and there to taste, better
> than any pleasure, the bitter happiness of feeling themselves akin,
> frail and forgotten. (p. 188)

The lesbian's story is integral to the story of female individuation, and more
than Max's disapproval specifically of Amalia, it is his prescriptive sense of
normality which estranges Renée from him. For in the end, he is not just
condemning lesbians but also the special ties between women that offer the
most viable hope of sisterhood. Revealing too is Colette's use of melancholy
not to suggest a compromised or compensatory feeling that arises from lesbian
love itself, but a sadness imposed by an oppressively uncomprehending and
unappreciative social context. What is reprehensible is not the touching
melancholy or bitter happiness of the lesbian, but the phallic viewpoint which
distorts and condemns an essentially nurturing behavior as abnormal and
immoral. Colette's words and Renée's decision to part with Max ring clear with
the pertinence of this minor lesbian episode to the overall problematic of
female identity choices that forms the core of *La Vagabonde*.

This same sense of naturalness carries over in explicitly lesbian terms in the short story "Habitude," published in the collection *La Femme cachée* (1924). A brief sketch running a little over three pages, the vignette is a post-mortem of a lesbian relationship that has come undone: "They broke up in the same way as they had become close, without knowing why."[11] The first paragraph is an important exposition, especially for what it leaves out. At no point is the affair of Jeannine and Andrée singled out as exceptional simply because it is lesbian. Rather, the narrator accepts the same-sex love affair as a given which needs no comment. Furthermore, the narrator attributes the decline of the affair not to any inherent instability of minority love, but to the same kinds of dynamics that cause heterosexual relationships to fail. One cause is reputed to be Jeannine's indiscretions not about the lesbian nature of her affair with Andrée but about revealing too casually Andrée's embarrassing real name, "Symphorienne"; another version holds that Andrée's abuse of her greater age and the sex roles of dominant and passive that begin to infiltrate the couple's interaction both bring the affair to its end. Moreover, the break seems mutually agreeable and calm in its effects. When a chance encounter takes place, the nostalgia and regret that Jeannine feels centers not on the specifics of Andrée or their relationship, but rather on the companionship and comforting habits that their affair brought. The end of lesbian love proves to be no different from the end of heterosexual love, for it dwells on the loss of security and solidarity, now replaced by solitude. Though hardly a dramatic statement on the part of Colette, it is nonetheless daring to assert that, at least insofar as the participating individuals are concerned, there is little to distinguish the coming and ending of lesbian love from its heterosexual counterpart. It is like all love, natural and unconscious to the lovers involved.

The theme of the fraternity of wanderers and vagabonds is returned to momentarily in *La Fin de Chéri* (1926). Once again, lesbianism evokes a sense of solidarity and collectivity. This time, however, in contrast to *La Vagabonde*, it is a question of a male-female alliance. One of the few respites Chéri finds in his tormented exile from love is in the company of the older woman Camille, a lesbian:

> It astonished him to find her worthy of respect because she was plain and simple, and when he was alone in her company for the first time and far away from town-life, it began to dawn on him that a woman burdened with some monstrous sexual deformity needs must possess a certain bravura and something of the dignified courage of the condemned.[12]

Chéri's observation is couched in terms that are hardly just or flattering to Camille, who is herself accused of being unkind because of "frustrated femininity."

Yet the passage has a certain touching quality, however attenuated by particulars. Colette seems to be suggesting that there is something to be found in common between a man who has been forced to abandon total sovereignty and so become vulnerable and a woman who has had to overcome the social constraints placed on her existence. This shared marginality of roles which are modified without being wholly abandoned appears all the more likely given the appeal of androgyny to Colette; she often stated her preference for men who develop a weakness that opens them up to nurturing and being nurtured, and for women who develop a strength and resilience in the social and personal spheres. This also helps to explain Colette's fascination with masks and theatrical behavior, usually in the form of tranvestism and cross-dressing. For her, roles had to be altered, not simply reversed and adopted. She could not altogether give up thinking in terms of masculine and feminine — in part because of her personal preferences and in part because of sociohistorical circumstances — a trait for which more contemporary lesbians-feminists such as Jane Rule in *Lesbian Images* can easily reproach her. Hers is a liberal rather than radical critique of sex roles, as this passage shows, but it was not without daring in its time and pertinence to our own.

So far we have seen that Colette returns to lesbianism usually on a personal plane. Any macrocosmic meaning must be interpreted from *Les Vrilles de la vigne, La Vagabonde, La Fin de Chéri,* and "Habitude." With the novella "Mon amie Valentine," however, Colette shifts her discussion to the social plane.[13] Using the episodic exchanges between herself and a disagreeing friend as a vehicle for communicating her own views on motherhood, marriage, female fashion, and countryside existence, Colette inserts a section which deals with a lesbian dinner club and bar. Reproached by Valentine for being seen frequently at the bar run by Sémiramis, the narrator defends the bar, its notorious lesbian owner, and the clientele of "young men with long hair and women with short hair."[14]

At first her defense is couched in largely impersonal terms, with Colette explaining the realities of the bar in order to expose Valentine's tales as inaccurate rumors. The bar, she remarks, provides a relaxed atmosphere where homosexual men can, in the company of accepting equals, surrender up the stereotypical behavior that marks them in a heterosexual social setting:

> Yes, you'll find a large number of young men who aren't the slightest bit interested in women. At dinner-time they feel at home there, they're resting. They're gathering strength for supper. They don't need to waggle their hips, call out shrilly, wave handkerchiefs moistened with ether.... (p. 116)

Finding such male companions "nice" and "unaffected" (p. 117), Colette tries to convey the ambiance of the bar with a certain objective detachment.

Finding that she has sustained Valentine's interest, Colette then finally brings herself into the discussion. It is significant, moreover, that she begins to defend this social institution in personal terms when she shifts the topic from homosexual men to lesbians. "I've the courage to tell you now that I find pleasure, while I'm having dinner at Sémiramis's place, in looking at women in each other's arms, waltzing well" (p. 119). Colette uses her sensuous descriptions of the women to convey and reinforce her own approval and attraction, and this homosexual episode of the novella ends ironically with her conventional interlocutor agreeing to meet Colette later that same night at Sémiramis's bar. It can hardly be called a conversion, but both her rational explanations of homosexuality as a social phenomenon, with codes and institutions of its own, and her personal admissions make for a convincing defense. She has found the lesbian part of "la femme cachée," the hidden or suppressed part of a woman's identity that serves as a prefatory controlling metaphor for the collection of vignettes collected under that same title. In that respect, the structural and thematic insertion of lesbianism in "Mon amie Valentine" corresponds to the psychological and sociological place that Colette assigns to it.

Compared to some of the Claudine episodes or to *Le Pur et l'impur,* the lesbian moments in these various works can hardly be called glaring, which is perhaps one reason why they have gone relatively unnoticed and undeveloped by critics. Yet even if they are not among the most noteworthy moments in Colette's corpus, they are revealing all the same. They show that Colette's interest in lesbianism passed with little interruption from her early to her mature works, and that her return to the subject transcended Willy's influence. They also prove that Colette's vision of lesbianism, whether on a personal or social plane, is always integrative, that treating it divorced from other women's issues remained for her as much a distortion as omitting it altogether. Finally, these works demonstrate both a thematic and a stylistic evolution, a progress in ethical stance and esthetic structure that would culminate in the work which Colette herself thought might one day be considered her masterpiece — *Le Pur et l'impur.*

Le Pur et l'impur

First appearing as *Ces Plaisirs* in 1932, *Le Pur et l'impur* (1941) is probably the one work which stands to benefit most from the Colette revival, for it previously proved to be Colette's most awkward and resistant text. It is a text in turmoil, a difficult work filled with complexities in narrative structure and discourse and with the endless subtleties, ambiguities, and even contradictions of its many anecdotes. Yet no small part of its contemporary importance is tied to its apparent impenetrability, for it stands as proof that Colette is no simple confessional writer who entertains her readers but never troubles them. *Le Pur et l'impur* is perhaps the clearest evidence that Colette is not just a story teller but a story maker. Advocates and adversaries alike find it nearly impossible to make unqualified statements about the work, to stand in complete agreement or disagreement with its treatment of minority sexuality.

The mixed narrative voicing, the absence of nature, the episodic discontinuities, the juxtapositioning of characters and narrative asides — for these and other reasons, *Le Pur et l'impur* seems, when compared to Colette's other writings, a curious work which stands apart from the mainstream of her career. For many readers, the oddity of the work is heightened by the full attention that Colette gives to homosexuality. But Colette's previous treatment of this same theme suggests that, at least in this respect, *Le Pur et l'impur* is not so much a radical departure as a radical consolidation. Its thematic distinction — not to be confused with its narrative and stylistic innovations — lies not in breaking new ground but rather in carrying to their logical outcome, in a form that is too visible and unequivocating to be dismissed as unimportant or secondary, the earlier strands of lesbianism in Colette. In *Le Pur et l'impur* the lesbian Colette does not allow herself to be overlooked or underrated.

The carry-overs in *Le Pur et l'impur* are evident. Although Colette significantly shifts her emphasis, giving lesbianism the dual privileges of forming the bulk and core of the work, the text is still integral in its design. Male homosexuals receive major narrative attention and, in one case, full narrative approval. We enter the text and the theme of purity and impurity, moreover, through the tale of Charlotte and her well-intended illusions and through a consideration of Don Juan as a representative male imperialist of pleasure. Finally, comparisons between homosexual and heterosexual bonding are either overt or never far removed from the narrator's mind and words.

Another of Colette's continuing interests centers on the inversion of sex roles and the abolition of what are, for her, the distinctive features of female identity. It is this worry which inspires her misgivings about mannish women and "unisexuality," voiced most vociferously through Amalia X's strong remarks about "pseudo-men," and which generates her disapproval of the oppressive absorption or fusion of two women who lose their individuality to the tyrannical "we" such as in the case of the "Ladies of Llangollen."

A third abiding concern for Colette is the issue of nurturing, the heritage of Sido and the decisive female virtue, that she can or cannot discern in various couples. It is just this trait which endears the narrator Colette to the old poet-scholar who makes a harvesting trek to Touraine with his younger male lover. And it is also this trait which, when it collides with the denial of femininity, as in the case of La Chevalière, creates ambivalence on the part of the narrator and confusion for readers who want clear-cut value judgments from her.

The impact of these and other legacies from Colette's earlier treatments of lesbianism is, however, enhanced by two aspects of *Le Pur et l'impur* which merit special attention. The first is Colette's consciousness of her topic and text; the second, the work's implicit metapsychological and sociological dimensions.

For all its maxims, *Le Pur et l'impur* is not a thesis novel. Its organization is more dramatic than didactic. Yet if Colette is not truly systematic in her stance as a *moraliste,* neither is she simply intuitive. She casts her thoughts in a typically informal and undogmatic form, but there can be no doubt about the consciousness she has both of the process of writing and of the context of her subject matter or purpose: "I hope to add my personal contribution to the sum of our knowledge of the senses. . . . I am betraying a tolerance that some will condemn as strange. . . . I find it in me to see in homosexuality a kind of legitimacy and to acknowledge its eternal character."[15] These are not the statements of someone who simply stumbled on the issue of minority sexuality and then incorporated it, whether casually or exploitatively, in her writings. They demonstrate Colette's serious intent to legitimize people and behavior which were severely stigmatized by the social standards of her time.

It is easy to read the work as culminating in a certain failure when Colette admits, "The word 'pure' has never revealed an intelligible meaning to me" (p. 175). But Colette's conceptions, however vague, of purity and impurity are wholly idiosyncratic and have little to do with the normative morality of society. It is wrong, then, to link the purity of the characters and behavior in *Le Pur et l'impur* with their legitimacy. Whether pure or impure, each has a right to exist free from the strictures of prescriptions and condemnations.

But Colette adds more than personal acceptance as her contribution to an inquiry into homosexuality and lesbianism. Even though her remarks hardly constitute a rigorous critique of minority sexuality, they do cohere and often seem to prefigure, though by no means completely, much of the recent research into homosexuality and many of the contemporary attitudes of lesbians and feminists. Moreover, conscious as she is of her purpose, Colette is always the literary crafter, working her messages into the very fiber of the text.

Colette's itinerary of characters, for example, is a highly varied one, including the aristocratic and socially engaged but sensually removed La Chevalière, the decadent and self-destructive poet Renée Vivien, the cynical and earthy actress Amalia X, and the pastoral and quietly passionate ladies of Llangollen. All of these women live out their lesbianism in different ways; and more than just providing Colette with the kind of colorful characters she always cherishes, they suggest the continuum and variety of lesbians when viewed as a social class.

Drawing her lessons from experience, her own and others', Colette clearly sees how rigid and reductive stereotypes can be. The contrast of her characters is not simply entertaining or the result of Colette's own rich life which crossed all kinds of economic, social, and psychological divisions. Without receiving systematic formulation, such contrast anticipates many of the points that

Simone de Beauvoir would make about the lesbian in *The Second Sex*, a work which seeks to establish the theoretical underpinnings of the experiential truths we find in Colette. By the end of *Le Pur et l'impur*, it is difficult not to perceive a lesson that emerges from the work as a whole, a lesson which Beauvoir summarizes when she remarks:

> The association of two women, like that of a man and a woman, assumes many different forms; it may be based upon sentiment, material interest, or habit; it may be conjugal or romantic; it has room for sadism, masochism, generosity, fidelity, devotion, capriciousness, egotism, betrayal.... The truth is that homosexuality is no more a perversion deliberately indulged in than it is a curse of fate. It is an attitude *chosen in a certain situation* — that is, at once motivated and freely adopted.... Like all human behavior, homosexuality leads to make-believe, disequilibrium, frustration, lies, or, on the contrary, it becomes the source of rewarding experiences, in accordance with its manner of expression in actual living — whether in bad faith, laziness and falsity, or in lucidity, generosity, and freedom.[16]

Indeed, Colette's elusive use of purity and impurity may even be seen as an early version of situation ethics and moral relativism which is tied not only to a sense of motherliness, but also to Beauvoir's use of authenticity and similar existentialist vocabulary.

Of course Beauvoir's critique is largely philosophical and political. But further sociological and psychological research, especially that of Kinsey and his followers, has confirmed the observations of Colette and the assertions of Beauvoir. There simply exists no method or need for determining the cause of lesbianism or predicting the behavior of individual lesbians. The lesbian subculture is heterogeneous and pluralistic, defying strict categorization. In her own narrative fashion, Colette shatters stereotypical thinking about homosexuality and lesbianism quite a while before serious sociological research provided more objective ground for doing so. To be sure, today's readers may find the success of Colette's project somewhat compromised by her ideas about purity and impurity and by her reluctance to accept certain forms of female virility. But her achievement stands on its own merit and must be recognized: social clichés give way in Colette to individual notions; and determinism, whether in the form of sin or illness, yields to choice and preference. On both counts, Colette advanced minority sexuality toward its modern reassessment.

Although she was integrationist rather than separatist in her viewpoint, Colette also anticipates the current lesbian-feminist coalition. Viewing women as more tolerant of personal difference, she sees that the disparity between homosexual and heterosexual men is much greater than that between lesbians and heterosexual women. For that reason she would probably concur with Beauvoir's remark that "it is erroneous to distinguish sharply between the homosexual and heterosexual woman."[17] Colette realizes, moreover, that the alternative and sheltering sovereignty of lesbian alliances is valuable for what it cultivates in the lesbian as a woman more than as a lesbian. It may involve female eroticism, a personal and physical sovereignty of sexual fulfillment: "A woman finds pleasure in carressing a body whose secrets she knows, her own body giving her the clue to its preferences" (p. 111); or it may involve female society and female language, such as the sequestered cellar in Montmartre where La Chevalière's circle gathers and where "in the admirable quickness of their half-spoken language . . . every message from woman to woman became clear and overwhelming, restricted to a small but infallible number of signs" (p. 78). For Colette, lesbianism is clearly a privileged path to discovering the realities of womanhood. Her sense of a lesbian-feminist coalition is not yet political, except implicitly, but it is physical, psychological, social, and linguistic. In Colette's world, once lesbians escape both male domination and masculine masquerading, a welcome confrontation with femaleness inevitably occurs. Her lesbians are not exiles from the woman's condition but insiders who carry crucial lessons for their sisters.

One of the most remarkable points at which Colette's consciousness of her topic and text converges with the implicit sociological dimensions of her work is her critique of Proust. Praising Proust as an author whose own perspective as a male homosexual generates "the dazzling truth that guides us through Sodom" (p. 131), she reproaches him for imposing his vision of male reality onto female reality and for mistakenly portraying a lesbian Gomorrah as possessing the same kind of powerful institutional sovereignty that men hold in a phallic and patriarchal social order:

> This is because, with all due deference to the imagination or the error of Marcel Proust, there is no such thing as Gomorrah. Puberty, boarding school, solitude, prisons, aberrations, snobbishness — they are all seedbeds, but too shallow to engender and sustain a vice that could attract a great number or become an established thing that would gain the indispensible solidarity of its votaries. Intact, enormous, eternal, Sodom looks down from its heights upon its puny counterfeit. (pp. 131–132)

Colette's implication is clear: homosexuality is a comparatively weak tie between the sexes. The closer bonds involve majority sexual politics, with homosexual men related to a male power structure and lesbians to the general condition of women. It is this same argument which Beauvoir will advance within the framework of alterity in *The Second Sex*, which Rochefort will give fictional form in *Les Stances à Sophie*, and which has come to form one of the working assumptions of the contemporary women's movement.

Colette singles out Proust for criticism, but her remarks can easily be read as a larger indictment of the way that lesbianism and the woman's situation in general have traditionally been perceived and passed on by men. Avoiding strident and prescriptive polemics, Colette is nonetheless calling for an end to the distortions that have arisen because women have not had their own say about themselves. Colette herself is too modest, perhaps too artistically and rhetorically calculating to announce such an ambition for her own work. But with a momentum that builds throughout her career, Colette's writings securely stake out her claim as one of the first and still most commanding tellers of the woman's tale.

As Colette herself demonstrated from the early *Claudine* novels to *Le Pur et l'impur*, the lesbian's story is a central, not peripheral, part of that tale. Colette openly and frequently admitted her preoccupation with love and nature. It would be hard to name two themes more traditionally evocative of "feminine writing," and there can be little doubt they helped to attract her early critics and to make her a classic in her own time. But Colette had, perhaps unwittingly but possibly consciously, set herself a test which allowed her to transcend the limitations of tradition. Historically, minority sexuality is the extreme point at which concepts of love and nature come into conflict. For Colette, however, such a conjunction posed no dilemma. It became, on the contrary, a productive source of her progress both as woman and writer. Over a period of nearly fifty years, and through a wide variety of themes and techniques, Colette persisted in passing the test of love and nature with barely a faltering step. The lesbian Colette is today an essential part of the classic Colette.

Notes

1. For an excellent general discussion of lesbianism in French literature prior to Colette as well as a pioneering analysis of Colette's lesbianism, see Elaine Marks, "Lesbian Intertextuality," in *Homosexualities and French Literature*, eds. George Stambolian and Elaine Marks (Ithaca: Cornell University Press, 1979), pp. 353–377.

2. For further discussion of the eighteenth century, see my essay "Homosexuality and the French Enlightenment," in *Homosexualities and French Literature*, eds. George Stambolian and Elaine Marks, pp. 161–185.

3. George Steiner, "Eros and Idiom," in *On Difficulty and Other Essays* (New York: Oxford University Press, 1978), pp. 116–118.

4. For additional information about the lesbian in popular fiction during the early years of this century, see Jeannette Foster, *Sex Variant Women in Literature* (Baltimore: Diana Press, 1975), pp. 201–217.

5. An outline of the major trends and events of feminism in Colette's time can be found in Michèle Sarde, *Colette, libre et entravée* (Paris: Stock, 1978), pp. 164–170.

6. Colette, *The Complete Claudine*, trans. Antonia White (New York: Farrar, Straus & Giroux-Noonday Books, 1976), p. 6. All references to *Claudine à l'école* (*Claudine at School*), *Claudine à Paris* (*Claudine in Paris*), *Claudine en ménage* (*Claudine Married*), and *Claudine s'en va* (*Claudine and Annie*) are to this edition.

7. *Sex Variant Women in Literature*, p. 200.

8. Ibid.

9. Elaine Marks, *Colette* (New Brunswick: Rutgers University Press, 1960), pp. 175–177.

10. Colette, *The Vagabond*, trans. Enid McLeod (New York: Farrar, Straus and Giroux-Noonday Books, 1975), pp. 181–182. All references to this work are to this edition.

11. Colette, "Habit," in *The Other Woman: A Short Novel and Stories*, foreword by Erica Jong (New York: New American Library-Signet Classics, 1975), p. 91.

12. Colette, *Chéri* and *The Last of Chéri*, trans. Roger Senhouse (New York: Penguin Books, 1974), p. 160.

13. "Mon amie Valentine" was published posthumously in the collection *Paysages et Portraits* (Paris: Flammarion, 1958). The story bears no original date of publication, but the war scenes it contains would suggest that it was written sometime during or perhaps shortly after World War I.

14. Colette, "My Friend Valentine," in *The Other Woman: A Short Novel and Stories*, p. 116. All references to this work are to this edition.

15. Colette, *The Pure and the Impure*, trans. Herma Briffault (New York: Farrar, Straus & Giroux-Noonday Books, 1975), pp. 55, 147. All references to this work are to this edition.

16. Simone de Beauvoir, *The Second Sex*, trans. and ed. H. M. Parshley (New York: Random House-Vintage Books, 1974), pp. 468, 473.

17. Ibid., p. 466.

9 *The Vagabond:* A Vision of Androgyny
ERICA M. EISINGER

Anxious and veiled, never born, the androgyne wanders, astonished,
begging softly . . . (Le Pur et l'impur, IX, 63)

La Vagabonde reveals Colette's persistent concern with the question of
psychosexual identity. *La Vagabonde,* in the tradition of the French *roman
d'analyse,* recounts a renunciation of love. From a contemporary feminist
perspective which seeks to eradicate sex roles and strive toward a vision of
psychic wholeness or androgyny, the theme of renunciation of love in women's
writing takes on new significance. A refusal such as that of Renée Néré in *La
Vagabonde* may reflect a revolt against androcentric relationships and a search
for personal autonomy. Renée's project can be viewed as the struggle to
establish an androgynous identity after an intense experience of sexual
polarization: her choice of vagabondage becomes a specific rejection of the
traditional female sphere of house and family for the androgynous world of
freedom and creativity.

An androgynous interpretation of *La Vagabonde* integrates this novel with
Colette's lifelong examination of sexual ambiguity. For Colette, men and
women, girls and boys — like other natural creatures, the plants and animals
which normalize her world — operate outside the boundaries of rigid sex
classification. Colette consistently sought the unity behind creation: "There is
only *one* animal," she often said.[1] Whatever the division — flora or fauna, male
or female — Colette resisted imposed duality and embraced a vision of
wholeness which has much to offer contemporary students of androgyny.
Androgyny has been defined as the existence, real or ideal, of psychic unity
within the sexes. Androgyny comprises the notion that an individual, regardless of sex, can aspire to the full range of human potential. Although Colette

95

never articulated a complete philosophical position on this or any other matter (indeed she said that general ideas suited her as little as hats with feathers), one work, *Le Pur et l'impur*, is an investigation of what Colette called "true mental hermaphrodism."[2] And her fiction is infused with a unique androgynous vision: one that is not static, but in process throughout the life stages; one that is fully sensual, embracing the widest range of sexual preferences; in short, a vision which celebrates female strength and creativity. "You understand," wrote Colette in *Le Pur et l'impur*, "a woman who remains a woman is a complete being."[3]

It is Colette's inspiration to see androgyny not as "a static image of perfection,"[4] but as a dynamic series of life stages. The pattern of Colette's fiction can be seen as the journey of a "pure" protagonist away from the androgynous paradise of youth, through the impurity of rigid sex assignment, and back toward an ideal which unifies male and female. It is axiomatic for Colette that the closer the creature to a natural state, the more androgynous. Thus a woman will experience androgyny in phases: first in the gender-free world of childhood and adolescence, then in the liberating world of work such as the music-hall, and finally through time, in the androgynous harmony of aging.

La Vagabonde illustrates Colette's concept of androgyny as prelapsarian, as a recollection of adolescent purity, to be renewed through the dual disciplines of work and solitude. *La Vagabonde* recounts Renée Néré's search for self-definition which is discoverable through a liberating chastity. Renée's task, the restoration of her androgynous identity, is accomplished on three levels: through the recovery of contact with an earlier, natural creature, the strong, sexless adolescent Renée; through the validation of her present self, the Renée of the music-hall; and through acceptance of a future Renée, and implicitly, of advancing age.

The novel begins with Renée at thirty-three, recently divorced from a tyrannical painter husband, a disguised Willy, and earning her living on the music-hall stage as a mime and dancer. Into Renée's fragile equilibrium intrudes an aristocratic admirer, Maxime, who forces Renée into a genuine self-recognition. The novel transcribes not simply the choice between love and freedom, but Renée's growing awareness and acceptance of her unique androgynous nature and creative gifts. The cold, empty solitude of the opening chapters reflects less the absence of a man in Renée's life than Renée's isolation from her own self, from the source of her creative energy, which is her vibrant contact with the physical world first experienced in youth. The early scenes show Renée alone at her mirror, which highlight her isolation and her growing sense of panic at advancing age. Renée has after all only a limited number of years in which to earn her living as a music-hall performer. Hence the importance of make-up which masks her years, yet hides Renée from herself. "Can that be you?..." she asks the mirror reflection. Renée is unrecognizable to herself at the novel's opening because she has lost contact with her genuine being. It is not her youth which she seeks to recover in the mirror, but her freedom. Renée senses that she belongs elsewhere, "in a land I have forsaken," in Colette's famous phrase. The lost paradise is the paradise of androgyny; the country to which Colette's women seek a safe return is the androgynous world of their youth before the fall into sex roles.[5]

It is the subtle memory of a cherished childhood close to nature which restores Renée to psychic wholeness. Her exile from her natural state of unity with creation is symbolized by her urban exile. It is precisely when Renée physically leaves the capital and returns to the land of her childhood in the novel's final section that her decision to refuse Max becomes inevitable. To refuse the security of love and choose the awful freedom of vagabondage, Renée must first replace the narrow optic of the mirror with the open vista of the train window. For it is through the train window, a symbol of movement and process, that Renée sees her true self in her youthful double, a young girl with eyes "ageless, almost sexless," who recalls Renée's early freedom.[6] The restoration of her youthful persona enables the character to look forward to advancing age with equanimity, even with pleasure, as a renewal of psychic wholeness.

Renée's search for androgyny infuses the setting, characterizations, plot, and imagery of La Vagabonde, none of which are rigidly sex-specific, and all of which promote role reversal or role transcendence. Each element of the novel's structure contributes to strengthening Renée's acceptance of her androgynous identity; each enlarges the protagonist's and the reader's conception of androgynous possibility.

La Vagabonde is one of three novels set against the background of the music-hall.[7] The music-hall plays a critical role in the affirmation of Renée's androgynous identity for the theatre is a lesson in role, a deliberate masquerade, where the tentative divorcée can try on parts and discard them. On the stage, all is pretense, travesty, impersonation.[8] The music-hall for Renée is an apprenticeship in androgyny. Like the writer, the great stage performer, Colette suggests, needs to be both masculine and feminine, like Marguerite Moreno, Colette's interlocutor in Le Pur et l'impur, whose strong, sexless features can suggest the total human experience.[9]

The music-hall offers a milieu where the vulnerable, wounded Renée can heal, where she can move from the exclusively female world of marriage and domesticity, into the male world of work and activity. Here Renée gains strength and confidence through earning her living, traveling, seeing the world independently, meeting her former social class on a new footing — in short, the music-hall provides an initiation into the abandoned realm of androgyny.

The music-hall even more than the theatre is a world of marginality. Yet the music-hall is invariably positive in Colette's writing; whatever is potentially degrading in the life of the artiste becomes heroic for Colette. On stage Renée is an object, after all. But even her semi-nudity becomes a statement of virility,[10] a display of muscular control, of discipline, and power. Her beauty on stage, which renders her vulnerable to male affronts, is neither fragile nor ornamental: it is athletic. She turns these suggestive performances into celebrations of movement, of rhythm and beauty — all the qualities of her writing. So the music-hall becomes a literary apprenticeship as well, and reinforces the affirmation of artistic vocation which enables Renée to refuse her admirer.

The silence of the mime play further suggests a primaeval, animal-like quality which Colette associates with purity. The mime can be sex-free because no voice betrays gender. To talk is to fall into the trap of sexual polarization. Renée admires the stoic reticence of the *artistes*, their wordless camaraderie. In contrast, Max will talk too much, using words as a trap to capture Renée in a prison of rigid gender definition.

The music-hall provides an opportunity for Renée to meet men freed of the humiliation of unequal sex roles. In the world of the stage, men and women experience each other as coworkers, comrades, not as lovers or enemies. The exhausting physical labor of the theatre provides a reprieve from love, like the *retraite sentimentale* of the natural world, a sublimation of sexual tension. The stage demands a commitment, Colette implies, which is superior to the demands of love.

The theatre requires both men and women to earn their livelihood by virtue of their physical attributes. Both sexes put on make-up, exhibit their bodies, receive propositions, and fear the loss of their ability to please. Stage life equalizes or neutralizes sexuality. In the camaraderie of hard work, men and women lose their modesty, and also their coquetry. Entering the world of the *artiste* from the outside, Renée Néré's admirer, and the Blue Lieutenant in *Mitsou*, are shocked at the easy acceptance of nudity and intimacy.

The music-hall performers share the fine physical development of Colette's youthful androgynes: lanky, slim-hipped creatures whose bodies betray no age or sex. They share the moral healthiness of adolescents though their work may bring sickness and even death. Colette admires the steady heroism of these *artistes* — so many with asexual names: Jadin, Mitsou, Bouty — who triumph over hardship, illness, discomfort, poverty, and exploitation.

But the freedom of the music-hall is illusory. The stage cannot function as a permanent resting place for the creative androgynous person, because its demands are finally ruinous. The stage provides a temporary respite from the battle of the sexes, the endless "pursuit" which is the title of the mime play performed by Renée and Brague. The stage experience is literally a rehearsal for freedom, a *répétition* like the nightingale's song in the title story of *Les Vrilles de la vigne:* the stage teaches transformation, rebirth, for Renée whose name means rebirth. The experience of performing provides a bridge for Renée Néré, which spans the sexual abyss of maturity and connects the older self with the remembered world of adolescent androgyny. The music-hall renews Renée's concept of autonomy, brutalized in marriage and divorce, and permits her to restore faith in her own incomparable vision, to pursue her true vocation as a writer.

If Renée feels at home in the hermaphroditic world of the music-hall, it is because of her fundamental receptivity to sexual ambiguity, both in the domain of sex-linked attributes and sexual preference. The name Renée, so apt to incarnate renewal, also recalls Colette's friend, the Sapphic poet, Renée Vivien, who is profiled in *Le Pur et l'impur*. Indeed it is the appearance in the novel of Amalia Barally, another character out of the pages of *Le Pur et l'impur*, which sharpens the rift between Renée and Max, for Renée views the lesbian Amalia with tolerance, and even attraction. Androgyny represents for Colette a widening of options and naturally includes homosexuality. Although Colette takes pains in *Le Pur et l'impur* to disassociate physical and psychic bisexuality, androgyny is clearly linked with acceptance of, and participation in, bisexual experience.

Renée can understand attraction to both men and women for she combines within herself both the stereotypical "masculine" traits of ambition and activity and the "feminine" attributes of warmth and nurturance. Like Léa in *Chéri* whom she anticipates, or like Claudine whom she recalls, Renée as an archetypal Colette hero is simultaneously virile and vulnerable. She wears man-tailored suits and loose-fitting kimonos. She has a head for figures, and a sensitivity for feelings. In her marriage, where she was a victim of sexual tyranny, she nonetheless wrote three novels.

It is her love for work and independence which unites her with her comrades in the theatre, while idleness assimilates Max to the female role of courtesan. Even the name, Renée Néré, suggests self-containment, while the ornamental superfluity of "Maxime Dufferein-Chautel" points to his contingency and uselessness.

The supporting characters, particularly the two confidants, Hamond and Margot, reinforce the sexual ambiguity of the central figures. Hamond shares with Renée a "feminine" inclination for subjugation in love. But unlike Renée who considers this attitude ignoble, Hamond never combats his weakness. Love for him, as for Max, is his whole existence, in Byron's phrase. For Renée, love increasingly becomes "a thing apart." If Hamond works, we never seem to know at what. His sole occupation is to serve as go-between, or procurer, to promote Renée's love affair, like the female *duennas* of courtly literature.

Margot joins with Hamond to watch over Renée almost as if they were surrogate parents, but it is Hamond who talks of love, and Margot who talks of money. It is Margot, moreover, who provides Renée with the crucial monthly stipend which permits her to exist independently as few divorcées could.

Such reversals of sex role or coincidence within one individual of cross-sex characteristics suggest an identity of the sexes, a view which frees the character from the confines of gender. Colette excels in alluding to the resemblance of the sexes even at the moment of the most intense role separation, in the love relationship. Renée and Max, so different psychically, are physical equals, identical in pleasure. They are significantly the same age. Colette's plots are likewise androgynous, that is, not gender-specific: what happens is equally appropriate for either sex. The story of La Vagabonde, or that of Duo or Chéri, to cite but two examples of Colette's fiction, is equally imaginable with the roles of male and female exchanged. The sex of the protagonists in Colette is often simply irrelevant. In the short story "Nuit blanche" we do not know the sex of the lovers — here women — until the last line. The sexual identity of the protagonists in another, longer story, Bella-Vista, is deliberately obscured, but once revealed, explains everything and nothing. Colette's novel about adolescent love, Le Blé en herbe, makes the same point about age as well as sex: these distinctions are fluid, like the sea against which Phil and Vinca's story unfolds. In the mystery of human relationships, sex, for Colette, is a blind alley.

In La Vagabonde, Colette manipulates the story line to provide Renée with a forum for movement and activity, while Max stays immobile and passive. At Renée's departure on tour, she is explicitly compared to a soldier leaving a sweetheart behind. The novel's structure neatly follows the curve of Renée's feelings for Max. When she is active and in motion and has work, in the first and third parts, she rejects Max. It is only in the novel's middle section, when Renée is out of work and stationary in Paris, that she allows Max to enter her life. The cycle of rejection-acceptance-rejection of the male admirer reproduces in reverse the basic cycle of androgyny which moves from adolescent acceptance to mid-life rejection to final readmission. The circularity of the pattern suggests finally a basic wholeness, or unity, the image of which is the sphere.

The initial change in Renée's feeling toward Max from indifference to attraction is directly related to her temporary assumption of the spectator role: it is when she sits backstage and watches Jadin's performance, and Max's subsequent admiration, that she experiences jealousy, which feeds romantic passion. The male assumes an all-important role in a woman's life, Colette implies, when she is denied access to mobility, to work, to self-fulfilling occupations. The moment Renée is herself on stage, or traveling, Max recedes into unimportance. It is not the distance which separates Renée from Max in the final part of the novel that is devastating to their love, but the physical act of travel itself, which reopens the world of visual experience to Renée: locomotion brings perception.

The androgynous message of La Vagabonde is expressed in the novel's controlling visual imagery. For the vagabond is also a visionary; Colette here takes the Sido injunction "Look!" as a moral imperative. In La Vagabonde to see means to be in control of one's own creative powers, to possess the treasures of the natural world with one's own eyes, to live the solitary experience of the artist. Conversely, to be seen implies an appropriation of oneself, a loss of creative energy, the transformation into a sexual object.

Renée's lucid moments, in solitude, in front of mirrors or open windows, are previews of the final self-realization. The self Renée discovers behind the mask of the heavily made-up music-hall *artiste* is the writer. The two professions are alike; both are creative and rhythmic. The small circle of light of the desk lamp under which Renée writes (Colette's own *fanal bleu*, her blue lantern) reproduces the stage spotlight, symbolic, in turn, of the artist's self-generated illumination which is represented by the sphere. (Colette herself collected luminescent spheres on her writing table as talismans of the vision of unity she was transcribing.)

In contrast to the glow of the creative act, love for Renée Néré imposes darkness. Max is described as somber; he casts a shadow over Renée's radiant creativity as he wishes ultimately for her to stand in his shadow. From the first, Max's contact with Renée has been visual only; for him, *voir* (to see) is synonymous with *vouloir* (to want). "That man wants nothing good for me; he just wants me."[11] Renée is astonished that one can fall in love merely by looking at someone. She is impatient when Max attaches more importance to the play of light on her hair than to her words. The crucial moment of reversal, when Renée sees Max as a spectacle, alerts her to his basic unworthiness.

Renée is perhaps one of the first career women in literature, a new creature for whom love and work are equal pulls. Passionate love exposes one to the risk of living forever on stage in front of someone's admiring gaze. In her first love, Renée served as the painter's model, literally *his* vision; with Maxime Dufferein-Chautel, she is similarly a visual object, an apparition. Both men, one kind, one cruel, seek to appropriate Renée's own light, to bathe her instead in the "banal dawn" of domesticity. Beyond his innocent air of the bourgeois paterfamilias, Renée correctly senses in Max the master, who, in giving her everything, would steal from her her most precious possession, her own "incomparable vision (*chimère*)."

Renée rejects Max, finally, in the name of her artistic vocation. In a Proustian moment of privilege, looking out of a train window by the sea at Sète, Renée awakens to the urgency of possessing the marvels of the earth through her own eyes. Renée recalls an earlier self, a queen of the earth, who belonged to no one but herself. Renée's rejection of Max is also a rejection of a limiting definition of femininity, which would subjugate a woman's whole being to a man and to her biological capacity to bear children. For Renée who knows friendship with men on terms of equality, Max is almost an indecently masculine man; he is too "virile" to suit Renée, in spite of his courtesan-like idleness. In short, he is a man, which means an enemy, not a friend.

Renée rejects Max in the name of freedom, the freedom to see: "I refuse to see the most beautiful countries in the world reflected minutely in the amorous mirror of your eyes. . . ."[12] Renée is free: to travel, to earn her living, to write, to be alone, but not to love. The strong androgynous persona cannot survive, Colette seems to believe, the onslaught of intense sexual passion. The fear of the loss of integrity leads Renée to choose a self-protective chastity. The solution to seek the self in solitude is often the only viable alternative for the sexually mature woman in Colette's universe. But the retreat from love is only temporary. With advancing age it is possible for the women in Colette's world to regain the full androgynous paradise, that is, peace with themselves and with men, who become no longer enemies, but as in adolescence, other selves. Acceptance of male-female love comes after the acceptance of the androgynous self; and it comes late, after the long, sleepless night of sexual embattlement, at dawn, *la naissance du jour*, which is a new beginning.

Renée's refusal of love and acceptance of her androgynous identity do not make of her any less a sexual creature. Psychic genderlessness does not imply asexuality for Colette. On the contrary, the sexuality of the androgynous creature is enhanced by the positive attraction of ambiguity: "a strong seductive aura emanates from a being of uncertain or dissimulated gender."[13] Renée's struggle to resist Max does not come from any moral imperative to eschew sexuality. Renée never repudiates the strong physical attraction she feels for her admirer, which she takes as a sign of a healthy sensuality. But she rejects submissiveness, and a desire which would make of love her master. The god the vagabond serves is Chance.

Renée's rejection of Max is not a renunciation, but an affirmation of her unique, androgynous self. Though fragile, this self demands a more worthy partner than Max. In sacrificing Max, Renée is, in fact, losing very little, merely the comforting temptation of an adoring mediocrity. He does not read; he is not analytic; he can hardly appreciate Renée's gifts; he could not understand her reluctance to bear a child, nor her dedication to her craft; he could not accept the appeal of homosexuality as Renée does. In short, he is not an androgynous man. Renée rejects Max in part because she fears his domination, but also because she fears he is unworthy. She rejects Max, very simply, because she loves her work, and finds in that calling a superior passion.

Colette sees androgyny as an option for "certain strongly-organized beings."[14] It is a privilege but also a burden. Often misunderstood, the androgynous creature may be condemned to solitary "vagabondage," as the search for a worthy partner proves fruitless. For the androgyne, single-sex individuals, men and women, are but half-equals. "He retains the right, even the duty, to never be happy."[15] As Renée Néré's itinerary shows, beyond ordinary happiness lies perhaps the greater pleasure, the recognition of special creative powers made possible through the renewed contact with the androgynous paradise of the natural world.

As the very structure of *La Vagabonde* shows, the life of an exceptional woman is cyclic; stages of rebirth and productivity follow periods of sexual polarization and sterility. The periodic flowering of the rose-cactus which the wise Sido knows to treasure above the ephemeral pleasures of human relationships, the lesson of *La Naissance du jour*, is anticipated by Renée's choice of celibacy. Creativity is firmly associated with androgynous self-sufficiency: the creative process is one of self-insemination. To attain her freedom and give expression to her artistic vision, Renée must recapture the psychic wholeness of her youth; she must shun the narrow definition of female purpose as centered on house and family. She must, in fact, choose the opposite: vagabondage, the homeless existence of the wandering androgyne.

Notes

1. In Maurice Goudeket, *Près de Colette* (Paris: Flammarion, 1956), p. 35.

2. Colette, *Le Pur et l'impur*, in *Oeuvres complètes* IX (Paris: Flammarion, 1948–1950), p. 51.

3. Ibid., p. 83.

4. Cynthia Secor, "Androgyny: An Early Reappraisal," *Women's Studies* 2, No. 2 (1974), p. 164.

5. Colette says of her own youth that she experienced: "la secrète certitude d'être une enfant précieuse, de sentir en moi une âme extraordiniaire d'homme intelligent, de femme amoureuse . . ." "Miroir," *Les Vrilles de la vigne*, in *Sido* (Paris: Hachette, 1901), p. 204.

6. *La Vagabonde*, in *Oeuvres complètes* IV, p. 94.

7. The other two are *L'Envers du Music Hall* (1913) and *Mitsou* (1919).

8. The story "Gribiche" opens with a male impersonation, an ironic travesty, since Gribiche dies an exclusively female death, of a septic abortion. *Bella-Vista*, in *Oeuvres complétes* XI, pp. 193–229.

9. Colette recalls Sarah Bernhardt's criticism of another performer's art as failing to combine masculine and feminine qualities. *Colette, Earthly Paradise*, ed. Robert Phelps (New York: Farrar, Straus & Giroux, 1966), p. 290.

10. During her own stage career, Colette bared a breast during a performance, which she calls in *Le Pur et l'impur* "l'arrogance intermittente de ce qu'une femme possède de plus viril," p. 118.

11. *La Vagabonde*, p. 25.

12. Ibid., p. 233.

13. *Le Pur et l'impur*, p. 63.

14. Ibid., p. 51.

15. Ibid., p. 63.

10 Colette and Art Nouveau
CLAIRE DEHON

Between 1880 and 1910 Art Nouveau, or "Modern Style," exercised a profound influence on artistic creativity in France.[1] It penetrated architecture, interior decoration, and the design of everyday objects. Although it inspired several painters, its impact on French literature and music remains undefined. Authors and composers did not associate themselves explicitly with the movement, and scholars have generally followed their example by neglecting to seek out currents of sympathy. In his recent book on Colette, however, Robert Cottrell suggests in passing that strong affinities did exist between Art Nouveau and the style of Colette.[2] This article aims to bring to light these affinities because a recognition of Art Nouveau in Colette's work will enhance our appreciation of her artistic creativity and ultimately situate her work in a definite artistic tradition — a yet unsolved problem. In a more general sense, such a study also suggests that Art Nouveau influenced all the arts more profoundly than has been previously recognized.

Obviously, investigating the relationship between Art Nouveau and the work of Colette presents certain unavoidable risks. In the first place, a comparison between two arts that employ different materials, and consequently arouse different sensations, always raises difficulties. A particular structure, for example, yields different impressions in painting and prose.[3] Moreover, critical vocabulary adds to the confusion, because words like "theme," "image," "color," "musicality," or "rhythm" are often used loosely. Finally, because Colette's literary career continued long after the popularity of Art Nouveau had faded, it may be difficult to distinguish between an authentic influence of the style and the fortuitous preferences of an artist.

Göran Hermerén's *Influence in Art and Literature* offers three necessary conditions to establish an influence between different works of art.[4] The first relates to time: the work which imitates must follow the work imitated. Second, some contact must have been possible between the inspiring work and the artist who is inspired. These two conditions are intended to avoid superficial coincidences. Third, there must be a great number of similarities between the works, including important stylistic aspects. With Colette, the first two conditions are easily met, because she began writing when Art Nouveau was flourishing, and because in her works she described objects designed in that style.[5] This study focuses on the third condition and establishes that she remained faithful to the style throughout her life. To show this I shall compare various objects in the Art Nouveau style with *Claudine à l'école* (1900), *Chéri* (1920), *La Fin de Chéri* (1926), and *Gigi* and its three accompanying stories (1944). These selections span the author's literary career and reveal the evolution of her artistic temperament. To be sure, not all elements that comprised Art Nouveau and Colette's style can be considered in this study. I shall therefore confine my attention to those aspects of her work that are most crucial in understanding her style: the choice of subject matter, the patterns that characterize her works, the so-called "feminine" traits, and her use of colors.

I

An investigation of the influence of Art Nouveau on Colette requires an appreciation of the salient features of the artistic movement.[6] One of its more interesting aspects lies in its attempt to give an artistic appearance to everyday objects such as houses, furniture, jewelry, vases, door-handles, and even suspender-buckles. In their desire to make products of industry comparable to hand-crafted objects, the artists of Art Nouveau rejected the imitation of established styles and sought new fashions. Certain techniques helped to make this possible: the use of iron in architecture, and refinements in glass-making and pottery production. The movement was also characterized by an ornamentation that concealed structure, by asymmetry, flat colors, two-dimensional designs, "feminine" elements (curving lines and representation of female bodies), and an interest in things precious and rare — a curious element in a style that claimed to carry art to the masses. These characteristics of Art Nouveau, together with its dynamism, reveal an affinity with the baroque; in both styles attention is always directed toward secondary elements, and each object — each line — undergoes a continuous metamorphosis.

Notwithstanding its originality, Art Nouveau was inspired by several artistic trends of the time. The mark of the Neo-Gothic has been found in its surface structure; the Neo-Rococo appears in the "plastic treatment" of the entire work and in the often inflated fashioning of every detail; the Neo-Baroque is found in the "dramatic opposition" of areas of light and shadow and in the fluidity of the shapes that melt into one another. To these influences must be added those of the Pre-Raphaelite painters (feminine forms and floral decoration), Neo-Celtic painters (lacework and gallic motifs), and Japanese art (asymmetry and fragile creations).[7]

Despite its relatively short life, Art Nouveau enriched the arts, partially because of its search for modernity through the choice of subject matter. Similarly, *Claudine*, *Chéri*, and the short stories — like most of Colette's works — are purposely modern in the sense that they deal with familiar matters in a vocabulary that is frequently quite ordinary and sometimes even close to slang (*Gigi*, pp. 9, 17; *La Dame*, p. 105; *Claudine*, pp. 28, 31).[8] A new school, examinations, a quarrel, the transformation of a girl into a woman or of an ordinary woman into a heroine, dreams incited by illness or war — all of these form a part of an everyday world from which everything extraordinary has been eliminated. Conforming to Colette's conviction that heroism is banal, her characters are for the most part not at all remarkable. They belong to a middle class neither brilliant nor shabby, and their fates hold neither great unhappiness nor boundless joy. Details render them very "real" (for example: the precise and unflattering description of Andrée's eyes or the physical portrayal of a Léa who has grown old and flabby [*Gigi*, p. 22; *La Fin*, p. 212]).

The subjects in Art Nouveau decoration and paintings are also familiar ones. Instead of giving his "Muses" divine attributes, Maurice Denis represents them as three *Parisiennes* resting beneath trees. The products of Gauguin's "Breton period" reveal the same concern for reality while at the same time transforming it through an original composition and an audacious use of colors (Hamilton, color plate 22; Abbate, p. 13). In imitation of the Nabis (painters who tried to unite Nature and abstract ideas), the painters and designers of Art Nouveau chose common flowers or insects for subject matter and they represented them with a very precise realism: the floral decoration on a Daum vase resembles a botanical illustration; a dragonfly and a butterfly on another one by Gallé are worthy of an entomological textbook (Battersby, plates 33, 34).[9]

However, in Art Nouveau and Colette, the realistic impression is contravened somewhat by asymmetrical, irregular, and unexpected constructions. In the guise of a girl's diary, *Claudine* falls into two unequal parts, the first concerned with matters of the heart, the second dealing with examinations and a visit by a governmental official. The thread of the story is interrupted by digressions that are apparently superfluous to its development (*Claudine*, pp. 45, 59). Moreover, the novel conceals in its many asides some revelations about its author, her life, and her emotions. *Gigi* begins *in medias res* and ends without apparent reason, like the "slice-of-life" style favored by the naturalistic writers. But the fairy-story theme — the prince marries the peasant girl — contradicts the structure and introduces an ironic twist. The effect obtained is a misadaptation of a subject to its support (here, the text) and it calls to mind several Art Nouveau objects, among others Lechu's candelabras, Allion's ashtrays, and even a pair of boots of the period (Battersby, plate 17; Schmutzler, p. 156). On the one hand, splendid female bodies draped in revealing veils serve as ordinary bases for practical items like a candle-holder or an ashtray. On the other, a boot comes close to becoming a work of art in itself because of its decorative style. This method uses both ridicule and irony: in the first instance the notion of beauty has been debased, and in the second an ordinary object has been exalted. In *Gigi*, this tension between beauty and vulgarity carries the reader effortlessly from reality to dream.

The structures of *L'Enfant*, *La Dame*, and *Flore* also illustrate the interplay of dream and reality in Art Nouveau. *L'Enfant* is based on dream visions that swell and shrink, on the intrusion of reality into imagination and vice versa. At times it becomes difficult, if not impossible, to distinguish between the two. In *La Dame*, a narrator, some comments unconnected with the plot, several possible interpretations, and some brief asides lead the reader to believe that the author was unable to choose one central idea and that she has let her pen wander at will (*La Dame*, pp. 96–97, 103–104). *Flore* contains a disorderly collection of reflections on various gardens and on the time-lapse filming of a flower coming into bloom. The imbalance and irregularity of the structures draw the reader along a twisting, unpredictable course. The gate of Guimard's "Castel Beranger," or a poster by Mucha portraying a woman use the same type of devices (Ponente, p. 176; Guerrand, ill.): the bars of the gate bend and straighten themselves without apparent cause, and in a similar way the hair on the woman's head curves and stretches out so that one cannot tell if it is still her hair or an extravagant decoration.

These developments, which upset our idea of balance and which seem to pull our imagination in all directions, serve the same function for Guimard, Mucha, and Colette. They transcend the subject while at the same time raising it above everyday reality. And here appears a phenomenon identical to the one seen in *Gigi*: the lowering of the work through realistic details is counterbalanced by an elevation toward abstract beauty resulting from accessory ornamentation. This ironic intermingling produces an esthetic tension in which lies the stylistic richness of Art Nouveau and Colette.

While moving in this way from reality to dream and back again, the elements that make up these works are ceaselessly being transformed. The bars of the gate or the hair become enfolding spirals, growths, monstrous serpents. In Colette, subject matter, characters, objects, and words never remain fixed. Many of the works that appear to have been written for one reason contain other motives as well. *Claudine* mixes licentious elements with childhood memories. Behind the luxurious lives of a demi-mondaine and a gigolo, *Chéri* reveals the misery of two hearts perfectly suited to one another but irrevocably separated by life's circumstances. In *Gigi*, the reader tends to become more interested in the exterior events than in the rapid growth of a girl into a woman. The glorious dreams of the child in *L'Enfant malade* conceal his struggle against paralysis, and *Flore* hides a poetic art behind its reflections and memories. Characters are metamorphosed: Mademoiselle Aimée into a bird; Dutertre into a wolf; the servant into a lute or a violoncello; Madame Armand into a cupboard; Tigri-Cohen into a monkey; while Gigi appeared to be an "archer," a "clumsy angel, a boy in skirts" (*Claudine*, pp. 39, 33; *L'Enfant*, p. 71; *La Dame*, pp. 97, 102; *Gigi*, p. 10).

Objects, too, undergo unexpected transformations: a lock of Léa's hair "crawled down her neck like a little dry snake" (*Chéri*, p. 150); a letter opener resembles a "sparkling landscape of mint" (*L'Enfant*, p. 29). The whole physical world around the child is transformed: he "watched calmly as the chorus of shapes and colors arose within him" (*L'Enfant*, p. 77). The very words lose their firmness: "J'ai l'air d'un zébu. Mais z'ai bu, oui, z'ai vien vu [...]"; "Chryse Saluter-Médure," "Alyzie Effanti," "Lysie Infantil" (*L'Enfant*, p. 81). Voices become lines: "The voices [...] all blend into straight lines and curved lines — one curved, one straight — a dry line — a wet line" (*L'Enfant*, p. 68). Sounds become concrete: "hunch-backed sounds carrying echoing flasks on their heads, on their beetle-backs, pointed sounds like the snout of a mongoose" (*L'Enfant*, p. 83). Of course most of these alterations of reality illustrate the mental state or the fantasies of a feverish child, but the technique emphasizes the notion that there is no real barrier between dream and reality. So Garnier's bed becomes a giant butterfly; Charpentier's lectern becomes a delicate vine; a flower sculpted by Angles becomes a portrait of Cléo de Mérode (Guerrand, ill.; Abbate, p. 140; Battersby, plate 19).

The so-called "feminine" aspects of Art Nouveau and of Colette's work succeed in a similar way in combining reality and dream. Traditionally, "feminine art" makes use of pale colors and curved, soft lines; its subjects are frequently animals, flowers, pale women with languid glances and ethereal expressions; it traditionally has neither energy nor clarity. Without discussing the pertinence of the adjective "feminine," we can note here that woman, or rather her image, dominates both Art Nouveau and the works of Colette. She serves as an inkstand as well as a candle-holder and an ashtray; she decorates lamps, jewelry, vases, ornamental plaques; her mysterious smile is found in Mucha's posters and in the sculpture of Raoul Larche; in fact she appears everywhere.

Naturally women are found in all of Colette's works, but they do not have the disembodied and superior air of the women of Art Nouveau, who — pale and mysterious, with faraway look — seem to belong to a dream. In Colette, women wear hair-curlers; they have circles under their eyes; they are described more realistically (*Claudine*, pp. 224, 225; *Gigi*, pp. 26, 28–29). From a plastic point of view, the Art Nouveau feminine forms evoke a rather cold sensuality (Guerrand, ill.), whereas for Colette, the body has both its pain and its glory, and it calmly accepts sensuous pleasures (*L'Enfant*, pp. 88–89; *La Dame*, p. 97; *Gigi*, pp. 40–41; *Chéri*, p. 39). Her female characters dare to assert their personalities and their desires; they face life with courage and they reconcile their dreams with reality. Yet their humble qualities and their quiet way of solving problems transform them into heroines and through this elevation, they join the dream women of Art Nouveau.

The faces of Art Nouveau women do not express their feelings or their mood; their impersonal appearance renders them mysterious. Sometimes cats symbolize mystery, and Colette is simply conforming to accepted usage in associating Mademoiselle Aimée and her sister with this animal (Claudine, pp. 21, 64, 115). These "cat-women," apparently unaffected by ordinary sentiment, represent independence, guile, and sensuality. Charming, they attract attention, but they remain as enigmatic as the women of Mucha.

Colette pays attention to details of furniture and clothing, and especially to color (Léa's dining room, Chéri's clothes, Chéri, pp. 23, 50; Tante Alicia's salon, Gigi's dress, Gigi, pp. 33, 34; the general appearance of Madame Armand, La Dame, p. 97). Mademoiselle Sergent's dress is clearly Art Nouveau: "a dress of black silk [...] [embroidered] with large bouquets, slender garlands along the hem, branches climbing up the bodice, all in silks of faded violet shades" (Claudine, p. 212). Or again, when Claudine returns from a garden: "I have mauve clematis petals in my hair, leaves on my dress, a little green insect and a ladybug on one shoulder, and my hair is all out of order" (Claudine, p. 160). She reminds us of Botticelli's painting Spring, a very feminine figure but one that is as other-worldly as the women of Mucha.

Despite these examples of idealization in her female characters, on the whole Colette created her women more realistically than did Art Nouveau. Her male characters, however, are more imaginary than the heroines. The best example is Chéri who, because of his cold and distant beauty, represents the fin de siècle male ideal. Slender, beardless, between adolescence and maturity, he recalls the youths of Minne or Maillol (Schmutzler, pp. 107, 134). Colette describes Chéri's apparent insensitivity in such phrases as "he remained as mysterious as a courtesan," "an Asian Prince" with an "inscrutable look," "Chinese," "Negro" (Chéri, pp. 47, 50, 78). Sometimes he embodies mystery like a god or an idol (Chéri, p. 46; La Fin, p. 271). The inhumanity of his beauty makes him a creature apart, between heaven and earth. At certain moments he appears as a "seagull," or as "a winged figure, gliding, asleep in the sky" (Chéri, pp. 27, 152).

We see in this character the tendency of Art Nouveau to locate beings or objects between reality and dream. Thus Chéri has within him some pragmatic elements (he manages his fortune competently), but these are opposed to idealistic elements like his beauty (Chéri, p. 32). This dichotomy is resolved for him by suicide, while Colette's heroines overcome the dilemma by accepting their eclipse (La Seconde), the end of their hopes (La Dame), or the coming of old age (La Fin).

To give her characters their realistic or dreamlike appearance, Colette never described them completely or logically, but chose some aspects of their personalities, however trivial. This interest for unimportant details is shared by both Colette and Art Nouveau. In Colette it appears in description of physical or mental particularities (the physical deterioration of Léa, *La Fin*, pp. 211–212), and in her heroine's gestures or reflexes, which we never encounter in so-called masculine literature (for example, the passage in which Gigi's grandmother explains how to sit modestly, *Gigi*, p. 8). In Art Nouveau, detail is pervasive; the most ordinary objects of daily life are embellished, as seen in the Daum and Gallé vases (Battersby, plates 33, 34), in houses, furniture, book-bindings, doorbells, silverware, fans, clothes (Battersby, plates 14, 25, 38, 44, 45).

Along with the focus on detail, Art Nouveau and Colette share a circuitous approach to reality. Colette acknowledged that her condition as a woman forced her to avoid "the simple truth that is like a flat melody without modulation," and to be "content in the midst of half-truths, half-silences, half-lines" — in short, to ignore the direct and logical exposition of a "masculine" esthetic (*La Dame*, p. 110). Her informal tone only seems careless; it disguises the writer's labor, lively intelligence, and breadth of learning. The desire to conceal artistry is not found in Art Nouveau, which, on the contrary, took pleasure in exhibiting skill. However, the decoration and the secondary detail do draw one's attention from the center of the work and therefore may hide its "real" meaning. The ambiguity of some objects like the portrait of Cléo de Mérode (is it a woman or a flower? [Battersby, plate 19]) suggests that Art Nouveau might not have said the "simple truth" as Colette called it.

Colette and Art Nouveau reflect similiar tastes in the kind of artistic materials each employed and in the preciosity of their juxtaposition. Examples are many: a dressing-table made of sycamore wood inlaid with bronze; a metal lamp with a shade made from a shell; a diadem made of old bronze and decorated with semi-precious stones; a sculpture in oxidized silver-plated metal on a pedestal of opalescent glass (Battersby, plates 5, 23; Abbate, p. 143). Colette mentions rather than describes Art Nouveau objects: Claudine possesses notebooks covered with "metallic moire," pencils of rosewood, lacquered pencil-boxes, mahogany and ebony rulers (*Claudine*, p. 146). In literature, an unusual word, an exotic image, or a complex construction serve as precious materials. Here it is primarily a question of names of precious stones or flowers, like "oncidium," "stanhopea," "trichophilia," or of composite words: "cahiers-prétextes," "bras-rémiges," "plume-couteau," "figues-améthystes" (*Flore*, pp. 139, 152; *Claudine*, p. 119; *L'Enfant*, p. 66; *Gigi*, p. 10). Unusual combinations of materials result also from a mixing of tones, and in Colette, the elegant, the vulgar, and the childish intermingle.[10]

In the plastic arts and decoration, color plays an essential part in the style. The Art Nouveau shades are often warm: gold, green, yellow, bronze, dark oxidized silver. The preferred woods are light: sycamore, cherry, wild cherry.

Georges Feure, Mucha, and Edouard Benedictus liked dark reds, pale greens, blue, mauve, and delicate yellow — with little violent contrast. The Gallé, Daum, and Argy-Rousseau vases are also of soft colors that sometimes blend into one another (Battersby, plates 33–36; Abbate, p. 124).

These generalizations, which do not exclude other tones, are established easily enough for the plastic arts, but not so in literature. To obtain an objective basis for judgment, one must only select the adjectives of color without making use of the fact that a ruby is red unless the author expressly says so. The use of colors in *Claudine* lacks the coherence that we encounter in Colette's later works. But already we find blue and rose, colors of dreams and joy, and an opposition of black to white (*Claudine*, pp. 56, 58, 65, 71). White signifies youth, innocence, purity; black symbolizes night and mystery (*Claudine*, pp. 20, 41, 118, 129, 142, 151).

It was I. T. Olken who explained the use of color in *Chéri*.[11] Blue and rose accompany Léa, while Chéri appears in white and black — colors of fate, "romantic colors of night and death" (*La Fin*, pp. 162, 244, 283). A statistical study of the adjectives of color on the short stories produces interesting results: Colette used white most often (56 times), followed by blue and black (45 times each), and rose (44 times). We cannot help noticing that blue dominates *Gigi* (18 of 30 color adjectives), and that the shades vary widely: "dark blue like wet slate," "blue like evening," "dull blue," "lavender blue," "navy blue," "shadowy blue" (*Gigi*, pp. 9, 32, 34, 37, 51, 52). White predominates in *L'Enfant* (14 of 24 color adjectives) but it is contrasted to other colors: "sea-green," "periwinkle blue," "Bordeaux-wine color," "moonlight," "opaline," "*septicolores*," and "the color of springtime grass" (*L'Enfant*, pp. 63, 66, 74, 77, 81, 86, 90). Black permeates *La Dame* (14 of 19), but here too several indefinable tints soften the impact: "milky," "flat-white," "snowy blue" (*La Dame*, pp. 97, 100, 101). The color rose constitutes 21 of 41 color adjectives in the last short story, and it is contrasted with shades like "greenish-white," "the color of dried blood," "dark blue like a bruise," "aluminum-white," and "wine-rose" (*Flore*, pp. 136, 139, 142, 143, 170).

The four basic colors symbolize the content of the short stories: *Gigi* is a "flowery blue" tale; a sick child and his innocence call for white; the attempted suicide of Madame Armand suggests black; and rose, in *Flore*, evokes happy dreams. To avoid the banality of a rigid system, Colette contrasted these colors with unusual nuances — and so paralleled Art Nouveau once again. The drawings of Georges Feure based on greens, yellows, and browns, or the pink and blue dining room by Collet illustrate this search for subtle color and the desire to create a whole atmosphere based on it (Battersby, plates 1, 49–52).

As noted above, other elements of Art Nouveau, such as the Neo-Celtic, the Neo-Gothic, the Neo-Baroque, Pre-Raphaelism, and Japanese art, influenced Colette as well. We find references to a Celtic period and an imaginary Middle Ages (*Claudine*, pp. 151, 242, 245). From the Baroque and the Rococo came the preference for the curving line, the flowery decor, the theatrical gesture (*Chéri*, p. 76; *La Fin*, p. 176; the suicide of Chéri, *La Fin*, pp. 282–285).[12] Apart from an allusion to Ophelia, Pre-Raphaelism hardly appears at all, a fact that is not surprising in an author as sensual as Colette. She shared with Rossetti, however, a taste for rose and blue. The influence of Japanese and Chinese art is revealed in the asymmetry, in the artistry of the descriptions, and also in characters like Chéri, who is compared to an "Asian Prince" who wears Japanese robes and who enjoys decorating his salon with Chinese vases (*Chéri*, pp. 47, 50, 122; *La Fin*, pp. 172, 270).

II

All these similarities demonstrate that Colette's esthetic ideal resembled that of Art Nouveau. It remains to be proven that she stayed conscientiously faithful to it until the end of her career. One of the last short stories, *Flore et Pomone* (1944), establishes this in an indirect manner. The text seems to be an inconsequential accumulation of memories; however, in it, Colette reaffirmed her esthetic preferences by associating the making of a garden with artistic creativity.[13]

The most striking elements of the implicit comparison between Colette's horticultural preferences and the esthetic of the works studied here are found in a curvilinear structure. In *Flore,* Colette asserted that as a child she preferred gardens designed with curving lines, paths interrupted by "great flowering masses" (p. 145). Already in *Claudine* (and with some self-mockery), she admitted her attachment to curves and indirect exposure of thought. This is demonstrated by a song Claudine loved:

> Along the same slow curve,
> Implacably slow,
> Rises in ecstasy, falters, and falls
> The complex present of slow curves.
> In an identical autumn the curves duplicate each other,
> Your sorrow parallels the long evening of autumn,
> And flattens the slow curve of things, and your brief skips.
>
> (*Claudine*, p. 59)

The author said also that she did not like to allow "a glorious landscape to enter freely into my house, through all openings" (*Flore*, p. 145). For Colette, a rigid or uninterrupted structure has little charm. And great, profound ideas must not constantly pervade a work, nor a too-refined artistry be allowed to immobilize it. Similarly, blending essential details with others that appear to be superfluous contributes an unexpected note and adds to a natural tone.

Colette provided an ironic definition of style while talking about gardens:

"From the time it begins to please us, style is nearly always the bad taste of our predecessors." Furthermore, she would like to do without it, because it is too "predictable" (*Flore,* p. 168). Her ironic attitude did not prevent her from shaping and controlling her material: as a certain disorder "can only be achieved with the help of the pruning shears," the gardener, like the writer, learns how to trim and eliminate (*Flore,* pp. 133–134, 145).

Colette preferred common flowers to orchids and other rarities (*Flore,* pp. 139, 171). A profusion of colors and their distribution gave her infinite pleasure, but she felt uneasy in a garden where one sensed too much human control (*Flore,* pp. 139, 167, 151). All this meant that she chose common words as literary raw material; she varied settings, subject matter, and tones, and she sometimes concealed her artistic labor, letting her imagination carry her along.

Colette continued the comparison between gardening and writing in her reflections on French, Moroccan, and Parisian gardens, and the chateaux of her childhood. Those sites serve as points of departure for imaginary voyages made necessary by the tragedy of war and the boring aspect of the garden at the Palais Royal where Colette lived. The gardens in *Flore* represented escape from daily life and its fears, like the "Paradou" in Zola's *La Faute de l'abbé Mouret.* At the same time the symbols allowed observations on the French people, the Midi, Brittany, Parisians, and aristocrats (*Flore,* pp. 134, 144, 141). Such a method suited Colette well: starting from a trivial subject — a flower, an animal, an insignificant woman — she proceeded to comment on human society. This indirect manner had the advantage of eliminating any pretentious or bitter note and avoiding confrontation with her readers.

In the midst of war, the memory of oranges evoked sunshine and warmth. They stood for abundance, and they called forth a number of sensuous comments on their flesh, their taste, and their scent (*Flore,* pp. 153–155). Passages on summertime, pears, and apples all serve to extend the parallels between artistic creativity and the creativity necessary to design a beautiful garden.

Thus, through this implicit comparison, Colette reaffirmed her artistic inclinations. They had changed little since her earliest writings, and they closely approached Art Nouveau. The number of parallels between the two fulfill the three above-mentioned conditions put forth by Hermerén: Colette's work was conceived at the same time as or after Art Nouveau; the author knew of the movement; the number and the breadth of similarities — of inspiration and form — make coincidence impossible. These temporal and spatial circumstances and similarities establish the important influence that Art Nouveau exercised on the writing of Colette.

This influence, however, should not imply that Colette's style remained stagnant. Although only a few aspects of Art Nouveau appeared in *Claudine,* later they grew more frequent and more completely integrated into her works.

In her first novel Colette used uneven and asymmetrical organization; she referred to Art Nouveau objects and began to make use of colors to symbolize a well-defined concept. Subsequent works show a development of these traits. Art Nouveau elements are found again in familiar decors or in a hero like Chéri; structures sometimes become complicated by apparently unnecessary ornamentation. Concerns traditionally characteristic of women and veiled confidences enter to enrich the work. A variety of images, symbols, comparisons, and memories is used simply to render the text more beautiful. Finally as in Art Nouveau, the integration of all these elements produces an overall effect where secondary details play an important role in the esthetic balance.

After 1910, the interest in Art Nouveau diminished as artists looked elsewhere for inspiration. Interior design became simpler, lines straightened, and floral details disappeared. Nevertheless, the union of arts, craftsmanship, and industry affected our perception of our surroundings by making familiar objects beautiful as well as functional. In the same way, Colette employed a complex and ornamental style for fairly ordinary events and characters. By doing so, she raised what might have been merely popular novels to the level of literary works.

Because Art Nouveau influenced Colette, one can place her now in a definite artistic tradition. But in order to consider that style and Colette's in a broader context, it remains to be proven that Art Nouveau influenced other writers such as Proust, Gide, Valéry, or even Maeterlinck. The decorative prose of *Les Nourritures terrestres* or of *A l'ombre des jeunes filles en fleurs*, the preciosity of Valéry's poetry, the mysterious and impersonal characters of Maeterlinck could be examined as part of Art Nouveau's esthetic. These studies would enhance our understanding of Art Nouveau and most of all they would illuminate its relationship with symbolism, one of the most complex problems in the history of styles.[14]

Notes

1. In France the term "Modern Style" is usually preferred.

2. Robert Cottrell, *Colette* (New York: Frederick Ungar, 1974), pp. 25–28.

3. Etienne Souriau has reminded us in his work, *La Correspondance des arts* (Paris: Flammarion, 1969), that "the different arts are like different languages; imitation between them requires translation, reworking in an entirely different expressive medium, the invention of parallel rather than literally identical artistic effects" (p. 31). See also René Wellek and Austin Warren, *Theory of Literature* (New York: Harcourt, Brace and World, 1956), pp. 125–135.

4. Göran Hermerén, *Influence in Art and Literature* (Princeton: Princeton University Press, 1975), pp. 157–177. One should also consult Helmut A. Hatzfeld, *Literature through Art: A New Approach to French Literature* (Chapel Hill: University of North Carolina Press, 1969), to

gain an idea of methods used in comparisons of different works of art.

5. Sidonie Gabrielle Colette, *Oeuvres complètes* (Paris: Flammarion, 1949– 1950, 15 vols.), Vol. VIII, *La Seconde*. Colette here refers to the shop owned by Bing, which specialized in Art Nouveau objects (p. 219). And in Vol. XIII, *Gigi*, she describes an Art Nouveau object (p. 33).

6. For a clear understanding of this article, the reader should consult the following works on Art Nouveau:

Francesco Abbate, *Art Nouveau: The Style of the 1890's*, trans. Elizabeth Evans (London: Octopus Books, 1972).

Mario Amaya, *Art Nouveau* (London: Studio Vista, 1966).

Martin Battersby, *Art Nouveau* (Feltham, England: Hamlyn, 1969). This is the most essential book for an understanding of this article.

Roger H. Guerrand, *L'Art nouveau en Europe* (Paris: Plon, 1965). Since the illustrations are not numbered, reference to the photographs is made simply as "Guerrand, ill."

George Heard Hamilton, *Nineteenth and Twentieth Century of Art* (New York: Harry Abrams, n.d.).

Philippe Julian, *Dreamers of Decadence* (New York: Praeger, 1971).

Alastair Mackintosh, *Symbolism and Art Nouveau* (London: Thames and Hudson, 1965).

Nello Ponente, *The Structures of the Modern World* (Geneva: Skira, 1965).

Robert Schmutzler, *Art Nouveau* (New York: Abrams, 1962).

7. S. Tschudi Madsen, *Art Nouveau* (New York: McGraw Hill, 1967), pp. 58– 70.

8. Colette, *Oeuvres complètes*: Vol. I, *Claudine à l'école*; Vol. VI, *Chéri, La Fin de Chéri*; Vol. XIII, *Gigi, L'Enfant malade, La Dame du photographe, Flore et Pomone*. Later reference will be made as: *Claudine, Chéri, La Fin, Gigi, L'Enfant, La Dame, Flore*.

9. Wylie Sypher, *Rococo to Cubism in Art and Literature* (New York: Random House, 1960), p. 220.

10. In *Gigi*, for example, a childish style alternates with an elegant style (although the "elegance" has a dubious origin). Gigi uses baby words like *"teuf-teuf"* and *"tonton"* (pp. 17, 43), and Madame Alvarez conducts conversations worthy of her former profession (pp. 43– 45).

11. I. T. Olken, "Aspects of Imagery in Colette: Color and Light," *PMLA*, LXXVII, No. 1 (March 1962), 141– 148.

12. On this subject see Mari McCarty, "Theatrical Colette," lecture delivered in a seminar on Colette at the annual meeting of the MMLA, St. Louis, Mo., November 1976.

13. She uses expressions like "horticultural art," "the art of grafting," "the rhythm," "the style," "the order of a garden" (*Flore*, pp. 140, 141, 145, 166, 168).

14. This article was translated by Abigail Siddall whom I thank very deeply.

11 Colette and Ravel: The Enchantress and the Illusionist

MARGARET CROSLAND

Colette's writing, as her readers well know, is colored throughout by her awareness of the world of the senses. Her response to things physically seen, touched, and heard, quite apart from her reactions to thoughts and emotions, is one of the most distinctive elements in her work. At the same time it is her feeling for rhythm, harmony, and the general musicality of words that creates those beautifully balanced phrases and sentences, long and short, which make her prose into poetry without ever becoming that unsatisfactory thing, poetic prose. If her collaboration with Maurice Ravel reveals her as a professional librettist who might have ventured further into this field, any reader who enjoys music soon notices how much Colette obviously enjoyed it too. Spontaneous amateur music evidently remained in her memory most of her life and can be "heard" in a great deal of her most accessible and successful writing, while her own appreciation of many composers was one of the happier results of her hard-working *apprentissages* during her early years in Paris.

As a child in the village of Saint-Sauveur en Puisaye, some seventy-five miles from Paris, Colette would have had little opportunity for a sophisticated musical education, especially since her parents were far from rich, but of course in the late nineteenth century families made their own music. A reading of *La Maison de Claudine* and *Sido*, both of them written after she had composed the libretto for *L'Enfant et les sortilèges*, yields many clues about the part played by music in Colette's early background. She obviously inherited an awareness of it from both her parents. Among the items that her mother "Sido" obviously remembered with regret when she left her brothers' Belgian home at the time of her first marriage were "the piano, the violin."

And Sido, who had been born in Paris, would certainly have enjoyed some forms of music there. From *La Maison de Claudine* we also learn that Colette's father, who may have had Italian ancestors, had a "velvety baritone voice" which affected deeply their neighbor Madame Bruneau, who liked sad music. She thought that Captain Colette's voice was "theatrical," and Sido proudly hinted that he might have been a professional singer if he had wanted to. It is not surprising that Colette's brother Léo was an expert amateur musician at the age of 14 and "would transfer to the piano, without a single mistake, a melody or a theme from a symphony heard in the *chef-lieu*," this latter being probably Auxerre. There is a description in the same book of the music and dancing at a village wedding, and the last few pages of *Sido* describe how the two brothers escaped most of their sister Juliette's wedding by deciding to provide the music: "Our Aucher piano was taken to the church and mingled its pleasant, slightly reedy sound with the bleating of the harmonium. The savages [Colette's way of describing her brothers] bolted themselves into the empty church and practiced the Suite from *L'Arlésienne*, some piece by Stradella and another by Saint-Saëns specially adapted for the wedding ceremony." Colette's vivid memories of her two brothers come particularly alive for the reader today as much through music as anything else; she recounts, again near the end of *Sido*, how they would make up their own nonsense rhymes to well-known tunes, including Torelli's famous *Serenade*. And if most families produce amateur child musicians of some sort, it is worth remembering just how large a part of Colette's own memories in these two autobiographical books include music and singing. Perhaps this writer who remembered and wrote down so many lines about "un cachet de benzo-naphtol" or "le baume analgésique du pharmacien Bengué" did not find it too difficult to think up those curious lines for the Teapot or Arithmetic in *L'Enfant et les sortilèges*.

There may have been some music at Colette's own village wedding in 1893, although we know from her piece *Noces* that it was no festive affair. As she became accustomed, with difficulty, to her new life in Paris, she must surely have realized that nothing was more different from the music she had enjoyed in her teen-age years than the music to which she was now more or less forced to listen in the company of her husband, Willy (more correctly, Henri Gauthier-Villars), who was a sophisticated music critic seriously interested in all that was new and "trendy" at the time in addition to the classics which he obviously knew well.

Paris in the 1890's is perhaps remembered more easily today for music of the Offenbach type (this highly successful German-Jewish immigrant had died in 1880) than for the more serious work that music lovers could hear if they sought it out at the Conservatoire or the Colonne and Pasdeloup concert halls. Many more people would enjoy Charpentier's opera *Louise* in 1902 than Debussy's *Pelléas et Mélisande* in 1906, while lovers of Wagner, among them

Henri Gauthier-Villars, usually made the pilgrimage to Bayreuth in order to enjoy him to the full. The Wagner-lovers did *not* include Colette. She, as we know, introduced a caricature-portrait of her husband in the last two of the *Claudine* novels and again in *La Retraite sentimentale* of 1907, presenting him as the music critic "Maugis." Apparently Willy himself had invented and actively enjoyed this amusing but hardly flattering or attractive portrait of himself, but it must be agreed that Colette's handling of the figure is very funny. Hardly dated, even today, this portrait-caricature can still remind us of the exuberant and snobbish music critic whom most of us meet from time to time. He is a perennial and international figure, genuinely fond of music and often very erudite, even if self-absorbed.

Colette learned a great deal from Willy about writing generally and about that particularly difficult art, writing about music. He "organized" many young people, including journalists and would-be or budding composers, into writing the column *Les Lettres de l'Ouvreuse* in the newspaper *L'Echo de Paris*. These "apprentices," who were anonymous at least when they began writing, included even Claude Debussy, the critic Emile Vuillermoz, and of course Colette herself. Her memories of this work were not good and in her autobiographical book *Mes apprentissages* she told how she was forced to correct the proofs of these articles so late at night in the newspaper offices that she could hardly keep awake. However, she learned a good deal about music, both from listening to it and from hearing composers, performers, and critics talk about it. Obviously, we do not think of her as a music critic, but she looked at and listened to the composers with a novelist's eye and ear. It was the novelist who left us that unforgettable portrait of Claude Debussy in the late sketches *Trait pour trait* of 1949:

> One Sunday evening, after we had heard *Antar* played for the first time in France, unless perhaps it was *Schéherazade*, chance brought us together, and Debussy, obsessed and overwhelmed, was singing his symphonic memories within himself. He was humming like a swarm of bees or a row of telegraph poles, a searching and undecided murmur. Then the memory became precise and his closed face suddenly opened.
>
> "Wait! Wait!" he said very loudly. "Like this ... mmmmmmm ... and like that: mmmmmm ...."
>
> One of us caught hold of this remembered scrap of melody as it flew by and drew it out further.
>
> "Yes, yes," Debussy cried. "And while this is going on there are the cellos lower down, saying: mmm ... And the kettledrums, my goodness, the kettledrums, just a faint murmur which prepares us for the explosion of the brass, and ... and ...."
>
> He pursed his lips, then miaowing as he went on to imitate the

violins, he panted, torn apart by the timbres which vied for places in his memory. He continued to imitate the music by hammering on the piano with the poker, drumming on the window with his fingers and doing his best to recreate the xylophone and the celesta."[1]

It is a lively, comical picture and yet, without using a single musical term, Colette manages to convey something of Rimski-Korsakov as he sounded to people who had never heard him before.

Colette's contact with music was not limited to the concert hall and the opera house, for it should not be forgotten that she spent some happy, hard-working years on the music-hall stage where she appeared in mime-drama. There has been a good deal of speculation about the quality of her performance as a mime and it is probably safer to admire the old theatrical photographs of, say, Rêve d'Egypte (1907) or La Chatte amoureuse (1912) than to say she was highly accomplished, although some of her contemporaries found her performances deeply moving. Whatever her merits as a silent stage performer (her untrained voice, with the accent of Burgundy which she never lost, did not not help her as an actress), she can only have learned more about music, although admittedly not music of any high quality. The success of these odd little mime dramas must have depended almost entirely on the interplay between movement and music, although this latter was surely intermittent.

Yet only someone who had a true feeling for music could have written two memorable pieces about dancing that have not often been quoted. One is the article Ecole de danse which she wrote for Le Matin in 1914 and was later included in the posthumous collection Contes des Mille et un matins (1970); the other is one of her reviews which she wrote in the 1930's, published in La Jumelle noire, 1934–1938. Ostensibly the article was about the Ballets Jooss but it went beyond a mere notice:

> When the human spirit is possessed with misanthropy and turns away from man, detesting momentarily the sound of words, singing, and laughter, it can still bear, in fact, it seeks out, the spectacle of dancing. I imagine that we all go through these crises — fatigue, intolerance, sadness — during which time nothing appears to be empty enough. At these times it is not the theatre or the screen which can reconcile us with our own species. Only dancing, with its wings, its paradoxes and its conventions, its mimicry without depth, can give us any pleasure; I am no longer surprised that when I come tired and lifeless to an evening of ballet or even to one of those colorful music-hall celebrations, where words play a part as modest as it is unintelligible, I leave feeling better, and sociable.[2]

This quotation is one small reminder of the many elements which had made up

Colette's musical education. Her training had in fact been far from formal, but music had obviously been in the air when she was a child and she had been quick to learn from her practical experience in the concert hall and in theatres of all types. By the time of her second marraige in 1913 she had left the stage temporarily at least and was working mainly as a journalist. Three years later, in 1916, she received an unexpected offer which was to enable her to use this knowledge and to express herself as a poet working with a composer. She was asked by Jacques Rouché, director of the Paris Opéra, if she would write the libretto for what she herself described much later, in the *Journal à rebours*, as a "fantasy-ballet." The choice of subject was left to her and she found she had an idea for a kind of fairy-tale opera. She surprised herself by completing the work within a week, for as a rule she wrote slowly and painfully, complaining to all her friends about the tedious toil of composition.

At this point World War I was already two years old and had naturally changed her existence. She published no major novels at this period and risked German bombs to be near her second husband, Henry de Jouvenel, who had been mobilized. At the same time she enjoyed, when she could, the company of her little daughter, Colette de Jouvenel, who was now three years old and supervised at the family chateau in the Corrèze district by an English nurse. Colette's first title for her libretto was in fact *Divertissement pour ma fille* ("Diversion for my daughter"). Jacques Rouché of the Opéra liked her text, invited her to see him, and suggested various composers who might set it to music. He mentioned many eminent names, but she listened in polite silence until he mentioned Ravel, who was best known in France at that time for his one opera to date, *L'Heure espagnole*, and the ballet suite *Daphnis et Chloé*. Colette's hopeful and excited reaction left no doubt about her feelings, but Rouché warned her that even if Ravel agreed to use her libretto, he was unlikely to work very fast.

Colette not only enjoyed Ravel's music; she had met him personally as far back as 1900, when they had both attended the musical soirées held in Paris by Madame de Saint-Marceaux. Many years later, in the *Journal à rebours*, Colette wrote a memorable description of them. Composers, musicians, and serious *amateurs* would gather at the house every Wednesday for dinner, and the evening that followed provided entertainment of the most varied kind. The composers Fauré and Messager might improvise duets at the piano, trying to catch each other out by "sudden modulations" and changes of key. The Prince de Polignac, wearing a beige vicuña shawl, would listen and draw caricatures at the same time, while a female marmoset would eat up any cake crumbs that had fallen to the floor. Occasionally the musicians would go through the old music books in the house and sing sentimental songs from 1840 or so, and history was made for Colette at least when Messager arrived one evening with the score of *Pelléas et Mélisande*, "clasping it to his heart, as if he had stolen it."

The other rising star of these soirées was Ravel himself, who was two years younger than Colette. It was here that she first met him, and she remembered in *Journal à rebours* every detail of his appearance. "Side-whiskers ... of voluminous hair exaggerated the contrast between his imposing head and his tiny body. He loved striking cravats, shirts with ruffles." He wanted attention but he was sensitive, and often hurt by the remarks of music critics, who of course included Colette's husband. She realized that he was "perhaps inwardly shy [and] ... maintained a distant air, a dry manner." She did not become friendly with him, for indeed few people did so, but she was drawn to the young composer's music first by curiosity and later, to use her own words, by a slight thrill of surprise, the "sensuous and malicious attraction of a new art." It is significant that the same phrase could be applied to her own writing.

The libretto she wrote in 1916, however, appeared to be different from all her other work through its form alone. While it contains more of pure fantasy than anything else she wrote, it begins in the world of reality, moves into a singular type of fairyland, then returns to the real world again.

The outline of the libretto is now fairly well known, but that does not make it any less surprising or more credible. A naughty little boy won't copy his lesson — he hates everything and everybody. He breaks the teapot, hurts the squirrel in its cage, pours water on the fire, attacks the little people on the wallpaper, and takes the clock to pieces. Then he sees the furniture dancing; the teapot and the cup threaten him, and so does the fire. The fairy-tale princess has lost her magic power, for he has torn up the story book in which he first met her. A strange old man appears, personifying Arithmetic, and a whole choir of numbers chant multiplication tables, which are in fact all wrong. Two cats sing or rather mew a love-duet. The scene then changes to the garden. All the creatures who live there — the dragonfly, the bat, the frog and the squirrel — reproach the child for his destructive behavior and punish him. Suddenly the little boy sees that the squirrel has been hurt, and bandages his paw with a piece of ribbon. His own hand has been hurt, too. The animals want to save him, for they have been touched by his kindness to the squirrel. They call for his mother, the only person who can help.

It is a lyric fantasy, a poem with hardly any rhymes, a moral tale in fact. It might have been called pure escapism, for in 1916 most people were forced to give their attention to other things. Ravel at the time was driving an army truck at the front, and the copy of this libretto never reached him. The war came to an end, and it was 1919 before he eventually saw what Colette had written. He was the first to appreciate the freedom allowed by this fantasy and felt he could use it for what he called in a letter an "American operetta," presumably thinking of musical comedy. He began to think about setting it and told the author that he was writing notes, although not a note of music. He added that there might be some alterations, but no cuts. On the contrary, he suggested that the squirrel's little story might be expanded.

"Just think," he wrote, "of all the things a squirrel could say about the forest and how that would lend itself to music!"[3] His friend, however, did not catch his enthusiasm, and the squirrel had to be content with a few lines of prose. Colette responded more positively to another of Ravel's suggestions. Her original libretto had included a figure representing a cup of Limoges porcelain. The cup took part in the action and scolded the child, using strong local words — words such as "Fouchtra!" This not very musical expression can be clearly seen in the one surviving page of Colette's original manuscript version. But Ravel had a better idea. "What would you think," he wrote to his collaborator, "of the cup and the teapot in old black Wedgwood singing a ragtime?" To hear such a thing at the National Academy of Music seemed to him highly entertaining. Colette agreed. "A rag-time," she replied in March 1919, "of course!" And she hoped a terrifying gale would stir up the dust at the Opéra. So the teapot and the cup were given nonsensical dialogue that was half-Chinese and half-English. Ravel knew nothing of English and left this to Colette, who was no linguist, but at least heard it spoken by her daughter's nurse.

Ravel did not say much more to Colette about the text, although he pointed out somewhat coldly that he had no daughter, and therefore the title would have to be changed. She found him much changed, too, no longer flamboyant in any way, and he "touched everything with a squirrel's glance." He also asked if the cats could sing "mouain" instead of "mouau," or, as she was to write later, perhaps it was the other way round, she could not remember. In the final version of the libretto we read only "Duo miaulé musicalement." Colette's mother, the famous Sido, had told her when she was little that cats were divine creatures; not everyone could understand them. If, in this opera, all other animals could talk, cats must keep their age-old distinction by using a language strictly their own.

Other operas were long in the making, but few as long as this one. No fewer than five years passed after these early consultations. Colette then approached Ravel again, inquiring hopefully about his progress. In the end there seemed no possibility of a production at the Paris Opéra, but in March 1925 Ravel at last wrote to his collaborator with details of the première — it was to take place in Monte Carlo. A suite awaited her at the Hôtel de Paris, he said, where the food was indigestible and soigné. If she had a moment, he asked, could she write another verse for the aria addressed by the child to the Princess, "Toi, le coeur de la rose." However, Colette had to travel a good deal that year; she was acting in *Chéri* in the provinces and in Belgium, and perhaps this is why the text remains at seven short lines of lyrical prose.

Some music critics had misgivings about the collaboration between these two controversial artists, the enchantress and the illusionist, as the composer and critic Roland-Manuel called them. Ravel himself was prepared for criticism, especially about the mixture of styles in the work, but he stated in the biographical sketch he wrote that this would not worry Colette, while he himself didn't care a damn. The Monte Carlo production was a success, but the Paris audiences who heard the work at the Opéra-Comique in 1926 were taken aback. Some people found it funny, some were offended by the music-hall treatment of certain passages. The composer Honegger, one of the group known as "Les Six," believed that Ravel's handling of the famous cat duet was brilliant programme music, for he did not *imitate* cats, he used their mewing as a basis for his melodic line. Ravel did not attend the première because he was on his way to Scandinavia. But he read a review in the newspaper *Le Temps* and wrote to a friend that his opera seemed to have "taken a knock."

Colette, of course, like Ravel, was used to a mixed reception. Many of her books had suffered the same treatment on publication, and in fact still do, while in Britain at least critics still argue about the opera itself. Those who regard the work as a masterpiece realize that the libretto and the score could not exist independently of each other. If the writer and the composer had come together more or less by accident and did not seem too close personally, they did share several affinities, more perhaps than they knew themselves. They were perceptive artists who both possessed an ironic sense of humor, and in their respective mediums, they were each capable of virtuoso achievement. They both loved the mysterious elegance of cats, but at a much deeper level they related the world of animals to the world of humans. Colette in fact once wrote in "Paradis terrestre" (*En pays connu*) that her image of paradise or fairyland could not exist without animals. Ravel had already set to music those challenging prose texts by Jules Renard, the "Histoires naturelles," and composed *Ma mère l'Oye*, the Mother Goose suite.

Most of her life, ever since the Claudine books and the *Dialogues de bêtes* of 1904, Colette had written about animals, but she never wrote mere descriptions of them. She seemed to write from inside their minds, and through them she watched humans. During the first World War Colette was naturally horrified by the aggressive behavior of people, and in 1916, the year when she wrote the opera libretto, she published *La Paix chez les bêtes* — Peace among animals. Men were tearing each other to pieces, she wrote, but she believed they had established a new relationship with animals, giving back to them an earthly paradise which civilization had removed. She dedicated the little book to soldiers who had learned to live peacefully with animals, while one essay even contains a description of cats singing about love and war. Was this so far from *L'Enfant et les sortilèges*? I think not, for no one part of her writing was entirely isolated from any other. Her approach was usually indirect, and at the same time personal. She had watched her small daughter, she remembered herself as a child, she remembered her love for her mother. Ravel too had been deeply attached to his mother, and all his life he remained close to childhood through his passionate interest in fairy tales. Animals who help a willful child because suddenly he has helped them: it sounds sentimental, and

Ravel himself would never have looked for such a theme. But such is the controlled fantasy of its presentation that he accepted it gladly. Colette herself found tears in her eyes when she saw the opera and was aware that Ravel, although he always worked obliquely, had expressed much of his own personal tenderness in the music.

The enchantress then had melted the heart of the illusionist. When her own novels were dramatized she preferred to work closely with a professional playwright. Her collaboration with Ravel might seem on the surface to be more remote, but in reality it *was* close, for they shared so much that could only be expressed indirectly through their work. In a moment of light-hearted irony Ravel once wrote that he was transcribing a forlana by Couperin and would like to see Mistinguett and Colette dance it together in fancy-dress in the Vatican. But there is no doubt of his deep respect for her genius; in the opera the orchestra never dominates the voice. And as the reputation of the work spread, Colette herself thought only of Ravel: "The frogs croak and jump," she wrote in "Paradis terrestre" (*En pays connu*), "the bats squeak, the dragonflies waltz...In her gay little piece of magic the librettist had not imagined that an orchestral wave, starred with nightingales and fireflies, would raise her modest offering to such a pitch."[4]

Ravel died in December 1937 after a long nervous illness which involved loss of memory and the inability to work. When in 1945 the French violinist Hélène Jourdan-Morhange published a moving tribute to him, *Ravel et nous*, it was Colette who wrote the preface, regretting that this courageous man had left the musical scene with so much still unexpressed, "so many birds, guitars, dances and melodious nights." No doubt she remembered their meetings over the years and their one but eminently successful collaboration. She had described him earlier in *Journal à rebours* as composing beneath the "nyc-talopic," day-blind gaze of his cats, and now she wrote that only a cat could celebrate Ravel, the "affectionate master of cats from Siam." And who, except Colette and Ravel, could have collaborated on that unique opera, *L'Enfant et les sortilèges*?

Notes

1. Colette, *Trait pour trait, Oeuvres complètes* (Paris: Le Flammarion, 1950), Vol. XIV, pp. 191–192.

2. Colette, *La Jumelle noire, Oeuvres complètes*, Vol. X, p. 333.

3. This letter from Ravel and others quoted in this article are drawn from Roland-Manuel's *Maurice Ravel* (Paris: Gallimard, 1948).

4. Colette, "Paradis terrestre," *En pays connu, Oeuvres complètes* Vol. XIV, pp. 381–382.

12 The Theatre as Literary Model: Role-playing in *Chéri* and *The Last of Chéri*

MARI McCARTY

The writer is both actor and author, meaning that he or she conceives the novelistic text as both practice (actor) and product (author), process (actor) and effect (author), play-acting (actor) and value (author) —Julia Kristeva[1]

Colette the woman lived her life with a theatrical flair, and it is not surprising that her writings exhibit this element as well. Theatrical references surface at every stage of the text, from the basic level of the word itself to the overall ambiance of an entire book. In the process, they sustain a powerful dramatic illusion for the reader while at the same time providing the key to a new understanding of her prose.

Colette's characters are more than usually conscious of themselves as performers. They are constantly concerned with the way they will be perceived from outside. In addition to monitoring their physical appearance, Colette's characters calculate their words and movements in advance to provide the greatest possible effect for their spectators. Even when under the stress of a great emotion, they are eternally vigilant to the appearance and impact of their acts on their audience.

Many of Colette's characters are connected with the stage or draw their behavior model from the theatre. Farou in *The Other One* is a playwright, Michel in *Duo* a producer-director, Renée in *The Vagabond* an actress — and the list goes on. The dramatic tendencies are not limited to the professional actors in her books, however. Non-actor characters do not escape role-playing in their everyday lives, and, indeed, embrace it with enthusiasm. Calliope in *Claudine and Annie* is adept at a "theatrical entrance," and Minne, the

Innocent Libertine, wrings her hands "like a little girl who would play Phaedra." Passers-by watching a building occupied by bandits are electrified by the scene being played before them, and one bystander guards her "front and center seat" from a usurper who would take it from her ("La Bande," *Dans la Foule*). The Vagabond Renée Néré operates a reversal when she spies Max from the wings: "He has become the spectacle for me." This willingness to view others and oneself as a spectacle involves the reader as well in what can only be described as a systematic destruction of the traditional novel's notion of fixed character. In Colette, character is self-projection.

Chéri offers a particularly rich example of the theatrical tendency in Colette. Most of the novel is set in closed rooms (Léa's bedroom especially) or strictly defined spaces (such as Charlotte Peloux's garden) reminiscent of the confines of a stage.[2] The lighting intensifies the theatrical feeling: Chéri first appears in front of Léa's rose-colored curtains, as the streaming sunlight bathes everything in a rosy glow. Standing before a long mirror placed between two windows, Chéri is able to contemplate himself as if on a stage flanked by curtains, encompassed by a proscenium arch (mirror frame).[3] Later, his features are highlighted by Léa's rose-colored lamps, giving his mouth a rouged look. Significantly, when Chéri leans over the dining room table, "the sunlight playing upon the white tablecloth and the glassware illuminated him as if by footlights" (*Chéri*, VI, 57).

Indeed, Colette sees her characters as performers in the limelight. Perceiving all of humanity to be actors in the vast, mannered comedy of life, she endows each of her characters with the traits and accessories which befit his or her role. These roles are not arbitrarily assigned, but are specifically tailored to each character. Elaine Marks has noted the "types" which appear in the novels, making it seem "as if she were writing for a fixed cast of players: the adolescent, the demi-mondaine, the unoccupied male"[4] — but, in many cases, Colette has endowed these "types" with a seeming autonomy. Fascinatingly, they appear to have *chosen* their role, and are acutely conscious of playing it.

As the drama critic Eric Bentley has pointed out, there is no alternative to role-playing, whether in the drama or in real life: "The choice is only between one role and another."[5] As with any performing assignment, a consciously assumed role may be well- or badly acted. The most effective roles are those which exhibit certain aspects of the true personality, aspects which the individual wishes to emphasize. Other aspects, less attractive, may be left out of the role. Conversely, people wishing to appear evil, or to stand remembered for their eccentricities, may emphasize other traits; one fashion designer, for example, uses an "odious theatrical laugh" to intimidate his models (*La Chambre éclairée*, V, 437). It is important that the role be consistent in order to be believable. In addition, it must be checked constantly to insure that it has not been outgrown.

The best role-players are those who choose to play the role of themselves,[6] creating a second skin which corresponds exactly to their true nature in every facet but one: vulnerability. By excising vulnerability from one's role, one is less likely to suffer the intense emotional pain which life can inflict. When the role has become second nature, one can rest secure, at least temporarily, from great upheavals in one's existence. Carried to extremes, this protective role can become a cocoon shutting one off from the world's joys as well as from its griefs; but assumed with intelligence and awareness, such a role allows much emotion to penetrate it, without for all that leaving one's raw nerves exposed to every attack of the Other. This defense, Colette finds, is necessary, and, indeed, salutory.

The situation in *Chéri* is extremely conducive to role-playing. Léa is a "grande cocotte," one of the successful courtesans of Paris at the turn of the century. Her profession demands that she play a constant role in her dealings with men.[7] Indeed, many of the courtesans of the day were also stage actresses. Léa thinks that her relationship with Chéri is just another interlude in which she plays her role with a younger man; she will find that such is not the case. For Chéri's part, he has become accustomed to a certain behavior by his long liaison with Léa, and enjoys playing the role of child to her mother-figure — as a courtesan's son himself, he has grown up in a theatrical atmosphere. The two of them will find during the course of the book that the roles they have played for years are no longer valid. Léa must come to grips with the onset of aging and all its attendant changes, and Chéri will try to abandon the psychological role of child.[8] Léa's role is a healthy one, being based on a strong self-image, and will ultimately withstand the test by accepting an inevitable metamorphosis; Chéri's more inadvertent role will prove unequal to the challenge, as is evident in *The Last of Chéri*.

Léa's role consists in maintaining a gracious equilibrium by careful attention to her appearance. The presence of any spectator, including her own reflection, recalls her to this noble demeanor. Her home is filled with mirrors, the better to see herself objectively. Even while eating alone in the dining room, she scrutinizes herself and her mirrored surroundings. When she finished, "she had ample time to note the 'Madame is beautiful' in her butler's discreet glance, which did not displease her" (p. 23). She never lets down her guard when she is with someone else. When Mme Peloux, Chéri's mother, suggests they relax in kimonos, Léa refuses: "These disheveled afternoon siestas disgusted her. Her young lover had never seen her untidily dressed, nor with her blouse undone, nor wearing slippers during the day. 'Naked, perhaps,' she always said, 'but squalid, never'" (p. 29).

Mme Peloux is herself an accomplished performer, whose role has been known to change according to the age and behavior of her son. Once Chéri became old enough to go out on his own, Mme Peloux took up her new part with gusto: "'Ah, for us mothers, life is such a cross to bear!' — and passed painlessly from the state of the happiest-of-mothers to that of the martyr-mother" (p. 33).

Unfortunately, Mme Peloux's ability to thus change her role with the times is done in the wrong manner for the wrong reasons. Instead of allowing her son to grow and become an adult, she has kept him a child by her motherly attitude which alternates between smothering and laissez-faire. Léa's subsequent tutelage serves to reinforce Chéri's childlike qualities. The difference in ages has led to a natural division into mother/teacher Léa versus child/pupil Chéri. Chéri alternates between the pouting "schoolboy," the mischievous scamp, and the grateful child seeking security from his "Nounoune."

After Chéri's marriage, Léa must put on a mask of contentment to forestall prying by Mme Peloux. When Léa realizes she is in love with Chéri, it rocks her role to its foundation. The part she has fashioned for herself required that she be a beloved but independent woman who never allowed herself to fall in love, since she would then have to relinquish her total command of her emotions. Her search for an outward change of scenery will not change this inner problem.

For his part, Chéri is completely disoriented after his marriage. His role as Léa's pampered young lover is the only one he can remember, and he is unable to change it now. In *The Last of Chéri* Colette will refer to Chéri as a tormented actor parading before a cruel audience; now, with his young wife Edmée, Chéri may be likened to an actor who is outgrowing his juvenile type-casting but refuses to accept the inevitable. When, crying, Edmée accuses him of still loving Léa, Chéri is at a loss as to his response. Léa never cried before him, and therefore never taught him the appropriate reaction. Nevertheless he remembers Léa's lines from the scenes they used to play together, and "he tried to imitate the tone and words of the voice whose power he knew so well" (p. 86).

Conscious, just as Léa was, of his appearance to others, he maintains a superior position by his outward demeanor: "the secret lay in the way he carried his head, the sureness of his stance, the easy grace of his shoulders and arms . . ." (p. 89). But this act is only mechanical during Léa's absence, and it is not until her return that he becomes revitalized. When Chéri sees Léa's lights ablaze in her home, Colette uses a nearby streetlamp almost like a spotlight recalling him to his former role.

As for Léa, her momentary resolve to sink unresistingly into stereotypical old age is shaken by a visit from Charlotte Peloux:

> She had seated Charlotte Peloux in a deep armchair, in the soft light of the silk-panelled room, just like the old days. She herself had automatically taken the high-backed chair which forced her to pull back her shoulders and keep up her chin, just like the old days. (p. 119)

Erect and gracious, she meets Mme Peloux's cruel insinuations with equanimity. For her part, Mme Peloux knows how to make the most of her ammunition, by the careful use of props and pauses: "She broke off and lit a cigarette, as clever as an actress at this kind of suspenseful pause" (p. 120).

Léa is ready for her, secure in her ability to withstand the onslaught as she has before. Her outward appearance will remain serene, strengthened by years of discipline. As if to emphasize the return of her role, a warm light returns and bathes the participants and the curtains which flank them. Léa has again resumed her part in the play, and feels strangely happy in the role of herself:

> All this must be taken up again since it's Life, it's my life.... Let's begin again, since it's been decreed. Let's do it cheerfully, since it's so easy to sink back into the comfortable grooves of the old life...
> (p. 120)

A remark about Chéri causes her to redden, however, and the light she welcomed only a minute ago now exposes her emotion to Charlotte Peloux, whose eye is ever watchful. Nevertheless, when Charlotte leaves, Léa is exhilarated by their rivalry, which she knows will keep her alert and careful about her looks.

The ache she feels at losing Chéri is still there, however, and to assuage it, she tells herself that she might not say no to a new young lover. What follows shows one of the most fascinating characteristics of a Colettian role: its remarkable ability to summon spectators which provide the needed impetus for performance. Although completely alone in her room, Léa still maintains her role for the benefit of an *invisible*, but powerful, audience: "She carefully smiled a mysterious and provocative smile, to delude the phantoms which could be hovering around the dressing table and the formidable bed gleaming in the shadows" (p. 130). These ghostly spectators prevent her from letting down her guard.

When the doorbell rings at midnight, Léa's immediate and instinctive gesture is to powder her face. The application of makeup will bolster her role in the face of the caller, whoever it may be. Chéri bursts into the room, and after a moment of surprise, Léa is again in control of herself; it is easier to finally play a scene with Chéri than to have played it with phantoms all these months. She is ready for a flawless performance: "The wild beating of her heart had subsided, allowing her to breathe easily again, and she wanted to play her role without a mistake" (p. 134). But Chéri protests her quickness to turn everything into "melodrama," and falls at her feet, crying with joy, searching for his accustomed spot nestled against her. He begs her to recite the familiar litany of her mother/lover role, the scolding words delivered in an indulgent tone. Drinking them in blissfully, he entreats her to repeat the lines over and over. He has come home to his "Nounoune."

For Léa, the joy is so great that she forgets the discipline of years and makes the fatal mistake of dropping her role. The next morning, thinking Chéri still asleep, she opens the curtains and is plainly visible in the light. She who remained faithful to her part even when her only audience was composed of invisible phantoms has now let down her guard before her lover. Chéri sees her without defenses: "Not yet powdered, a meager twist of hair at the back of her neck, double chin and wrinkled neck, she was rashly exposing herself to the unseen observer" (p. 145). She leaves the room, and at her return "he was grateful to note that in those few minutes Léa had done her hair, put on some makeup, and splashed herself with her familiar scent" (p. 146). But the damage has been done. When she departed from her role, he was shocked from his. Sensing that she is losing him, Léa resorts to weak banter. "But at the same time she knew that her voice sounded weak and false: 'How badly I said that...just like bad theatre...'" (p. 148).[9] In her happiness, Léa had forgotten that Chéri is as much a spectator as he is her lover; now it is too late. To remind us of the theatrical nature of their scene, the sunlight streams in from between the curtains, exposing Léa's wrinkles in the cruel light. Forgetting the lines she should speak, Léa falls back on a stock scene of jealousy. It is a part that does not suit her, and Chéri brings her back to herself by exposing this unworthy role: "Is that the way for Nounoune to speak?" (p. 151). He then recalls Léa's kindness, her sense of style and grace, "that wonderful way you have of talking, of walking, your smile, the classy way you act . . ." (p. 153). Léa listens to this and accepts the fact that all this is of a past era. Chéri has seen the old woman she has become. With great nobility she sends him back to his wife and to the youth he has never known. It is her greatest performance.

Still, when he hesitates in the courtyard she has a moment of vain hope:

> "He's coming back! He's coming back!" she cried, raising her arms. An old woman, out of breath, repeated her movements in the oblong mirror, and Léa wondered what she could have in common with that madwoman. (p. 158)

The madwoman in the mirror represents the future role of ridiculous old woman she has been trying to avoid. At the same time, she realizes that one may age without being grotesque if one lets go some of the no longer seemly attributes of youth. The mirror has enabled her to see herself from outside. In spite of her pain, she is already lucid. As Chéri walks away, "Léa let the curtain fall" on the portion of her life he represents. She will no longer be able to play the beautiful courtesan, and she refuses to play the aging and ridiculous courtesan. Not wishing to appear the madwoman in the mirror, she will drop the coquettish part of her image, while retaining the sense of pride and dignity that has served her so well. That she achieves this goal is apparent in *The Last of Chéri*.

For Chéri, the decision to end the affair with Léa may have seemed to indicate his liberation from the childish role he had thus far played. But *The Last of Chéri* shows that such is not the case. Throughout the sequel, mirrors will serve as a stage upon which he will see himself hopelessly locked in his part of aging juvenile actor.

In *Chéri*, Léa used mirrors to strengthen and confirm her demeanor, and the book both begins and ends with mirror images. Léa's glance at her reflection fortified her role by reinforcing her acts at moments of triumph; it also informed her when the role's usefulness had ceased. As for Chéri, his role was more unconscious, since he was content to simply *be* the handsome man he saw in the mirror. Léa used makeup and accessories to make her outward self conform to her inner state; conversely, Chéri's outer beauty was the determiner of his inner life, and thus of his actions. His appearance decided his conduct.

This youthful role is doomed, of course, by the passage of time. Gradually, Chéri sees the mirror as his enemy, since it is beginning to show him tiny wrinkles appearing in his hitherto perfect face. In *The Last of Chéri*, the mirror image of an older Chéri is so shocking to him that he divorces himself from his reflection. He refers to "the image of Chéri" in the third person (p. 184), giving it autonomy. With its dim blue light, surrounded by the frame as if by a proscenium arch, the mirror-stage shows him the actions of a stranger. Chatting with wounded soldiers in a hospital, he feels like an unwitting actor in a "patriotic play" beyond his control (p. 186).

When he discovers Edmée's infidelity (significantly, in a scene played before a mirror), he finds it impossible to arouse any emotion in himself. He has become a passive spectator of a play in which there is no part for him. With Dr. Arnaud taking over his role as sexual companion to Edmée, Chéri withdraws into his own one-character play, with somber lighting and dark curtains supplied by Colette.

Chéri's visit to Léa is the center of the plot and of the text. After seeing her, Chéri's vague uneasiness becomes crystalized in a worship of the past; as to the text, the visit takes twenty pages in almost the very center of the work. After the visit, the rest of the book seems to accelerate. This impression is caused not only by the text on its level as signifier (the chapters, shorter and quickly read, seem to multiply), but also on its level of signified (two weeks go by between the chapter at Léa's apartment and the next one).

For Chéri, the visit offers a possible solution to his malaise, but it proves to be the shock which will lead ultimately to his suicide. This chapter is also the one most inherently "theatrical," since both he and Léa are playing roles as well as seeing themselves in an exterior manner. But they have both changed, and cannot resume their erstwhile parts. Chéri finds Léa's transformation shocking, and she, jolted by the surprise she sees in his eyes, becomes more animated. Chéri is not fooled: "He suspected Léa of putting on an act of hearty and epicurean geniality, just as a fat actor on stage plays 'jovial' characters because he has grown a paunch" (p. 222). Chéri himself speaks with a "false voice," but his bantering tone is belied by his face, which woodenly refuses to smile on command.

Beneath the surface posturings are the actions Chéri would like to perform, but cannot. These impulsions are so strong that, denied the ability to be expressed openly, they create an extraordinary event. Astounded, Chéri sees his image acting autonomously, kneeling and gesticulating before Léa:

> He was astonished to find himself seated in a carefree posture, his legs crossed, like a handsome young man with bad manners. For inwardly he was watching his double, kneeling, hopelessly lost, waving his arms, baring his breast, and crying out incoherently. (p. 219)

In the end, Chéri realizes that his hopes for a retrieval of the old Léa are illusory. With a wrenching effort, he separates himself from his double and makes a seemly exit from Léa's apartment.

Chéri goes home to his bedroom "as blue and dark as a stage night" (p. 239), which Edmée, too, perceives as a stage:

> All of a sudden, Edmée felt satiated by the *spectacle*: the shadow of the *curtains*, the palor of the sleeping man and the white bed lent to everything the romantic coloring of night and death. (p. 224, italics mine)

That they see this room as a theatre is significant: it is of course in the bedroom that Chéri and Edmée play out their conjugal farce. The futility of a recapture of the past is brought home to Chéri with a jolt when he again confronts his image in the mirror. Thin, hardened, with "tragic" eyes, Chéri sees himself as his "public" sees him, and realizes that his career is over. Abandoning all responsibility for his acts, he is no longer anxious to control his role:

> Once his cigarette was alight, with a little encouragement he would have strutted like a peacock in front of an invisible public, and taunted his tormentors with a "Good, isn't it?" ... He was beginning now to enjoy his extreme state of detachment....

From this, it is only a small step to the finality of death.

The Last of Chéri is the progression into darkness of one who has tired of playing his role. In the novel *Chéri*, Chéri welcomed the light instead of fleeing from it: the first passage of that work shows him in front of a mirror, basking in sunlight streaming through pink curtains. In *The Last of Chéri*, the war having intervened, Chéri wishes to "close the curtains" (p. 187), to shut out the too-white light, and welcomes the progressive shadowing of his mirror-stage. Finally, in the Pal's apartment, he no longer feels viewed by an audience; the dark curtains are perpetually drawn, and he is alone. Theatrics are no longer necessary: his short-lived effort to excite himself into crying "Nounoune" embarrasses him, since there is no longer any need to think of his public personality.

Like many others of his generation, Chéri has come back after the war to a world whose demands for performers have changed. The spectators no longer have any use for an aging "juvenile." His career in reality is over, and he finds that a mirror-stage is not enough to sustain him. His eyes unable to bear the bright lights, his youthful makeup fading, he can only ring the curtain down.

In *Chéri* and *The Last of Chéri*, Colette seems to be saying that role-playing can be salutory if the part is well chosen. The wrong role will lead to bad acting, "bad theatre"; conversely, no role at all leaves one defenseless, a victim, since one is unprotected from the cruelties of life. By accepting one's part gracefully and playing it with dignity, one can succeed. Those who decry Colette's supposed lack of "moral depth" have missed this evidence that she holds each person strictly accountable for his or her own actions.

Beyond this, however, what can we make of Colette's insistence on the theatrical? The popular concept "All the world's a stage" is not new — but no other novelist has ever infused an entire life's work with the depth and breadth of theatrical metaphor we see in Colette. In the final analysis, I think Colette is saying that it is time for an entirely new understanding of the process of literature. No longer can we employ the time-worn model of literature as "a painting of reality," or as "a mirror moving along a road." The new literary model must include the action and movement of *theatre*. Colette exhorted writers to make their readers see and hear, through dialogue, what their characters were doing. In the last century, the French poet Mallarmé wished to draw poetry in this direction; now, in the twentieth century, Colette must be seen as the prime mover of the novel toward this goal.

French critic Julia Kristeva sees the literary text as being produced by "the person who is both *subject* of the book (author) and object of the spectacle (actor)," because the message of the text is both discourse and representation. Kristeva states that "textual work recalls *theatre* space and the order of *heiroglyph,* as well as their fundamental complicity."[10] She goes on to find in theatre the key to all written work: "This incomparable theatre is visibly the metaphor of textual practice."[11]

Having sensed this inherent theatrical quality of prose, Colette went so far as to make it overt. For her, the form mirrors the essence of the content, the techniques reflect that of the themes: the essential theatricality of the text itself.[12]

Notes

All references to Colette's works are taken from the *Oeuvres complètes* (Paris: Flammarion, 1948–1950), 15 vols. All translations are mine.

1. Julia Kristeva, *Semeiotike: Recherches pour une sémanalyse* (Paris: Editions du Seuil, Collection "Tel Quel," 1969), p. 124.

2. Elaine Marks has likened Colette's settings to the *lieu unique et clos* of French classical tragedy. See Elaine Marks, *Colette* (New Brunswick, N.J.: Rutgers University Press, 1960), p. 67.

3. For a discussion of the mirror's distancing effect, see Paul Schilder, *The Image and Appearance of the Human Body* (New York: Science Editions, John Wiley & Sons, Inc., 1964), especially pp. 50, 52–53, 84, 224.

4. Marks, p. 68.

5. Eric Bentley, quoted in John P. Siak, "In Praise of Privacy," *Harpers* 250, No. 1497 (Feb. 1975), 106.

6. This recalls Margaret Crosland's judgment that Colette's life was a consummate performance in which she was "acting the role for which she had been cast. The role of course was that of herself." Margaret Crosland, *Colette: The Difficulty of Loving* (London: Peter Owen, 1973), p. 172.

7. This connection between acting and prostitution was not lost on the Church, which long denied salvation to performers on the grounds that they were no better than prostitutes. In this vein see Maurice Druon, writing in *Lettres Françaises* (12–15 août 1954). He accuses the Church of denying Colette a religious funeral for the same reason that it refused one to Molière.

8. Chéri's sexual role is ambiguous, since he displays androgynous qualities. His beauty and his interest in jewels are often highlighted by Colette as being "feminine."

9. Léa has fallen into the trap that in the theatre lies at the extreme of so-called "method acting": if an actor is so involved in his role that he forgets the audience, he is no longer acting. As Diderot noted in his *Paradoxe sur le comédien* (1773), an actor must maintain an awareness of the audience in spite of the unbridled emotion he is portraying. His technique keeps his brain clear, reminding him of proper body placement and voice projection, even as he appears to be lost in feeling.

10. Kristeva, pp. 124, 236. Italics are hers.

11. Ibid., p. 237.

12. For a complete discussion of the theatricality in Colette's works, see my *Colette: Theatrical Aspects of the Novel* (Doctoral diss., University of Wisconsin–Madison, 1977).

III. Generation: The Production and Texture of Writing

13 Writing, Language, and the Body
YANNICK RESCH

The mere mention of them [the springs] makes me hope that their taste will fill my mouth when my time comes, and that I may take with me that imagined drink. (Sido, VII, 182)

There is no doubt that nature lay open to Colette in all its sensuous dimensions. Seeing it was not enough; she had to touch it, feel it, and taste it. A voluptuous desire for annexation by means of the caress, a wish for possession or even absorption lies at the root of all true knowledge. The sensuous holds sway over intelligence, perception over meaning.

But to "dream" reality is to allow the body, which is itself space, milieu, and mirror, to speak and to desire. Many passages in Colette's work stress the body's "hunger" for the material world, its need to take possession of it:

> "Never touch a butterfly's wing with your finger." [...]
> "But only just lightly! Perhaps this will be the time when I shall feel under this particular finger, my fourth, the most sensitive, the cold blue flame and the way it vanishes into the skin of the wing — the feathers of the wing — the dew of the wing ..." (*Break of Day*, 24)

In this section from *La Naissance du jour* the narrator, who is none other than Colette herself, conjures up, in a pseudo-dialogue with the beloved and absent Sido, their shared attitude toward life. A dialectic of identity and difference marks each step of their relationship. In contrast to Sido, who knows that it is "in abstinence and only in abstinence" that true possession lies, Colette experiences a compelling urge to "succumb to temptation," to give herself to the pressing desire to appropriate beauty by physical contact with the material world. But identity and similarity are instantly reestablished through the common image of mother and daughter as two great lovers: "For a 'great lover' of her sort — of our sort — there is not much difference between the sin of abstention and that of consummation" (*Break of Day*, 24).

The intensely carnal relationship of the self with the world passes, therefore, through the mother. The influence of Sido's personality is clear. She so dominated Colette's sense of self as to create an imbalance in her identification with parental models. Many passages about Sido testify to a repressed paternal image: "It seems strange to me, now, that I knew him so little. My attention, my fervent admiration, were all for Sido and only fitfully strayed from her" (*Sido*, 175). This repression was to dissolve gradually in the act of writing, which allowed the author's self to take on progressively what is owed to the father:

> It takes time for the absent to assume their true shape in our thoughts. After death they take on a firmer outline and then cease to change. "So that's the real you? Now I see, I'd never understood you." (*Sido*, 186)

The evolution of the self and the search for a balance in the self's status in the world and in regard to others constitutes the deep substance of Colette's fiction, which records step by step the growth of a triumphant and serene femininity. Throughout this process, certain constants prevail: the predominance of female figures, the search for a model close to the maternal figure, the rejection of sharply individualized heroines in favor of a character created out of a collection of themes that focus on a basic lust for life.

But even more than characterization, it is the structure of the narrative that bears witness to this obsessive search. In the novels, especially those written during Colette's mature period, after 1920, we discover a narration model centered on a triangular situation which almost always recounts a crisis in the life of a couple. The situation always involves one man and two women. One woman is older and is characterized by her maternal instincts; the other, younger, fills the role of the rival. Colette's self is associated with each of these female figures.[1] It should be noted, moreover, that the self tends to become more masculine over a certain period. Male "heroes" make their appearance in *Chéri*, *Le Blé en herbe*, *La Chatte*. This tendency reaches its culmination with the death of the hero in *La Fin de Chéri* and *Duo*.

The preceding analysis results in the following pattern presented here diagrammatically:

Chéri	Léa	Chéri	Edmée
Le Blé en herbe	Mme Dalleray	Phil	Vinca
La Fin de Chéri	La Copine ("the Pal") (substitute for Léa)	Chéri	Edmée
La Seconde	Fanny	Farou	Jane
La Chatte	La Chatte (substitute for Mme Amparat)	Alain	Camille
La Naissance du jour	(a) Sido	Vial	the narrator
	(b) Colette	Vial	Hélène

La Naissance du jour [In the first combination (a), Colette occupies with regard to Vial a filial role dependent on her mother. In the second triangle, the rival becomes the young Hélène while Colette takes the position of the maternal role (b).]

Duo	Maria	Michel	Alice

(The maid-servant, Maria, of "Monsieur," ends by establishing a bond of friendship and complicity with Alice.)

Le Toutounier   The return of Alice to her two sisters who are also living out a triangular situation.

Julie de Carneilhan	Julie	her ex-husband	Marianne

These narratives tend to underline the fact that the self — whether masculine (as in *Chéri* or *La Chatte*) or feminine — experiences a certain fascination for the female figure most resembling the mother figure. This leads us to believe that the representation of the mother is essential in the constitution of the self, which can be defined only in relation to the maternal figure. The language of the body is first and foremost to inscribe the presence of Sido. What characterizes the mother is her instinct, her complicity with living things, her "presence" in the world, and her eternal youth. In order to understand how Colette's self is inscribed in the text, it is necessary to have firmly in mind these various evocations of Sido: always faithful to herself to the end of her days, impervious to old age because each instant requires her to be brand-new, always a figure of energy and permanence.

It has often been said that Colette abandons abstract analysis of feelings and emotions in order to concentrate on what reveals them: a nervous "tic," a stronger smell, a complexion that changes color. But how, actually, does she go about focusing on the "signs" of the body? How does she reveal what these signs betray or what they hide? How does she make the body "speak"?[2] Colette seeks less to outline psychologically complex characters than to suggest figures which resemble or contrast with each other in relation to a basic model, a model entirely directed toward the instinct of self-preservation.

The characterization of these figures conforms less to an individualization and more to a variation, a modulation on certain themes. A precise symbolism of colors and smells[3] allows us to divide the characters according to their ability to develop in themselves the life-instinct or the death-instinct. *Chéri* provides a good example: the golden pink of Léa's body and of her apartment is opposed to the whiteness of Chéri and the cold colors that surround him.

Certain colors reappear from narrative to narrative: the amber coloring, the vermilion of the cheeks of Léa, Julie de Carneilhan, and Alice; and the pale and sickly flesh-tones of Chéri, Michel, and Alain. By its connotations, color associates the body with life or sickness, with vitality or lifelessness, and divides the characters along lines of Energy/Inertia, lines which, in terms of the main characters alone, amount to an opposition between man and woman. Variations of color indicate fatigue, anger, the onset of old age, and more generally the emotions of the character: rouge on the cheeks becomes wine dregs; lip-coloring shades off into whitish mauve; joy and anger make blood rush to the cheeks.

Colette stresses the permanence of a color by means of frequent references in the text, and highlights the values it conceals by juxtaposing it with an abstract epithet. Variations and combinations of color invite the reader to perceive, beyond changes in the psychology of the characters, the resulting modifications in relationships and situations. A similar device is apparent in the choice of smells and perfumes which not only anticipate and prolong the body's presence but also mark its changes and metamorphoses.

The vocabulary of the body creates figures of good health, of the body's "dynamism": the neck "envelopes a bundle of muscles," the breast is "high" and "light," the buttock "muscular." Beauty lies in physical strength and vigor; complexion, the ruddy complexion of country people, of people who live in the open air, confirms it. With age the body wrinkles but does not subside into flaccidity or ruin. The evocation of Sido impervious to age and praised in death for having "already conquered her eternal twilight of the morning" (*La Naissance du jour*, VIII, 27) serves as the model for all female figures, through which the self is defined.

A form of beauty based on naturalness emerges and predominates: little use of make-up, few attempts at enhancing or changing one's looks, few sessions in front of the mirror. Settled in front of the mirror, this type of woman does not play the "coquette" but faces her imperfections and defects squarely. The body occasions no complacency: it does not attempt to draw attention to its owner any more than it seeks to seduce by opening itself to the look of others. This absence of narcissism is accompanied by an easy manner and a freedom of gesture which may appear provocative to others, even indecent, but which is no more than the consequences of the liberation of women in the face of the prejudices and taboos of their time.

It is on the subject of nudity that Colette has most clearly shown women's determination to escape from their role as object. The female body, caught for a moment emerging from the bath, or in the mirror, or crossing a room beneath the embarrassed gaze of others, seems to be innocently unaware of the codes and rules which determine what may be exposed and what may not. This freedom from inhibition among Colette's women is all the more apparent to the reader because male nudity, and the narcissistic self-awareness it denotes, is accompanied by feelings of guilt. As example we have Alain's dream in *La Chatte* in which he is afraid to cross a town square because he is naked with only a tie around his neck. The notion of femininity that emerges from these examples is in opposition to the generally accepted one of the fragile, vulnerable woman. These particular characteristics are attributed, in Colette, to men who become in the eyes of women a "male object."[4] Men are slightly feminine and meretricious, especially when they, like Chéri, have no opportunity of aspiring to a "rank in the animal aristocracy."

Figures of strength and health, descriptions of the body may also present figures of desire. Through the senses the body takes possession of the world. Hands play an important part in Colette's work: the chubby hands of children; the wrinkled, working hands of Sido; the beautiful, idle hands of Léa; the fine, delicate hands of Chéri; the criminal hands of Camille; hands like flowers with nails; hands covered with hair. The hand defines the character physically and socially, even becoming a substitute for the person, expressing the ideas and behavior of its owner. A man's hand inspires tenderness and compassion in a woman — she sees in it disarming vulnerability and childishness — whereas the female hand, by contrast, like the look, is an area of domination. A finger becomes inquisitorial, extracts confession, forces a dialogue. It is the "yoke" that Chéri shakes off, or the maternal consolation that Alain solicits.

In short, hands, at once firm and gentle, are almost always the substitute for the maternal figure. A whole vocabulary of loving behavior describes this ambiguous link with the mother. The hand "fondles" ("palpe"), "pats" ("ta-pote"), "feels" ("tâte") the male body curled up against the woman's shoulder. There is no need to describe the amorous situation as the hand adequately indicates to the reader that in such situations it is the woman who nearly always takes the initiative, and often in a maternal fashion. The virile aggres-siveness of Camille who touches Alain with "impatient hands" while he "lets himself go" ("tandis qu'il se laisse faire") is reminiscent of Léa who "pats [Chéri's] young body . . . with the irreverent pleasure of a nanny" (*Chéri*, 38).

Men are the object of admiration and desire: their muscles and more generally the whiteness of their skin are to be admired, as is the femininity of their lips. They need take no greater initiative than to let themselves go, to let themselves be loved, thereby rapidly becoming objects of consumption. The pleasure of touching leads to the desire to bite or nibble the body of the loved one. Masculine characters are frequently compared to enjoyable foods. There is the remark of Julie de Carneilhan: "I can't bear veal, lamb or kid, and I can't bear adolescents" (*Julie de Carneilhan*, 165). Then there is Chéri whom Léa places among those "little sweets" that she allows herself and from which she anticipates "a good case of indigestion." A whole vocabulary confirms this comparison. She "fattens him up," "stuffs him," and Chéri, subjected to this delicate and tender nourishment, surrenders to it like a small child.

The link between sexuality and nourishment has no longer to be proved. Colette's work provides a highly convincing analysis of the relation between the two, often associating men, in their refusal to chew and digest, with that "naughty suckling child" which Léa could never bring into the world. Other thematic associations are suggested between excessive greed and anorexia, which show the roles of man and woman reversed in love relationships.

Everyone eats well in Colette's narratives. A good, although not excessive, appetite is "de rigueur." A well-chosen cuisine is savored. Women are "gour-mettes" rather than "gourmandes." They give great care to the choice of dishes and to what goes with them. One need only witness the refinement of Léa who, for a luncheon of delicate fish and pastries, "replaces a Bordeaux by a dry Champagne," or the delicate taste of Alice who suggests a drop of Beaujolais "to give pleasure to the cheese." Gustatory pleasure is marked by moderation, by respect for food. One eats in silence; Léa "savors" her coffee, "chooses *chasselas* grapes one by one," and considers her meals a "recreation."

For all of the female figures, eating is a celebration, a treat not only for the palate but for the eye and nose, for the whole body. Their pleasure begins with the setting of the meals, always airy places made more spacious by mirrors and cosily furnished. Their pleasure extends into the choice of china, with beauti-ful porcelain and crystal echoing each other harmoniously in shape and hue: "a crown of five white plates circling a black crystal vase with floating pink water lilies — the same pink as the table cloth." Noticeable here is the play of colors and the choice of materials which allow for effects of transparency and luminosity. Even a frugal meal deserves great care: Léa enjoys "June straw-berries, served, with their stalks, on a plate of Rubelles enamel as green as a tree-frog after the rain" (*Chéri*, 12). The reader becomes aware of the pleasure derived from this "corps à corps" with food. Léa displays "the strong teeth of a gourmande"; she pats her "joyous stomach" and "presents a gourmande's face." These descriptions are reminiscent of Sido who "happily sat down to table, spoon in hand."

The joy provided by food is linked to the fact that women experience a feeling of physical and moral well-being in the act of eating. In *Le Toutounier* the Eude girls who, for lack of money, "picnic" all year long, are particularly aware of the flow of energy created by a balanced, healthy diet: "Columbe blossomed (*refleurissait*) through the good offices of red meat and honest wine." "Refleurir" is the word which captures the physical expansion that accompanies the art of eating well. For eating is not only a pleasure but a remedy, the ultimate remedy against sickness. We should remember that the appetite of Colette's heroines is symbolic of their lust for life. The world is seen as digestible or, more specifically, as something to be savored. In *Chéri*, the old woman Lili is "greedy" for painting and painters, and in *Duo* Alice feeds herself on air, rose bushes, and "café au lait." Many are the examples which describe female characters' hunger for life.

Good health, however, can be affected by what Léa calls her "moral indiges-tion," by a kind of suffering which, although it gives rise to physical disorders, is almost invariably linked to love. There is no other remedy for this "mal de coeur moral" than good solid "lusty" food. Nervous tensions caused by emotional discussions, quarrels, and separations are always stabilized by eating: "In a few moments boiling milk, black coffee and the butter lying at the bottom of the well would fulfill their healing office" (*Break of Day*, 111). This quotation shows how the narrator of *La Naissance du jour* regains her strength following a sleepless night and an exhausting discussion with Vial. Similarly, Léa finds solace after a difficult afternoon at Charlotte Peloux's in "a cup of thick chocolate beaten up with the yolk of an egg, some toast, and a bunch of grapes" (*Chéri*, 61). After Chéri's departure she plans a trip to the south "to eat the cooking of garlic and sunshine." Alice, too, knows that by eating she will be up to facing a crisis: before admitting to her husband that she has been unfaithful, she exclaims, "we need some good nourishing food," and when Michel falls ill, she reacts by sitting down to a solid meal of stuffed cabbage.

Food plays a therapeutic role as well as underlining women's determination to resist all forms of aggression whether physical or psychic. With the onset of old age, women develop closer affiliations with food. With the end of amorous conflicts, a friendship with men begins which is devoid of aggression and coincides with a change in diet: "When one stops liking a certain kind of cannibalism, all the other kinds leave of their own accord, like fleas from a dead hedgehog" (*Break of Day*, 37). Old age is marked by a return to vegetarianism. Moreover, in matters of food it is women who are capable of reviving in men a taste for life by teaching them the art of good eating. Indeed, men, unlike women, are incapable of extracting from food the energies necessary to weather crises and griefs. Men are shown as lacking appetite; they eat poorly, they nibble at their meat or indulge to excess; Chéri "stuffs" himself with cherries and goodies. His childhood is a tale of "a glut of sweets" alternating with "hunger pangs." While men give in to anarchy and excess in matters of food, Colette's women find in it means to develop their sensuality, to bring calm to their lives, and to resist all manner of trials.

Nourishment occupies a central place in Colette's fictional universe not only because of its associations but also because of what it reveals of the maternal relationship. The only true food is derived from the mother. An overall "reading" of the function of food reveals the predominance of foods that one might qualify as "soft foods" over the "solids": foods such as cream, ice cream, creamy sauce, cream cheeses, and easily absorbed fruits like strawberries, peaches, and melons. The best example is provided by what Léa feeds Chéri, essentially soft and milky things. "Like a gourmet farm girl," Léa chooses the fruits in season for Chéri, symbolizing the good mother in contrast to Charlotte Peloux, who is termed "devouring" by her son. For even though Charlotte is rarely seen at table, her taste for alcohol and her aggressiveness are well known; with her, the pleasure of eating is seemingly replaced by a voraciousness which does not even spare people: "she bit at random, excited by the proximity of so tender a victim."

As for carefully cooked foods, Colette, in the manner of Sido, presents them simply flavored with olive oil and provençal herbs. In *La Naissance du jour* we are treated to "four little chickens split in half, beaten with the flat of the chopper, salted, peppered, and anointed with pure oil brushed on with sprig of *pebreda* serving as aspergillum; the little leaves of the *pebreda*, and the taste of it, cling to the grilled flesh" (VIII, 34–35). At this, the narrator's stomach expands with pleasure. Furthermore, it is apparent that she attributes to this smooth sauce ritualistic and religious significance.

Colette's identity as it appears through the above themes is based on a deep commitment to life, an extraordinary ability to recover from afflictions, mostly those due to love, and a firm desire to retain a certain independence from men ("le cher ennemi"). These, too, are the characteristics of Sido.

It would not be totally accurate, however, to reduce this sense of self to an obsessive search for the maternal image. *La Naissance du jour* emphasizes her desire to be different, which, while it occasions feelings of guilt, is also necessary for the evolution of the self:

> For it would never have occurred to her that from a youthful face there could emanate a perturbation, a mist like that which floats above grapes in their vat, nor that one could succumb to it. (*Break of Day*, p. 23).

How pure are those who have never forced anything open! To bring
my mother close to me again I have to think back to those dramatic
dreams she dreamt throughout the adolescence of her elder son, who
was so beautiful and so seductive. [...] If only I could see her thus,
and could she but understand me well enough to recognise herself in
what she would most strongly have reproved! (*Break of Day*, p. 25)

These passages illustrate the complex relationship which links the narrator to
Sido. In a first stage the narrator evokes the purity and innocence of Sido, who
is characterized by her tendency toward "abstinence." She contrasts to this
her own urge to consume, while at the same time emphasizing the similar
nature value of their amorous behavior; both Colette and Sido are great lovers.
Then, in a second stage, Sido, who has been to that point glorified, is reduced
to more human behavior, closer to that of the narrator who, as a result,
consents to accept what she has inherited from her mother.

This complex link with the mother is found especially in the places im-
printed with the maternal presence. The countryside wet with fog, a field
damp with dew, a garden choked by fragrant vegetation, hidden springs, the
lapping waves, the blueish milkiness of early dawn: all these places describe a
space mediated by the body, variations on the properties of a "felt" space,
rather than the precise description of geographical space with its precise
dimensions. These properties are rendered only in terms of emotions and
feelings: "The whole warm garden was nourished by a yellow light flickering
with red and purple. I could not say if this red, this purple came from a feeling
of happiness or an optical brilliance" (*Sido*, VII, 181).

The world is there, apprehended through the body, filled to the brim with
flavors and perfumes which shift back and forth in infinite *correspondances*.
The reader is invited to a feast of the senses where everything moves, whispers, and spurts, where everything is endowed with a dynamism which serves
to regenerate surrounding nature. It appears quite clearly that this space is
associated with the mother and that it possesses the same qualities. Nature is
conjured up in continual flowering, with all the characteristics of the womb.
Sido is the central figure in this closed and protected domain, the garden. The
garden is always shown in relation to Sido:

I could only have been content with a Sido standing in her garden,
between the hydrangeas, the weeping ash and the ancient walnut-
tree. That was where I left her when the time came for me to take
leave alike of happiness and my earliest youth. I did see her there
once again, for a fleeting moment [...] And there I am sure she still is,
with her head thrown back and her inspired look, summoning and
gathering to her the sounds and whispers and omens that speed

faithfully towards her down the eight paths of the Mariner's Chart. (*Sido*, 173–174)

Sido makes the garden exist by her presence, by her labors, and by the privileged status she enjoys with flowers and plants. This relationship appears as a dialogue in the text: "She maintained that its pulpy pink flowers, veined with red, reminded her of the lungs of a freshly-killed calf" (*Sido*, VII, 180) indicating thereby that nothing in nature can be described without her.

At the same time, this space mediates between mother and daughter. Sido's handing down of her power allows Colette to discover the originality of her identity: "It was on that road and at that hour that I first became aware of my own self, experienced an inexpressible state of grace, and felt one with the first breath of air that stirred, the first bird, and the sun so newly born that it still looked not quite round" (*Sido*, 156).

The earth is shown in its richness and in its generosity. It exalts the person who works it: "When you open up the earth, even for a mere cabbage-patch, you always feel like the first man, the master, the husband with no rivals" (*Break of Day*, 79). The earth is not only turned and ploughed but irrigated and bathed in dew and rain. An interesting collusion between leafiness and fluidity demonstrates the constant association in Colette's sense of self between the earth and the mother on the one hand, and between the sea and the mother on the other. Water, presented in various ways, appears as the privileged place of renewal both physical and moral.

The discovery of the self and of identity, using this relationship with the natural world as its starting point, is possible only because of Sido, who is the source of all things. Once these relations are established through the mother, Colette never fails to express the deep bonds that unite her with the material world: "It smells so good at ground-level"; "gardening attaches one's eyes and spirit to the earth."

For the narrator of *La Naissance du jour* the morning bath purifies and at the same time revives the body. There is in fact a double birth because the chosen moment is the beginning of the day when "the milky blueness begins to rise up from the sea" (*Break of Day*, 21). Moreover, it is once again Sido who is sought out and approached in this privileged dawn relationship: "She might [recognize me] if she came back at break of day and found me up and alert in a sleeping world, awake as she used to be, and I often am, before everyone" (*Break of Day*, 6). Colette has finally discovered her identity. The mother, evoked, summoned, inscribed in the text by means of the pseudo-dialogue with the narrator, has fused with Colette's sense of self; she has now only to transcribe "that which, like a poet, she seized and abandoned."

However, in the space given value by the mother, Colette gives special emphasis to certain elements: night, wind, and water. On the one hand, the space of day is dominated by the mother, a secure space which Colette turns to as she enters old age; on the other hand, there is nocturnal space inhabited by reveries of love which cast a spell over the narrator just when old age forces her to leave it. *La Naissance du jour* presents, above all, a poetic variation on these two spatial dimensions.

In contrast to the daytime, devoted to work, night operates in the text as the space of desire: "I am capering around Vial tonight in the way that a filly plays up before the start" (*Break of Day*, 64). Nighttime is entirely occupied by amorous meditation: "How good it is, in the depths of such a night, to contemplate seriously something that is no longer serious!" (*Break of Day*, 63). Night "gives herself to the earth as to a secret lover, quickly and a little at a time" (*Break of Day*, 53).

Just as blue, with its suggestions of cold and insubstantiality, symbolizes dawn, so pink heralds the night. Given this color's symbolism in the other novels, it connotes not only heat but also eroticism: "flamboyant sunsets," "rays of fire," "ruddy bands" (*Break of Day*, 49); all the suggestions of twilight are directly associated with amorous pleasures, which the narrator savors as she goes over her past life.

Wind, in its role as bearer of music, of perfume, and of the very throb of life, becomes through its power and violence an erotic element: it is "the strange tormentor"; it makes the provençal cook "groan under its weight" (*La Naissance du jour*, VIII, 17); it violates the narrator's refuge, bringing with it "a singular hommage of withered petals" (VIII, 17–18). The wind is essentially nocturnal and it disappears with dawn. Colette is especially sensitive to the ambivalence of the wind which both fondles and destroys, waking the body to fragrance and desire.

The wind inspires meditation: "The wind habitually cools my thoughts, turns me away from the present and back in the direction of the past." The mistral and the evening draughts penetrate the wide open house. For the narrator of *La Naissance du jour* the wind is beneficial and cooling, renewing the life and soul of the house and drawing together inner and outer worlds.

Finally, it should be noted that Colette in her evocations of twilight associates it spontaneously with dampness, with the evening dew and the wet ground. Water in its many facets is imagined as a place of rebirth and pleasure. In *La Maison de Claudine* "the child's hand, trailing in the grass, is suddenly aware of the evening damp" (*My Mother's House*, 24); in *La Naissance du jour* twilight is the time for watering the garden:

> After dinner I mustn't forget to irrigate the little runnels that sur-
> round the melons, and to water by hand the balsams, phlox and
> dahlias, and the young tangerine trees, which haven't yet got roots
> long enough to drink unaided in the depths of the earth. (*Break of
> Day*, 8)

Water is the liquid that nourishes not only the earth but also the body; the desire associated with the early morning bath, the thirst for sunbathed sea, the evocation of water inspires a twin reverie of penetration and birth. It is noticeable, for example, that it is after mentioning Vial and coming to the conclusion that men remain her most persistent preoccupation ("the oldest of my cares") that the narrator experiences the need to go into the sea not to plunge into it but to gather seaweed. The sensation she describes is that of the body bursting the surface: "where each movement of my bare legs breaks an iridescent film of pink enamel on the heavy blue of the water" (*Break of Day*, 69). Beyond this, the sea is frequently seen as "milky," reminiscent both in consistency and color of the maternal fluid. We understand also that the narrator's regret at having "missed the moment when the milky blueness begins to rise from the sea" (*Break of Day*, 21) is followed almost immediately by the need for sleep ("Shall I get up? To sleep is sweet") because sleep refers to childhood, to origin, and to the mother. The birth of day, the privileged moment of the mother, is dreamed by Colette as the source, and through the mother, as the place of rebirth. This double theme is inscribed in Sido's letters, thereby favoring the fusion with the mother.

The process of writing, language, and the body's spaces allow us to follow the itinerary of a woman's writing in which her sense of self is embedded. Through her female characters Colette has sought to define herself and to situate herself with regard to Sido. A dialectic of identity and difference accompanies this quest and is written into the description of female figures and of the space which accommodates them. It is possible to understand that within this demanding and passionate quest, the body plays a fundamental role. Parting from desire to desire, Colette's women learn how to liberate themselves from love and to forge a sense of peace which excludes neither the demands nor the imperious desire for beauty. The lust for life leads to a very carnal presence in the world, to the wish to "bloom" until death:

> Let me not forget that I am the daughter of a woman who bent her head, trembling, between the blades of a cactus, her wrinkled face full of ecstasy over the promise of a flower, a woman who herself never ceased to flower, untiringly, during three quarters of a century. (*Break of Day*, 6)

Notes

References to the 15-volume *Oeuvres complètes* (Paris: Flammarion, 1948–1950) include the volume number in Roman numerals. Translations by E. Eisinger and M. McCarty.

References without volume number correspond to the following English translations:

Break of Day, trans. Enid McLeod (New York: Farrar, Straus & Giroux, 1961).

Chéri and *The Last of Chéri*, trans. Roger Senhouse (New York: Farrar, Straus & Giroux, 1951).

Gigi, Julie de Carneilhan, Chance Acquaintances, trans. Roger Senhouse and Patrick Leigh Fermor (New York: Farrar, Straus & Giroux, 1952).

My Mother's House and *Sido*, trans. Una Vicenzo Troubridge and Enid McLeod (New York: Farrar, Straus & Giroux, 1953).

1. A psychocritical reading has been done by John Alix in his thesis "Superpositions chez Colette," (unpublished thesis, University of Aix-Marseille I, Aix-en-Provence, 1976).

2. See on this topic Yannick Resch, *Corps féminin, corps textuel, essai sur le personnage féminin dans l'oeuvre de Colette* (Paris: Klincksieck, 1971).

3. See Ilene Olken, "Aspects of Imagery in Colette: Color and Light," *PMLA*, LXXVII (March 1962).

4. See Marcelle Biolley-Godino, *L'homme-objet chez Colette* (Paris: Klincksieck, 1972).

14 Polymorphemic Perversity: Colette's Illusory "Real"
SUZANNE RELYEA

Signs wandering in the air, sometimes the words, summoned, deign to descend, flock together, settle – thus the little miracle that I call the golden egg, the bubble, the flower, seems to form: a sentence worthy of what it wanted to describe. (Mélanges, XV, 335)[1]

I

Until recently, both public and critical opinion have relegated Colette's work to the ranks of light reading. Citing her categorical refusal to consider the world through abstract forms of reference such as metaphysical systems or moral codes, commentators have qualified her narrative as purely descriptive. Indeed, Colette's own remarks encourage such judgments. In her middle sixties she advised the young Renée Hamon thus:

> Paint only what you have seen. Look for a long time at those things that give you pleasure, still longer at those that give you pain. Try to be faithful to your first impression. Don't make a fetish of the "rare word." Don't tire yourself by lying. The lie develops the imagination and imagination is the death of the reporter. Take notes — No, don't take notes. Beware of "embellishments," beware of indiscreet poetry.[2]

Colette is expressing a preference for the transmission of an apprehension of reality, acquired through direct experience, over invention. In fact, critics have been quick to point out that Colette lacks skill in designing and fleshing out multi-dimensional characters and in creating imaginative situations.[3] For the most part, her novels are linear love stories which, in however complex a manner and at whatever level of metaphor, draw heavily on and reflect personal experience. Her plots bear a striking structural resemblance to one another and her cast of characters reappears from novel to novel — the female and/or male adolescent beginning an erotic apprenticeship, the demi-mondaine, the stoic bourgeoise, ever wiser as a result of lovers' or husband's amorous duplicity, the egotistical man of leisure. Moreover, statements like those contained in her advice to Renée Hamon indicate a primary preoccupation with skilled, and therefore faithful, reproduction of the real, particularly of cherished objects and sensations. Words must cling determinedly to things, for things — birds, flowers, animals, love objects — are more important than words. Art is a tool, not a thing in itself, and its proper employ requires long, arduous apprenticeship. Small wonder, for the artisan's goal is none other than to reunite being (and especially that state of pure being which Colette associates with her childhood) and language.

At the same time, in the passage quoted as an epigraph, Colette suggests that the success of the storyteller's apparent labor of reconstruction depends on something far more mysterious than a simple mastery of skills. If the image is to qualify as an accurate "re-creation" of the object or sensation, then a miracle must occur: the words must consent to "flock together" to form "a sentence worthy of what it wanted to describe." Clearly there are strange forces involved, perhaps even muses — which makes the process a strange one: Colette wishes both to indicate things as things by re-presenting them in words and to reveal their poetic "essence." It is not simply a question of ensuring the referential value of a given articulation, but of poeticizing objects. It is my purpose to demonstrate that Colette conveys a convincing image of materiality at the same time that she transforms matter into a hyperbole of sensual *experience*. That is, things do not exist in and of themselves, but function as full, signifying events known through the senses of a speaking subject in the text, a voice which sometimes says "I" and sometimes veils itself in characterization. She works this magic by a process which I shall call the eroticization of the signifier. It results in a carefully controlled slippage of signifiers to the status of signifieds and, thus, to levels of metaphor not specified in the text, but on which our impression of sensuous contact with matter depends.

The character Chéri, in general not a particularly interesting fellow, draws us in because of his exceptional youth and equally extraordinary beauty. A literal incarnation, he re-presents his lover Léa's desire to the reader. While their initial referential value remains undeniable, the portraits of him to which Colette treats us hardly qualify as objective observation or as pure description:

> He was capering about in front of the sun-drenched rosy-pink cur-
> tains — a graceful demon, black against a glowing furnace; but when
> he pranced back towards the bed, he turned white again from top to

toe, in his white silk pyjamas and white moorish slippers.

He was standing in front of a pier-glass framed in the space between two windows, gazing at the reflection of a very youthful, very good-looking young man, neither too short nor too tall, hair with the blue sheen of a blackbird's plumage. He unbuttoned his pyjamas, displaying a hard darkish chest, curved like a shield; and the whites of his dark eyes, his teeth, and the pearls of the necklace gleamed in the over-all rosy glow of the room.[4]

Or, during the boxing lessons which Léa arranges for him and which she enjoys as she would a lavishly laid banquet table:

Léa smiled and revelled in the pleasure of the warm sun, of sitting still and watching the bouts between these two men, both young and both stripped.

How handsome Patron is — as solid as a house! And the boy's shaping up well. You don't find knees like his running about the streets every day of the week, or I'm no judge. His loins, too, are…will be…marvelous. Where the devil did Ma Peloux drop her line to fish up a child like that? The set of his head! A real work of art! And what a bad one he is! He laughs and it reminds one of a greyhound about to bite someone…[5]

The objectifying and, according to traditional definitions of sexuality and sexual identity, "feminized" quality of these portraits of male beauty is all the more striking in that one does not frequently encounter perceptions mediated by unabashed female desire in literature, even in works by women.[6] Chéri reduced to an erotic object is also Fred Peloux, an ordinary underdeveloped adolescent metamorphosed into an extraordinary work of art. The reader can never satisfactorily grasp for her- or himself the "real" character in question since, as the very change which older women effect in his name would indicate, Chéri remains largely someone else's fondled, fussed-over darling. Although the novel's conclusion suggests a Chéri embarked on his own course, Colette dispells any ambiguity about his potential autonomy in its sequel; *The Last of Chéri* makes it clear that, deprived of Léa's desire, he must sooner or later blow his brains out. Emptied of her excessive sensual energy, he loses his buoyancy and drifts slowly to the earth to lie helplessly devoid of meaning until his creator at last decides to end his quiet anguish.

Chéri, then, never succeeds in reclaiming his identity as Fred, but, even in his own eyes, remains Léa's "chéri." He also continues to think of her as his "Nounoune," but the relation lacks reciprocity; Léa not only recovers, albeit with considerable difficulty, from the loss of her Nounoune role after Chéri's marriage, but she also manages to forge a new identity which will render her dawning old age even more autonomous than were her courtesan years. Léa exists in, of, and for herself. She is the subject, the self of the novel. Chéri never accedes to real being; he *has* a function in Léa's life but *is* nothing, if not that function, even unto himself.

An object, a function, a work of art, a metaphor for a woman's desire, Chéri typifies the elusive signifier, which sometimes looks like a signified, in Colette's "purely descriptive" writing. There is a Chéri, a real character (signified) available in the narrative of the book of the same name; however, our experience of the "object" cannot be direct, for we only know him via Léa's sensuous appreciation (the chain of signifiers.) What's more, he himself functions as a signifier. The language should be a vehicle to carry us to him; but, far from attaining the transparency necessary to do so, it lies thick with Léa's eroticism. The very opacity of Colette's language draws our attention away from Chéri to it and thus, by analogy, to an image of the writer writing (Léa breathing libidinous life force into Chéri: Colette animating a love story with metaphor). The signifier "Chéri" indicates both a young man and a woman's desire; the former constitutes the text's referential aspect, its story. The latter constitutes its literal aspect, its self-reflecting opaque quality.

While Chéri represents an extreme of equivocated signification, the process by which we comprehend him is repeated virtually throughout Colette's works in her innumerable descriptions of fictional characters, real people, and the natural world. The complexity of that process lies in her consistent habit of fusing the signifying chain with reminders from the text's voice about its own erotic life — and life-giving — energy. So skillfully does she lead us into the voluptuous ambiance of her world that we readily mistake her senses for reality, the fragrant ambrosia of metaphor (a signified only recently slipped from the rank of signifier and capable of returning to it) for pure air. The text's process seems not to exist. "It's just a simple story," we think, "nicely told, to be sure, but lacking depth. *Chéri* is light reading." Such is Colette's magic, or rather her alchemy: the opacity of her language clears to transparency, accomplishing the impossible transcendence of its own weighty materiality. Prepared by her seductive manipulation of signifiers, we readily put aside the considerable distortion inherent in our preception of Chéri. We accept him as a possible fictional character, a thing in the world Colette creates around him. That passages describing him also speak to us of desire and of fictionalization itself — and, thus, in Colette's case, of the art of writing — we simply ignore.

If, on the other hand, we consciously focus on the process of signifying, we find ourselves faced with the issue of textual verisimilitude (*vraisemblance*). For our purposes let us invoke Todorov's understanding of the term:

> [...] one can speak of the *vraisemblance* of a work insofar as it at-
> tempts to make us believe that it conforms to reality and not to its own
> laws. In other words the *vraisemblable* is the mask which conceals the

text's own laws and which we are supposed to take for a relation with reaility.[7]

In order for Todorov's mask to function effectively, the signified must resemble the object referred to so closely that a blurring of the two occurs in the reader's mind. To qualify that process as magical is not to invoke exaggeration for emphasis. While recent scholarship is embroiled in controversy over the specific nature of the signified, there is little doubt that the latter can at least be described as forms rather than substances.[8] Saussure defined the signified as a concept, but did not identify it as the meaning of the signifier with which it is associated in any given instance. The process of creating *vraisemblance*, however, does just that. It requires that the reader agree that a form indicated by another kind of form, the signifier or acoustic image (which, unlike the signified, does have meaning) take the rules governing its participation in the production of meaning from real world matter, in the case of physical description, rather than from the interplay of signifiers within the text. There is, of course, the simple necessity of the reader's complicity, and we shall return to that perspective presently. First, we must examine the nature of the process of mask creation itself.

We are to assume that a form implies another form in a reader's mind and that readers accept that implication as a relationship with reality rather than an intrasemic or intratextual event. They pass through a signifier to a meaning which is presumed to be the truth and origin of the sign, that is, which authorizes the wedding of signified to signifier. Paradoxically the signifier both has meaning and is only the certifying origin's "visible mark," or "outer shell."[9] A simple notation, its sole function is to guide us to the thought, which itself retains an irrevocable privilege because of its assumed relation to reality. Thus belief in the *vraisemblance* of a text, character, or description would lead us to accept the signifier "Chéri" as a mere transcription of reality.[10] Meaning would become an *a priori* affair, established once and for all, by fiat of reality itself, the latter being a highly rational complex governed by strict, fixed conventions. The writer bows to the role of scribe.

Yet who among Colette's readers would qualify her work as transcription or reality as a rational set? On the contrary, critics have repeatedly emphasized Colette's "style," deeming it unique, idiosyncratic, remarkable for its ability to manage the world's chaos. In fact one would hardly wish to accept the above propositions as equivalents; the nature of *vraisemblance* is to show the reader a mask and elicit admiration for the excellence of its design and function. We do not take those skills and techniques which create an illusion of conformity to reality for an absence of such skill. We simply agree that Colette is adept enough at her craft to make it seem as though there were no craft involved. The reader knows *vraisemblance* is a mask but admires its very realistic quality.

Such admiration enhances one's enjoyment of the text, and indeed, suspension of awareness that there is any mask involved at all may be necessary in order for the reader to enter the text's play and participate in its meaning. However, it is regrettable that in Colette's case, critics have neglected to examine what Todorov calls "the text's own laws," commenting on her work as if they took her skillful invocation of *vraisemblance* for an inviolable relation with reality. In so doing we have done to her one of the things men have traditionally done to women: we have at once idolized and trivialized her. She is a sorcerer, a magic woman who holds the keys to her own unfathomable reality — which we are at a loss to articulate — a figure lauded and magnified beyond the propositions of serious consideration. We tend to view a magician's tricks as amusing, admirable, entertaining, and without depth. On the other hand, we tend to relegate the study of and responsibility for society's insoluble problems, among which we may count the entire realm of affectivity and sexuality, to those whom our culture defines as other, particularly women and writers. The dialectical, i.e., conflictual, relationship between feeling and perception and/or conceptualization is one such insoluble problem, and it is not surprising that readers have imagined Colette to be in possession of the secret of its comprehension. Indeed Colette's work encourages such mythologizing of her.[11]

However, the fact that she described herself as principally an observer hungry for the real should not divert us from focusing on the production of meaning within the text and in the text's relation to other texts. Her work consisted of a lifelong attempt to insinuate language, in fact a distinct "écriture," between herself and the world. Her efforts to create "a sentence worthy of what it wanted to describe" certainly parallel a wish to immortalize Puisaye and Sido, and perhaps to redeem the writer's departure from her childhood world. She chose the unattainable goal of dissolving time, and even metaphor, in a time- and signification-bound system, in language. The critic's task is all the better accomplished to the degree that she or he steps back from that goal.

Saussure's idea of the diacritical nature of meaning suggests one way of doing so:

> [. . .] in the linguistic system there are only differences. Or better: a difference usually presupposes positive terms between which it is established; but in the linguistic system there are only differences without positive terms. Whether we consider the signified or the signifier, linguistic systems do not comprise either thoughts or sounds which predate them but only conceptual and phonic differences which issue forth from them.[12]

This concept divests the signified of its privileged status, for it locates meaning in the interplay between the terms of a sign, or between signs, or between sentences, but always outside any given term and within the linguistic system itself. Rather than a prime mover itself unmoved, the ambiguous signified/referent thus becomes a cultural product subject to the same transitions as all critical and ideological concepts within the culture and linguistic system in question. Aptly named, it does indeed receive the impact of that which is meant, but only by virtue of its own referential quality. Signifieds refer the reader to other signs from which the former differ and to which they are, necessarily, in relation. This is not to say that the meanings produced by such networks of relations and interrelations are not governed by conventions; however broad the range, one can always delineate a spectrum of possible readings. Nevertheless, an understanding of meaning as differential and of limitations on reference as ideological — and accessory — phenomena is essential to an articulation of that process through which we come to proclaim that such and such a word, sentence, work is coherent or true, i.e., in accordance with our own version of that other text, "nature."

It is not my intention here to argue for or against the validity of this theory for linguistic systems in general. However, insofar as literature and specifically Colette's novels are concerned, it can be demonstrated that while the author attempts to make signifiers manifest signifieds, they most often exceed them, thus providing the energy for the term-to-term differential interplay which Saussure calls meaning. The proposition is a startling one, for it advocates resituating Colette's "stylistic" — and thematic — longings for transcendant meaning, placing them in a specific ideological context. It calls into question both characters and real world objects like the Puisaye garden insofar as their status as truths or origins which lie outside the realm of signifiers and their interplay is concerned; this in spite of abundant evidence throughout Colette's work that she experienced both life beyond childhood (outside her mother's house) and writing itself as exile from an original plenitude for which her entire opus records intense, if reserved, nostalgia. Thus, in her own terms, to say that her signifiers do not manifest appropriate signifieds would be to judge a necessary failure her long enterprise as a writer, to dissolve the golden egg, the bubble, the flower.

With these theoretical propositions in mind, let us return to Chéri preening before Léa's bedroom mirror. Since the scene takes place at the very opening of the novel, one might assume that it was designed in part to acquaint the reader with the character Chéri, or perhaps, since Léa is present, with his relationship to his mistress. If, following that assumption, we filter out the information it conveys, we find that: 1) A fluid composition in black and white, Chéri changes with the light; he sports dark hair, teeth as white as pearls, indeed, a pearl necklace, a nice chest, the grace of a demon, exceptional beauty and extreme youth. 2) The room in which he demonstrates "chiaroscuro" and his own physical perfection contains a mirror flanked by two windows, sunlight filtered through pink curtains and an ornate brass bed occupied by two magnificent arms ending in lovely langorous hands. In other words, there is a conspicuous absence of unthematized descriptive detail whose goal it would be to create what Roland Barthes has called a "reality effect."[13] Both Chéri's body and Léa's bedroom come to us devoid of gratuitous items which might denote some concrete reality, and which, if the author consciously resisted picking them up and integrating them into symbolic or thematic codes, would enable us to recognize the world we enter and orient us in it. On the contrary, while there is a paucity of statistical data about either the character or his space, what physical reality exists seethes with implication about Chéri, Léa, and their relationship. Faced with a passage purified of trivial gesture, insignificant objects, or superfluous dialogue, of elements which might assert the mimetic orientation of the text by signifying simply "we are the real," the reader immediately experiences an intense and sometimes confusing blurring-together of physical world, characterization, and plot.

Chéri's demand for the pearl necklace, obviously the property of the bed's occupant, speaks to us of his capricious nature and the balance of power in the relationship: Léa owns, Chéri covets (the latter will not begin to tap his own financial resources until after marriage to a peer). The pearls themselves suggest the transcendant quality of Chéri's beauty: he is neither male nor female, but an androgynous platonic form, a paradigm.[14] Like the flawless pearls which he says look better on him than on Léa, he embodies a certain artistic ideal, a gift of nature, savage, inscrutable, even barbaric, as Léa is fond of noting, yet fashioned by Léa's talented, experienced hand. The entire scene, black and white beneath a rosy overwash, resembles an old sepia print not unlike those photographs which cover one wall of the room in which Chéri will commit suicide. An ornate brass bed, arms which have protected him and hands which have caressed him for seven years, silk pajamas, and rich leather slippers all signify a highly studied, luxurious sensuality infused with unchallengeable power. Enclosed, overfull, the atmosphere suffocates the reader in lazy, voluptuous stimulation; everything points to everything else in a dense jumble of tautological signification.

Thus Chéri is hardly alone in his lack of autonomous ontological status. Like him, most of the materials which constitute the real in Colette's work signify something besides reality. They are never simply there. The objects in Léa's room and the entire world outside that room exist only as a demonstration of the story's course, that is, the course of desire. Things lack precision; they cannot just be, in, of, and for themselves. Places (Léa's townhouse and country retreat, Mme Peloux's salon, Italy, the Midi) either bring the couple together or tear them apart, but rarely interest the reader independently of the lovers. People also fulfill a thematic purpose, especially the flock of graceless, aging courtesans who regularly attend Charlotte's Sundays in Neuilly. In short, and whatever the appearances, the passage in question and the novel as a whole persistently equivocate their own hints at verifiable extratextual reference. Unlike Balzac's long lists of purely descriptive signs, the meaning of which is nothing other than their respective signifieds, Colette's sparse invocations of concrete reality lead us directly to other aspects of the text and nowhere clearly outside of it. Everything means something because, unlike Balzac, she uses words to indicate concepts about things rather than things. The meaning of reality can and does fluctuate, but concepts remain constant because she creates and controls them. Like the Puisaye garden, Chéri is less an existing reality than a cherished idea born of timeless longing. But it is important to realize that in Colette's work all "reality" shares Chéri's status.

Colette's world comes alive for the reader, then, but only on its own terms. It is a closed world containing largely immobile objects which we view on the same ontological plane, except when one of those objects, like Léa or the narrator in the Break of Day, provides the senses through which the reader understands the text's world. All of the text's objects take on meaning, and thus existence, by virtue of their reference to and differentiation from one another. Signifiers have a life of their own with respect to the world, but not with respect to the author's intention: to submit them to her own rigid authority. While there may be no ultimate meaning "out there," we certainly have one "in here," and language functions as a tool for the continual recovery, masking, and revelation of it. That said, we must go on to elucidate the connection between the internal coherence of a signifying system and the chaotic world of which it is trying to make some sense. While in semiotic terms the creation of meaning is an intratextual event, the laws by which a text produces such an event can only be understood with respect to the world from which they derive and in which they participate.

II

Signifiers "exceed" signifieds in Colette's work: forms, they correspond to that concept, in her case an ideal form, which she defines as their meaning. A peony is not a peony but an origin, a Platonic idea, which real world flowers strive humbly to imitate. The "real" peony exists in Colette's mind, in her desire, *and in language*, rather than in the world, and it is that form which she signifies when she writes. The interplay of forms to signify forms *is* the "poeticization of objects" which I mentioned earlier. However, peonies, handsome bodies, suffering, and the sea at dawn also form part of the reader's experiential reality, and she or he will more than likely assign referential value to Colette's signs. At the same time, in order to gain entry into Colette's universe the reader will participate in her persistent abstraction of the concrete. When Colette raises Chéri's knees to the level of poetic essence, readers both follow her to that level and retain the sign "knees" as pure representation.

This double-edged activity is precisely that semiotic dynamic fueled by an overloaded signifier. A pure form, a signifier can refer to other such ideals (a perfect face → immaculate silk pajamas → magnificent arms → Chéri's reflected image → pearls → pearl-like teeth, etc.) in an endless circle. A linguistic form with a meaning, it can indicate, even convert to a contractually shared concept or signified which cannot be grasped directly but requires an interpretant in the form of another sign (a synonym or paraphrase). While she intends to approximate being in language as closely as possible, to transform Derrida's time-bound "différance" into ever-present plenitude — or at least provide the illusion thereof — Colette in fact simultaneously confines us in her private empyrean of somewhat melancholy pure form, and releases us into a joyful interplay of possible meanings. Such interplay can only take place in that space opened by a verbal form that relates to other sequences (paraphrases or synonyms) whose trace it bears. Locked into the carefully prescribed meaning of Chéri's body or the objects in Léa's bedroom, we are also automatically and from the outset "caught up in the unmotivated play of developing symbols [. . . in] an active movement, a process of de-motivating rather than a structure given once and for all."[15] That is, we participate at once in a closed *a priori* set of pre-existing models, or Platonic patterns, and in a linguistic system which can only produce "conceptual and phonic differences which issue forth from it."

The process of "making sense" might be described as follows: attracted to a novel by its very potential for immersing us in a strange new world, a fictional world which at the same time includes and transcends ordinary experience, we must paradoxically reduce its strangeness in order to procure for ourselves the pleasure it promises. We can only assimilate it by retrieving the fiction whose very distance constitutes its charm. Insofar as Colette's work is concerned, we are most likely to do so by allowing ourselves to be seduced, by submitting to the authority of her desire and perceiving matter through her actively stylizing eyes. We never see Chéri except as Léa sees him or as he has internalized Léa's perception of him. Similarly Colette offers us her idea of the ultimate flower rather than putting us in contact with a particular flower, and, in our efforts to naturalize the text, we accept her idea as a representation of the thing, thus subscribing to her conventions in the process of interpretation. In so doing we equate Colette's set of paradigms with nature on behalf of itself. It can, of course, be argued that we always see the world only through the author's eyes, and this is so. Unfortunately we are likely to remain blind to the implications of that fact, to the specific historical, political, and sociological context of the writer's perception, and to assume ourselves in contact with a universal given: Nature. "Yes," we agree, "that's the way it is," when we might more appropriately notice that that's the way it is for a certain member, female or male, of a given social class and culture at a defined point in time. To confine our reading to the framework of Colette's own rather Cartesian set of conventions is to bind the real to a very specific, although hardly idiosyncratic, way of perceiving the world.

It remains that one cannot read without some set of conventions to guide the play of differences among signifiers and to structure the process of constructing meanings. What is essential is that we understand that necessity and the nature and implications of the maxims, prejudices, and values which govern our reading.[16] The need for them arises from our inability to understand any type of discourse except in relation to another type already familiar, legible, natural to us. In the presence of writing which does not approximate our vision of the world, which we judge *invraisemblable*, we are likely to simply translate back into what we define as natural language, ever presuming that it ought to be telling us something coherent and true. At another level, we may invoke and/or encounter in the text a pool of cultural stereotypes — generalizations we recognize as peculiar to a society, but which can organize the text for us, regardless of their tendency to oversimplify. Thus, for example, Colette gives us Léa who, "like any sensible woman in her fifties," must soon cease making love with young men, indeed with anyone. The path along which the story, and especially Léa and Chéri's dialogue, will offer us the least resistance originates with our understanding of certain prejudices with respect to sexuality and aging women. We can only make sense of and perhaps participate in Léa's disgust with the septuagenarian Lili's boisterous passion for an adolescent Italian prince if we accept that value as normative.

In order to better understand the values of the sign system in *Chéri*, let us turn for a moment to another of Colette's works. In a piece called "Orchid," a prose-poem included in her collection *For a Flower Album*, Colette offers up her "object" sealed from the outset in a tight network of metaphor, its reality almost entirely obfuscated for the reader:

> I can see before me a small, pointed wooden shoe, very pointed. It is made of some green material like jade, and on the tip of the shoe is painted in reddish-brown a minute nocturnal bird — two huge eyes, a beak. Inside the wooden shoe, along the whole length of the sole, someone — but who? — has sown a silver plant, slantwise.
>
> All around the small shoe are five asymmetrical arms, green, speckled with brown, diverging. A beautiful lower lip with a white foundation not unlike the tongue of an iris in form spread-eagled below them, stamped with a violet stipple, and the shape, yes, the shape of the pod of a cuttlefish, for in fact my orchid is an octopus: if not the eight arms, it does have the parrot beak of the octopods, the beak I called a moment ago the tip of the shoe.[17]

In order to render her orchid present to the reader she invokes over the course of the passage an octopus, a wooden shoe, a silver beard, an owl, and dried blood. Of an orchid other than the one before her she says it resembled "a bird, a crab, a butterfly, an evil charm, a sexual organ, and perhaps even a flower."[18] It is not surprising that such multimorphic substances should harbor unusual powers; the second orchid effortlessly seduces an experienced jaguar hunter, whose life is endangered when he lays down his gun to climb a difficult slope to pick it. A clement jaguar spares him, and the hunter subsequently becomes a devoted botanist. At the conclusion of this "portrait," Colette rhetorically wonders if the orchid "had forever engulfed him in the regions where a man, between two dangers, never fails to choose the worse." Like the hunter who has irreversibly locked himself into the embrace of a primitive elemental force, that of desire, we are seduced by the "nature" to which Colette refers, that is by a *certain reading of a text.* Closed off in such communion with power and beauty, the hunter, the narrator, fictional characters, and readers all find themselves dangerously alienated from the ordinary world of human experience, from what we usually call "the real."

Just so, we are alienated from orchids by Colette's orchid portrait. As was the case with Chéri's body and Léa's bedroom, there is no line or shape which does not form part of the tautological thematization of the world which is the passage's goal; there is no world, no orchid which is simply there and which could signify, "I am the real." At one point the orchid becomes a shockingly presumptuous imitation of an octopus, of a creature whose power to engulf is more explicit, less metaphorical than that of an orchid. The orchid seems able to serve only as a source of endlessly converging analogies, all of which signify what Chéri's body or Léa's room signify: the power of desire, seduction, possession and engulfment. The hunter is henceforth owned by the orchid, the course of his life dramatically altered, just as Chéri, owned by Léa's desire, will remain forever unable to carve out a free, autonomous existence.

Colette's nature, then, is a highly specific interpretation or reading of *what is natural.* It bears the marks of her time, her class, and her own and other peoples' attitudes toward her sex. That the whole of a woman writer's work — images, themes, characterization, plot, "style" — converges upon a single, fixed idea, that of primal erotic, if not clearly sexual, desire — this suggestion can and should lead us to ask questions about the role of women and writers in the late nineteenth and early twentieth centuries. In an attempt to elucidate the nature of that role I have posited a hypothesis: Colette took upon herself a dubious, monumental task, the personification of the Other for others, the role of unyielding retainer of the keys to life's most profound mysteries, specifically to that baffling enigma which is affect. That task was often urged upon women of her time by the period's literature, norms, practices, and prejudices. She therefore writes "like a woman," for it is "natural" for women to know about, to focus on, to live for desire. She is an unusual woman in that her women characters are more likely to dwell on and live through their own desire than that of others for them; on other counts, however, she conforms to current expectations about women and women writers.

Her assumptions about what is natural reflect not only expectations about womanhood, but also about women of the class of which she was part when she wrote any given work. It is assumed natural that a woman should be preoccupied with flowers. However, we would hardly find most of the flowers which appear in her album in working-class Parisian or rural peasant households. Roses, lilies, gardenias, orchids, camelias, anemones all suggest offerings of some price. In at least two cases, those of the roses and a lily, Colette in fact chides her daughter for extravagance when the latter bears her such gifts. The lily is associated with Mallarmé's poetry and Debussy's music, art forms largely available to and understood by people of some means, and only the initiated among them. The anemone belongs to the painter Redouté, tutor to princesses. As for more modest varieties such as lily of the valley, if they are less costly and less intimately bound to ruling class esthetics, the pleasure to be derived from them depends no less on a sense of participation in the joys of the chosen few. The narrator shares her First of May festival of the lily of the valley with a flower-peddling "dryad" who looks like Louis XIV and who invariably goes off alone into the "virgin forest" to harvest her plants. The narrator does not appreciate May weekends when the forest is "besieged" by uninitiated Parisian hordes with their automobiles, picnics, and ignorance of nature such that they pick the lily of the valley when it is too young, greenish-colored "like cauliflower."[19] The differentiation between knowledgeable, genteel — and usually solitary — appreciation of nature's gifts and popular consumption is clear. The narrator is not only a woman, but a woman of some class and distinction, one who singles out herself, and those with whom she affiliates herself, from the masses.

The point is not that Colette defines the world views of other classes, cultures, or the opposite sex as unnatural, but that her "nature" results from both a particular kind of signifier activity and values, assumptions, usages, and customs particular to her sex and class. Nature is not a truth but a text, a way to make sense of the extra-linguistic world which remains bound to ideology; once we isolate those conventions and textual practices by which it is so bound, we are free to accept or reject them for ourselves in our process of making sense of the work and thus to enjoy the intratextual creation of the text "nature" — in Colette's work a continual unfolding of desire.

Notes

1. Unless otherwise specified, all quotations from Colette's work are translated from *Oeuvres complètes* (Paris: Flammarion, 1948–1950).

2. Ibid., p. 371, Préface à *Aux îles de la lumière*, by Renée Hamon.

3. See Elaine Marks, *Colette* (New Brunswick: Rutgers University Press, 1960), Chap. 17, "Sorcery and Sagacity."

4. *Chéri*, trans. Roger Senhouse (New York: Penguin Books, 1974), p. 9.

5. Ibid., p. 33.

6. For an extensive study of Colette's eroticization and objectification of her male characters, see Marcelle Biolley-Godino, *L'homme objet chez Colette* (Paris: Klincksieck, 1972).

7. Tzvetan Todorov, Introduction to "Le Vraisemblable," in *Communications*, 11 (1968), pp. 1–4.

8. See Jonathan Culler, *Structuralist Poetics* (Ithaca: Cornell University Press, 1975), pp. 18ff.

9. Ibid., p. 19.

10. An extreme belief in *vraisemblance* involves subscribing to a strangely illogical if not patently tautological proposition: form to form relation ($s^r \rightarrow s^d$) equals form to substance relation ($s^d \rightarrow$ referent.) In the system of the novel *Chéri*, the notation C-H-E-R-I (s^r) operates bonded to the concept "Chéri" (s^d) — which is in fact Léa's concept — thus differentiating itself from all other concepts in the text; that is to say, the sign Chéri operates bonded to the character whom the author thus establishes as different from all other characters in the text.

11. For more extensive commentary on woman's function as a repository for men's unsolved and unsolvable problems (feelings of vulnerability and helplessness, sexuality, all strong emotions), see Jean Baker Miller, *Toward a New Psychology of Women* (Boston: Beacon Press, 1976).

12. Ferdinand de Saussure, *Cours de linguistique générale* (Paris: Payot, 1972), p. 166.

13. Roland Barthes, "L'Effet du réel," *Communications*, 11 (1968), 84–89.

14. Immediately following this passage Colette describes the couple as a woman draped in lingerie and lace and a male figure "seated like an Amazon on the edge of the bed." The novel contains many such allusions to Chéri's androgynous, or rather pre-gender quality. In truth he is sexually interested in neither men nor women, but in nurture. It would not be difficult to posit the thematic homology Sido : Colette :: Léa : Chéri.

15. Jacques Derrida, *De la grammatologie* (Paris: Minuit, 1967), p. 74.

16. Cf. Gérard Genette's definition of seventeenth-century "*vraisemblance*": a body of maxims and prejudices which constitute both a vision of the world and a system of values. *Figures II* (Paris: Seuil, 1969), pp. 73–75.

17. "Orchid," in *For a Flower Album*, Vol. XIV, p. 148.

18. Ibid., p. 150.

19. Ibid., p. 166.

15 The Anamnesis of a Female "I": In the Margins of Self-Portrayal
NANCY K. MILLER

Is it worthwhile I wonder, seeking for adequate words to describe the rest? I shall never be able to conjure up the splendor that adorns, in my memory, the ruddy festoons of an autumn vine borne down by its own weight and clinging desperately to some branch of the fir trees. (My Mother's House)

Opposite the first page of text devoted to the life and works of Colette in *Colette par elle-même* (Paris: Seuil, 1964) is a pen and ink drawing labeled: "Colette's birthplace." Beneath that caption, Colette has handwritten: "I would also like to die there...." Although in some sense all of Colette's work is attached — by a more or less visible umbilical cord — to that *place*, her first-person narrative *Break of Day* (*La Naissance du jour*) perhaps best demonstrates the specifically generic implications of that attachment. Thus while the heroine of *Break of Day*, the narrated "I," wonders whether the house she now inhabits is to be her last — "the one that will find me faithful, the one I shall never leave again? It is so ordinary that it could have no rivals"[1] — the house to which the narrating "I" proves faithful is not in the end hers, but her mother's. The ordinary fabricated house is textually evinced by the extraordinary (store) house of memory; and the "novel" by "autobiography":

> I tread obediently in the footsteps, stopped for ever, that traced their way from the garden path to the cellar, from the cellar to the pump, from the pump to the big armchair full of cushions, opened books and papers. On that trodden path, lit by a low sweeping sunbeam, the first of the day, I hope to learn why one must never put a single question to the little wool-seller — I mean to say Vial, but it is the same perfect lover — why the true name of love, that suppresses and condemns everything around it, is 'frivolity.' (pp. 132–133)

This anamnesis, however, this deliberate rememoration of an individual past, while ostensibly autobiographical in tone and content, is not *stricto sensu* autobiographical in *form*. That is, while the referent invoked — her mother's house — verifiably belongs to the biographical Colette's history and geography, its status here is not, however, a mark of autobiography as *genre*.[2] Rather, this inscription of childhood haunts which frames a meditation that is insistently "personal" and self-reflexive seems to signal the presence of another and archaic mode of discourse: that discourse of self-portrayal Michel Beaujour has named "l'autoportrait."[3] In its discontinuous presentation of a self, its anachronistic juxtapositions, its thematization of memory, of a memory figured in *space* and not chronology, its "poetic" organization — operating by homology and substitution — Colette's "fiction" seems unconsciously to mime a mode and model of literary production whose intertext would be, say, the *Essays* of Montaigne at one end and *Roland Barthes par Roland Barthes* at the other.[4]

But if rereading *Break of Day*, as I propose to do here, against the rhetorical strategies of the "autoportrait" resituates this self-reflexive fiction within a *non*-fictional literary continuum, in the final analysis does such a move account for the recollecting "I" in Colette's text? We know, of course, that genre itself is a fiction, in the sense that no single work ever realizes all the features of the model, the structure of which each text is but a necessarily incomplete variant.[5] Still, as I have argued elsewhere, any theory of textual production which in its categories does not interrogate gender is likely to provide an inadequate account of the female literary project.[6] The project of my reading is therefore double: To what extent does Colette's "I" in fact replicate the features of the "autoportrait" it seems to mime? To what extent does the gender of that self-inscription inflect or deflect from the genre?

It is the image in the mind that binds us to our lost treasures, but it is the loss that shapes the image ... (My Apprenticeships)

The title *Break of Day* and its well-known self-referential epigraph — "Do you imagine in reading my books that I am drawing my portrait? Patience: it's only my model" — even before the letter from "'Sidonie Colette, née Landoy'" with which the narrative itself opens, establish the maternal matrix as the origin of the fiction. It is a derivation, however, established by retroaction, when we learn that the original and sacred break of day is first that of the mother's "chaste, serene ghost" (p. 6); and when, at the end of the fourth chapter, the epigraph reappears in context, and we see that the model in question can only be the mother. The letter then confirms while seeming to announce the primacy of the maternal claim, indeed, of the maternal text. In this backward-looking construction around an "absent structure," Colette announces Barthes "by himself": "The self-portrait is haunted by a fantasy... of cultural community and stability, whose symbolic maternal register has been most clearly designated by Roland Barthes who places at the beginning of his book a photograph of his own mother, followed by pictures of the town, the house, the garden of his childhood, pictures from which he will develop his meditation. ..."[7] The self-portrayer constructs the "I" in the present tense, writing *to the moment* against this contact sheet of a past imaged in nostalgia.

Unlike the imperative of the autobiographer whose self must be *narrated* as a sequential logic of becoming articulated through the tenses of the past, "the formula of the self-portrait is: 'I'm not going to tell you what I've done, but I'll tell you who I am'" (Beaujour, p. 443). But how to *structure* this a-chronological self in writing, how to flesh out, as it were, a paradigm deprived of its projection onto a "natural" syntagma, of the *steps* that lead from then to now? Paradoxically these personal texts, these individualistic and idiosyncra-tic gestures obey another and non-narrational logic; what organizes these self-portraits is a rhetorical matrix with its own rules — rules, however, that are no more consciously present in the mind of the writer than the rules of grammar in the minds of most speakers. To draw one's portrait then, rather than to tell the story of one's life, is to reinscribe — inevitably, involuntarily — cultural commonplaces; to draw upon a collective thesaurus, a dictionary of the quotidian (in all its banality); to meditate upon the self as a writing self and an already written self; to withdraw and try to make sense of a human life in the shadow of death. [8]

Now this portrait of the self-portrayer may at first blush seem rather remote from the project at the heart of *Break of Day.* I would suggest in a first stage that it is not so much remote, as at an angle to it, an angle of sexual difference which derives from Colette's "take" on the culture and its privileged pur-veyors: the precisely self-conscious nature of a woman writer, who might say today, like Elizabeth Hardwick's narrator Elizabeth in *Sleepless Nights,* "After all, 'I' am a woman" — and say that, as Diane Johnson glosses the line, without injury but "with the knowledge that womanhood presents special difficul-ties."[9] These difficulties for "Colette" are overcome by remembering the woman writer in her mother. For "Colette" to say who she *is,* or as that ontology translates in the rhetoric of self-portrayal, what she *knows,* is to say, "I am the daughter of the woman who wrote that letter...I am the daughter of the woman who bent her head, trembling...over the promise of a flower" (p. 6).[10] For "Colette" to say who she is means to write for and against (but not in the terms of) the *literary,* hence patriarchal culture of the sort that informs the portraits of Montaigne or Barthes; she writes in terms, rather, of maternal *lore.* The text, the encyclopedia which has classified all there is to say, is first an oral heritage, and then a legacy by letters. The text through which "Colette" tries to write is her mother's discourse:

When I try to invent what she would have said to me, there is always one place at which I falter. I lack the words, above all the essential argument, the unexpected and equally enchanting blame and indulgence which fell from her so lightly, slow to touch and gently penetrate my clay, and then come to the surface again. Now they well up in what I write and sometimes they are thought beautiful. But I know well that, though recognisable, they are deformed by my personal notions, my limited unselfishness, my half-hearted generosity and my sensuality whose eyes, thank God, were always bigger than its belly. (pp. 27–28)

The daughter's "invention" falls short of its task, is a less convincing artifact because it is a rhetoric not grounded in the delicate workings of the mother lode, but in a *second* and tributary nature: "Between us two, which is the better writer, she or I?" (p. 141). That question, posed rhetorically after "Colette's" last reinscription of her mother's text, the last installment in *Break of Day* of her lesson by letter, has an obvious answer for "Colette": the better writer, far and away, is Sido. The wisdom and efficacy of maternal rhetoric come from an original and uninterrupted connection to the earth and the logic of its seasons, the daughter's rewriting to a garden traversed by the seasons of a sentimental journeying. "Colette" would have the sensual match the natural, but the analogy is always a faulty construction, a harvest destined to inferiority. As she exclaims, commenting upon another letter: "Oh, you hoarder of treasure! What I amass is not of the same quality, but whatever of it may endure comes from the parallel though inferior seam, mixed with clay . . . An age comes when the only thing left for [a woman] is to enrich her own self" (p. 34). And yet the daughter, belatedly, continues to write the paradox of enrichment through renunciation, to supply on her own, of her own, what is missing already and what she will come to lack.

At no time has the catastrophe of love, in all its phases and consequences, formed a part of the true intimate life of a woman. (Break of Day)

The project of the "autoportrait," we have said, is to explain who one is in the present tense. That is also the project of *Break of Day*, but its "I" is not that of the metadiscursive intellectual of Western culture meditating his status in the culture and the ultimate destination of his text. It is the "I" of a woman, a novelist and writer of love stories, an "I" bound to a specifically *female* anthropology. Colette's text thus operates a twist, a feminine orientation; her meditation is built around traditionally feminocentric commonplaces: not Man at grips with the allegories of Life and Death and the Book, with

Flaubert's *"Bêtise,"* but a woman in (and out of) Love:

> Love, one of the great commonplaces of existence, is slowly leaving mine. (p. 18)

> Shall we never have done with that cliché, so stupid it could only be human? (p. 21)

> I read a thought that I've read in one of my mother's last letters: "Love is not a sentiment worthy of respect." (p. 22)

> One of my husbands used to suggest to me: "When you're about fifty you ought to write a sort of handbook to teach women how to live in peace with the man they love, a code for life as a couple." Perhaps I am writing it now. (p. 22)

But this handbook of daily life (an intertextual grid in the "autoportrait"), this sum of practical wisdom dependent upon a thinking back through the mother, detours for its telling examples through a fiction in the present tense: the fragmentary love story between "Colette" and Vial. The love story, which begins only in the fifth chapter, does not however *structure* the space of *Break of Day*. It is derived from and juxtaposed to the more general reflection. It thus has the status of an *example*: an example of love's rules, like the "story" of Montaigne's falling off his horse in *Of Practice*. The interest of the narrative is not the love interest, but a psychological and "philosophical" one, a place to test a kind of death, to practice a leaving off from a kind of life: "Is that militant life over and done with then?" (p. 17). Still, the fiction *qua* fiction poses a problem in the determination of genre. Although Barthes (hand)writes on the inside cover of his "autoportrait," "All this should be thought of as being said by a fictional character" — thus underlining the impossibility of ever operating a coincidence between the hand writing the "I" and the "I" on paper — does "Colette's" novel with Vial ("la vie"?), her material figuration as a fictional character in a made-up story, radically alter the status of the organizing discourse of *Break of Day*? I think that we must recognize the "novel" as a feature that displaces this text of Colette's into the *margins* of self-portrayal, while reserving judgment for the moment on the project of the self-portraying "I" in Colette's corpus.

It is not certain that I have put an end to her portraits. It is not certain that I have discovered all that she has deposited with me. I'm starting late. But how could I find a better way to end? (Introduction to the Complete Works, Vol. VII)

In *Break of Day* (1928), well before the specifically meditative reflection on life, death, and memory of *The Evening Star* (1946), Colette seems to interrogate the possibility of transforming life into a continuous text — "an open and unending book," as she names it in the last line of that work — by the operations of memory. It is a transformation inseparable from a rewriting of the self through the mother's legacy. *Break of Day*, we saw, opens with a letter — the first of six — in which *Sidonie Colette, née Landoy* declines a visit to her daughter because she fears she might miss the blossoming of her pink cactus. This letter, written in the expectation of death, but structured by an essential if fragile verb of life — "fleurir" — is the material out of which "Colette's" meditation on renunciation — "the supreme elegance of knowing how to finish" (p. 142) — is constructed.[11] It is a meditation whose very last word is *oasis* — the *locus amoenus* of unexpected fecundity and reprieve. The letters are lessons to be learned by heart and practiced. Sido's letters, however, are generated by the imminence of a "natural" death she has in no sense chosen. She chooses only the modalities of approach, of *posture*. The difficulty, therefore, of imitating Sido's "protocole inflexible" (p. 123) resides in transcoding the urgency in a life not yet delimited by death: to philosophize is to learn to die. (In this sense *The Evening Star* constitutes the successful apprenticeship of the letters, for by its title, *Break of Day* proclaims the inevitability of beginning again, of continuity, but not of closure: the final punctuation is an ellipsis.) The parallel then results in an imperfect imitation, since the trajectories can never, by definition, coincide in time. Vial is not "the little wool-seller," nor is he so easily converted to a flower, except in a future perfect tense:

> It's good to learn such a lesson of behaviour. What breeding! I think I hear her, and pull myself together. Fly, my favourite! Don't reappear until you have become unrecognisable. Jump through the window and, as you touch the ground, change, blossom, fly, resound.... When you return to me I must be able to give you, as my mother did, your name of "pink cactus" or some other flame-shaped flower that uncloses painfully, the name you will acquire when you have been exorcised. (p. 140)

The project then of *Break of Day* is to *rename*: to transform through time and memory the aleatory of life and fiction into a new text punctuated by another order.

Sido's last letter — this one impossible to reproduce as an original because it is virtually illegible — would seem to be the pre-figuration of the *vita nuova* to which "Colette" herself aspires: "Two pencilled sheets have on them nothing more than apparently joyful signs, arrows emerging from an embryo word, little rays, 'yes, yes' together, and a single 'she danced,' very clear. Lower down she had written 'my treasure'" (p. 142). The distinguishable words, however, only assume meaning within the context of the dancing signs themselves; they are hieroglyphs, really, beyond the obligations of their habitual language of exchange. Sido's affectionate name for her daughter thus belongs not to the linearity of the past, but among

> strokes, swallow-like interweavings, plant-like convolutions — *all messages from a hand that was trying to transmit to me a new alphabet* or the sketch of some ground plan envisaged at dawn under rays that would never attain the sad zenith. So that instead of a confused delirium, I see in that letter one of those haunted landscapes where, to puzzle you, a face lies hidden among the leaves, an arm in the fork of a tree, a body under a cluster of rock. (p. 142; italics mine)

This letter then, the last, is not a mimetic object, not the *image* of her mother. The literal picture of death, "a head half vanquished, turning its dry neck impatiently from side to side on the pillow, like a poor goat tethered too short" (p. 142), is refused in favor of a semiotics of representation, a mapping of the imaginary. The landscape of a dismembered body is a discontinuous geography imaged only in memory.

In the antepenultimate chapter of *The Evening Star*, Colette describes hieroglyphs of her own. In her apprenticeship as a writer, at a loss for a word needed to complete a sentence, she would draw instead under and over the linguistic obstacle: "In place of the word murmur, I would have the sign caterpillar, which was much prettier."[12] At the end of her career, another form of ideogram offers itself: "Having for half a century written in black and white, I have now been writing with colored threads on canvas for what must be almost ten years ... My memoirs are inscribed in greenery that is blue, lilacs that are pink, and multi-colored marguerites. I shall begin a portrait of my star Vesper, embroidered from nature."[13] These inscriptions, like the last messages from Sido, are not strictly speaking communicative; intransitive signs, they attest instead to the *codes* of language as transmission. This writing is in its own way as perverted from a persuasive goal as that of the "autoportrait": "Obviously," Colette writes, thinking of her readers, "I am not counting on my tapestry work to win their hearts from now on ... *How difficult it is to set a limit on oneself* ... But if all I need to do is try, then all is well; I'm trying."[14] Embroidering from nature, Colette at last writes outside fiction: the pages of her memoirs are "deprived of ... the dialogue between imaginary characters, of the arbitrary conclusion which kills, marries, separates."[15] Beyond the closures of fiction and the *dead*lines of publication, Colette in retreat from the "novelistic event" covers pages without counting.

The last chapter of *The Evening Star* is a self-portrait of a writer. It opens on the "dawning" ("*poindre*") of a flower, a rose, and closes with the image of the end of a road in sight. At what she takes to be the end of her life and her career as a writer, Colette in her immobility still measures her self against the maternal model: "At the age I have now reached, was not Sido engaging in arm-to-arm combat with the great 'Prussian cupboard,' pierced by a bullet in 1870?"[16] But this very immobility proves to be the vehicle of the renunciation "Colette" sought prematurely at the end of *Break of Day*. There her writing is still bound to the time and timing of the novelistic, to a text dependent upon *plot*:

> That deep hunger for the moment which gives birth to the day must learn patience: the ambiguous friend who leapt through the window is still wandering about. He did not put off his shape as he touched the ground. He has not had time enough to perfect himself. But I only have to help him and lo! he will turn into a quickset hedge, spindrift, meteors, an open and unending book, a cluster of grapes, a ship, an oasis... (p. 143)

Beyond plot and the order of fiction, Colette at last lives the patience of Sido's lessons, lessons of old age bound to the alphabet of her *letters*: "You wrote to me that same day, a year before you died, and the loops of your capital B's, T's and J's, which have a kind of proud cap on the back of their heads, are radiant with gaiety" (p. 33–34). Like the "new alphabet" of the last illegible letter, the medium of Sido's message *is* the message. As Barthes writes in *RB*: "The alphabet is euphoric."[17]

In retreat at the end of her life from her former activities, like Montaigne installed in his idleness, Colette finds a "haven" in models for tapestry: "On a tombstone . . . there prays a dog made up of little squares, while all around the tomb there flutter cabalistic words like ABC, DEF, GHIJK, QRSTU..."[18] But if cross-stitching organizes the restless energy of a certain "superfluity," it is not an end in itself; rather it is the means to an ending, a "learning how not to write."[19] The hungry sensuality, and implicitly its writing in fiction, which in *Break of Day* was posed as a bodily inferiority against the balanced rhetoric of maternal discourse, is both transcoded and transcended in *The Evening Star*; yet a certain verbal appetite prevails intact: "There is a tired spirit deep inside me that still continues its gourmet's quest for a better word, and then for a better one still. Happily, my ideas are less insistent, they are quite accommodating as long as I dress them properly. They have grown used to waiting, half asleep, for their feed of fresh words."[20] The necessity of dressing one's ideas verbally is the *ethics* of the "autoportrait." Curiously, moreover, echoing the "runaway horse" with which Montaigne images his wandering mind — an impulse that must be "bridled" by writing — Colette codes her "pen and . . . needle, the habit of work and the wise desire to put an end to it" as "two horses in double harness." She concludes: "Oh, my slow coursers, try to pull together: I can see the end of the road from here."[21] But as all the self-portrayers discover, it is difficult to set a limit to the writing of the self. In *Le Fanal bleu*, three years after the publication of *The Evening Star*, Colette is not yet at the end of the road, "for writing leads only to writing. I am still going to write; I say this in all humility. For me there is no other destiny."[22]

When my father died, the library became a bedroom and the books left their shelves.
(Sido)

Between us two, which is the better writer, she or I? (Break of Day)

Upon her father's death, Colette, we could say, found her material: a dozen volumes, with handwritten titles, containing "hundreds and hundreds of blank pages. Imaginary works, the mirage of a writer's career."[23] The pages traced with "invisible cursive script" will be claimed by Colette as her "spiritual legacy."[24] Against this "proof of incapacity," the family resorted to various strategies of compensation.[25] Only the daughter Colette, usurping the prerogatives of the patronym in a lifetime of writing and naming herself, produced a visible text.[26] (Sido's writings, after all, are letters which exist only through her Minet-Chéri.) Amanuensis then to her father and mother, Colette's anamnesis is doubly filial.

The strange legacy of the paternal library, however, is perhaps the place we should retain as the locus of Colette's singularity and her inflection of the "autoportrait." If "the only real place to which the self-portrait . . . refers is the text, the book in its materiality, and language,"[27] then, metaphorically at least, we can say that Colette's text of reference *overdetermines* her eccentricity as a writer of self-portraits. The only completed page in the Captain's book is the dedication to his wife, the same Sido who writes to her daughter in *Break of Day*: "What a pity he should have loved me so much! It was his love for me that destroyed, one after another, all those splendid abilities he had for literature and the sciences. He preferred to think only of me" (p. 127). Colette, as Sido calls him in that letter, had a "woman's" career. His blank pages, one can only speculate, make "Colette's" writing possible, but at the same time, because they are destined to "feminine" silences, underwrite a filiation of marginality for his daughter's texts.

Although Beaujour is indifferent in his analysis to the *gender* of genre (it is an eventuality he never considers), it is clear that the culture whose rhetorical matrix produces the codes of self-portrayal in question is unself-consciously male, literary, and patrilinear. And as befits so phallogocentric a genre — in the most literal sense of the term — the self-portrait, he specifies, "always displays a theoretical (metadiscursive) dimension: a reflection on the means employed, and on the very possibility of the enterprise itself."[28] Colette's text, on the contrary, as her most casual readers can perceive, is coded by a rhetoric of selfhood, a culture that is female, para-literary and matrilinear. And its meta-discursive dimension proves throughout her work to be mater-discursive. Necessarily, then, her self-portraying enterprise betrays the absence of a *certain* self-consciousness. Thinking back through her mother, Colette's "I" does *not* suffer the fate of the "modern individual" whose "curse comes from the simple fact of his *birth*: rejected from the maternal breast, marked with the sign of the *ego*, condemned to wandering and conquest (the transformation of the world) or else to their obverse: interminable writing."[29] Unlike the male model of the genre, Colette's self-portrait is comfortably connected to the maternal body: "Patience: it's only my model." In the end, however, Colette cannot stop writing her self well after Sido has become a pre-text, "for writing only leads to writing" in the face of one's *own* death. In the margins then of self-portrayal "Colette" produces the "open and unending book" she had fantasized at the close of *Break of Day*: an endless rememoration of a female "I," unafraid of the commonplace called "frivolity."

For if I see no objection to putting into the hands of the public, in print, rearranged fragments of my emotional life, it's understandable that I should tie up tight in the same sack, strictly private, all that concerns a preference *for animals and – it's a question of partiality too – the child whom I brought into the world.* (Break of Day)

Rearranged fragments of the love plot, like Sido's rewritten letters, bear *material* witness to the protocol of negative synecdoche that codes Colette's project of self-representation. She will not tell all, and her readers are not to mistake the public, printed parts for the private integrity of a woman's life. They may look for what is missing, to find only what is already there to be read. But if Colette is not all there like Rousseau, neither is she partially there by literary analogy like Montaigne. Unlike the sons of the father, this daughter of the mother — and mother of a daughter — chooses to write of and from the garden rather than the library. She thus is indifferent both to predecession and descendance: the volumes on her father's shelf bore titles but their pages were blank; the garden goes on in her mind, even if words cannot account for the full meaning of its seasons. Outside genre and the library of an anguished production, the female self memorializing and memorialized goes on in her mother's *place*. Death does not interrupt the continuity of the maternal intratext, which continues to be rewritten by a daughter who neither can stop writing nor, by definition, finish her self otherwise.

Notes

1. *Break of Day*, trans. Enid McLeod (New York: Farrar, Straus and Cudahy, 1961), p. 8. Hereafter all references will be drawn from this edition and indicated parenthetically within the body of the text.

2. I refer here to the criteria established by Philippe Lejeune in his excellent study *L'Autobiographie en France* (Paris: Armand Colin, 1971). They will emerge implicitly in contradistinction to Michel Beaujour's criteria for "l'autoportrait" as outlined below.

3. In "Autobiographie et autoportrait," *Poétique* 32 (novembre 1977), 442–458. This article effectively adumbrates the argument of a full-length study, *Miroirs d'encre: Rhétorique de l'autoportrait* (Paris: Le Seuil, 1980).

4. I paraphrase here Beaujour's description of the modalities of self-portraying discourse, p. 443. Montaigne and Barthes are of course but two examples of the genre; the intertext is made up of both more archaic and more modern avatars.

5. I have loosely translated here Michael Riffaterre's definition of genre in "Système d'un genre descriptif," *Poétique* 9 (1972), 16, fn. 3. One could also say that any text is to the model what the part is to the whole; the problematics of genre is figured by synecdoche.

6. "Women's Autobiography in France: For a Dialectics of Identification," in *Women and Language in Literature and Society: A Feminist Perspective*, Sally McConnell-Ginet, Ruth Borker, and Nelly Furman, eds. (New York: Praeger, 1980).

7. Beaujour, "Autobiographie et autoportrait," p. 454; translation mine, here and throughout.

8. Summary of Beaujour's analysis, especially pp. 445–447 and 453.

9. *NYR*, 26, No. 10 (June 14, 1979), 7.

10. The solution of referring to Colette's Colette persona with inverted commas is Elaine Marks's in *Colette* (New Brunswick: Rutgers University Press, 1960), p. 212.

11. If the verb "fleurir" is indeed Sido's, the pink cactus is Colette's: Sido, in the original, spoke more prosaically (in her *acceptance* of the invitation) of her "sédum." This letter, like all the letters in *Break of Day*, was rewritten by Colette. Which of them is the better writer? See Michèle Sarde's recent biography, *Colette, libre et entravée* (Paris: Stock, 1978), p. 313.

12. *L'Etoile vesper, Oeuvres complètes* (Paris: Le Fleuron, 1950), Vol. 13, p. 304, translation mine. Future references will be drawn from this edition.

13. Translation by Derek Coltman as excerpted in *Earthly Paradise*, ed. Robert Phelps (New York: Farrar, Straus and Giroux, 1966), pp. 503, 504. This is an excellent introduction to Colette's "autobiographical" modes.

14. Phelps, p. 505; italics mine.

15. *L'Etoile vesper*, p. 303.

16. Phelps, p. 503.

17. *Roland Barthes par Roland Barthes* (Paris: Seuil, 1975), p. 158.

18. Phelps, p. 504.

19. Phelps, p. 505.

20. Phelps, p. 505.

21. Phelps, p. 505.

22. Phelps, p. 60, trans. Enid McCleod.

23. *Sido*, excerpted in Phelps, p. 60, trans. Enid McCleod.

24. Phelps, p. 60; *Sido, Oeuvres complètes*, Vol. 7, p. 220, italics mine.

25. Phelps, p. 60; *Sido*, p. 219, italics mine. Her brother used the blank pages of his father's mirage to write prescriptions; her mother tried to use them up in domestic tasks.

26. I am indebted to Christiane Makward for the connections she makes, and which I borrow from and develop here, between the father's name, his impotence, and Colette's name and subsequent career. Makward's paper, "Le Nom du Père: Ecritures féminines d'un siècle à

l'autre," was delivered at the Colloquium in 19th Century French Studies, October 1977, Columbus, Ohio. I would also like to mention here her essay in this volume, "Colette and Signs: A Partial Reading of a Writer 'Born *Not* to Write,'" which intersects my own at several important points.

27. Beaujour, "Autobiographie et autoportrait," pp. 454–455.

28. "L'autoportrait présente toujours une dimension théorique (métadiscursive): réflexion sur les moyens mis en oeuvre, et sur la possibilité même de l'entreprise." Manuscript version of *Miroirs d'encre*, n.p.

29. Beaujour, "Autobiographie et autoportrait," p. 453.

16 Image Structure, Codes, and Recoding in Colette's *The Pure and the Impure*

ANN COTHRAN and DIANE GRIFFIN CROWDER

Colette's *Le Pur et l'impur*[1] remains in many respects one of her least known works, in spite of the fact that she felt it might someday be recognized as her "best" book. Indeed, *Le Pur et l'impur* is a remarkable literary achievement by virtue of both form and content, for in it Colette explores the panorama of human sensuality through techniques which alter our conventional perceptions of this essential dimension of human experience.

Colette explains the purpose of writing *Le Pur et l'impur* in the text itself, modestly referring to it as: "this book, in which I hope to add my personal contribution to the sum total of our knowledge of the senses . . ." (p. 55). Her "personal contribution" is structured around a series of character portraits of people Colette knew during the *belle époque*, chosen to represent the various aspects of human sensuality as she perceived it. Among these are Charlotte, a woman who pretends orgasm in order to satisfy her young man, but who is actually concerned with holding her senses in check; the Marquise de Belboeuf (Colette's lover, better known as Missy and called La Chevalière in the text), a "platonic" lesbian shocked by the "salacious" expectations of other women; the poet Renée Vivien, portrayed as a person consumed by the senses; the famous Ladies of Llangollen, who established a "perfect" retreat lasting over fifty years; and a number of male homosexuals whom Colette frequently visited during the latter part of her marriage to Willy. The work concludes with a study of jealousy and its relation to the senses.

As we can see from the above description, *Le Pur et l'impur* treats all areas of human sensuality: male and female, masculine and feminine, heterosexual and homosexual. Cultural and social conditioning dictate that we consider these units as consisting of antonymous pairs. Not only is such an intepretation too simplistic, in Colette's eyes it is mistaken, for in *Le Pur et l'impur* she traces the multiple variations within a nonhierarchical spectrum of sensual behavior, where widely separated or opposed types actually share certain characteristics. It might seem difficult to imagine similarities between the lesbian Renée Vivien and the Don Juan-like Damien, but both show interest in the sexual act alone, and both are described as persons who "go too far." Similarly, Charlotte, the most "feminine" character according to Elaine Harris,[2] shares many characteristics with the "masculine" women of later chapters. Thus the series of character portraits, which to many readers seem only tenuously connected, constitute in fact an all-encompassing, intricately linked spectrum.

As the narrator of *Le pur et l'impur,* Colette's function is two-fold: she is both narrator-observer, and narrator-writer.[3] As observer, she structures the text around a series of anecdotes wherein the characters reveal through their behavior and attitudes the numerous forms human sensuality can take. The anecdotes are connected by assessive passages in which Colette explores more thoroughly the psycho-emotional features of her subjects' behavior. These passages establish in part the links between the characters in the spectrum, as Colette reveals their hidden similarities. In one such passage, Colette describes her own mental hermaphroditism (p. 60). She is thus, as narrator, in a good position to trace the intricate variations between the two "polarities."

But it is in her role as narrator-writer that Colette most clearly breaks down the polarized distinctions described above. Her unique vision of the senses is conveyed through a language seeking to express that which cannot be *intelligibly* defined or named. In the place of rational, logical explanations, Colette uses language which can best imitate the inexpressible: sensory images operate in the text to reflect Colette's perceptions. The expression of much of *Le Pur et l'impur*'s subject matter lies in the system of relationships which emerge as Colette combines the various sensory images into codes.

The term code generally refers to a set of related signs. The relationship between signs may be conventional, i.e., determined by our cultural and social assumptions, or textual, wherein the author establishes links by manipulating certain properties of literary discourse.

One important way in which the literary text reshapes our cultural and social associations lies precisely in its capacity to alter existing codes. That the literary text is able to recode conventional perceptions of reality is especially important in the analysis of *Le Pur et l'impur.* We shall thus concentrate in this study on Colette's textual combination of images into literary codes, and the resulting redefinition of reality. This particular use of the term code is roughly equivalent to the expression "image network," but it has the advantage of calling attention to the mechanism through which the code is created, as well as to the recoding process. Colette takes advantage of various properties of literary discourse — e.g., the possibility of establishing connections between signs sharing a common seme (unit of meaning), or juxtaposition of one unit of discourse (whether large or small) with another to equate metonymically or otherwise link the two — in order to combine images into codes. Since the images Colette links to form the various codes of the text often belong to different semantic fields, the literary codes she establishes in *Le Pur et l'impur* differ substantially from conventional codes.

The two major codes of the text, darkness and water, are of particular significance in *Le Pur et l'impur*, because they account for the predominant imagery in the work and show clearly how the literary text can recode existing systems. Darkness and water have long been associated with sensuality and with women, but by exploring their semantic potential or emphasizing certain features in the place of others, Colette significantly alters the conventional meaning of these two codes. We shall analyze each in detail to show the mechanism of code creation in *Le Pur et l'impur*, and to show how Colette restructures conventional notions associated with these images in order to offer new perceptions of sensuality in general, and of women in particular.

While the darkness and water codes are differently constituted in the text, Colette uses the same devices to establish each code. Briefly, the basic procedures for code creation are: denotation, connotation, juxtaposition through character, and node words.

Of these four procedures, only denotation relies on the obvious meanings of terms, where the active unit of meaning is immediately apparent. Thus words like "shadow" or "sea" refer directly to their respective semantic fields, darkness and water, for we all are consistently aware that shadows have a darkness component and that the sea is first of all water.

When Colette combines denotation words with terms from other semantic fields, the unusual juxtaposition results in new connotations. For example, in speaking of Charlotte's "foggy laughter" or of a "somber aroma," Colette extends the seme of obscurity to nonvisual items. (Usually, as the examples suggest, connotation as a code-creating procedure involves a Baudelairian type of "correspondance," whereby something normally perceived through one sense is represented in terms usually applicable to another sense.) Likewise, when sleeves or hair are qualified as "floating," they are incorporated into the water code. At times, the juxtaposition creates an oxymoron. For example, Colette describes the opium den as being as welcoming and inhospitable as a railway station (p. 16, our translation). By juxtaposing opposites, the oxymoron constitutes the most extreme type of linguistic formation capable of suggesting conflicting states and is instrumental in breaking down polarities.

A third procedure for combining signs into codes, juxtaposition with character, functions somewhat similarly to connotation but at another level of discourse. Here two or more terms are linked through their metonymic association with a character. Charlotte's deception takes place in a darkened room. Through their common relationship with her, the semes "obscurity" and "dissimulation" are related to each other and are integrated into the darkness code.

Finally, Colette uses node words to expand the semantic content of a given code. A node word is one which belongs to more than one descriptive system, because it contains a number of semes which may be activated.[4] As such, it can simultaneously belong to more than one descriptive system, and thus function as a point of transition or contact between codes, thereby creating even more complex relationships. The word "veiled" is an excellent example of the node word's capacity to expand codes: the term (or its grammatical equivalents) can be found in the various subcodes of the darkness code, referring to obscurity ("veiled lights"), to dissimulation (the androgyne, a creature of uncertain or dissimulated sex, is "veiled"), or to refuge (the Ladies' retreat "veils" the universe).

The four basic procedures described above function differently, but the result in each case is the same: to establish a system of relationships between images, i.e., to form codes. Likewise, while Colette's processes for selecting the darkness and water codes' constituent elements differ, the codes' textual operation is identical: the reshaping of conventional cultural associations.

Colette's thorough exploration of the semantic richness of a given concept — its potential to act as a seme in words belonging to otherwise separate codes — is best seen in the creation of the darkness code. The signifying power of this code in *Le Pur et l'impur* results from Colette's selection of certain potential semes from different semantic fields and their combination into a single complex code.

The darkness code includes five major subcodes: obscurity, dissimulation, enclosure, refuge, and identity. They are subcodes only in relation to the darkness code in this text — each could, in another work, constitute an independent code. This order is not arbitrary, but rather reflects the textual relation of the elements of one subcode to the next, as Colette expands the code to include more and more terms. The progression from obscurity to identity develops as images are linked with those from previously established subcodes. Linking occurs mainly through repetition of words containing common semes, through node words, and through juxtaposition with character.

The notion of obscurity dominates the first chapters of the work. The opium den in which Colette meets Charlotte is lit only by dull, reddish glowing lamps, and the encounter takes place at night. In this obscurity, Charlotte pretends to have an orgasm with the young man, thereby linking obscurity and dissimulation. The thematic relationship is made explicit at the linguistic level as well. Noting the similarity of Charlotte's laughter with the language of nocturnal birds, Colette compares the sounds Charlotte utters during the false orgasm to the sound of a nightingale, and adds: "No doubt this held Charlotte's secret prevarication, a melodious and merciful lie" (p. 18).

Obscurity and dissimulation are next linked through the predicates attached to the group of women in men's clothing, who, by their attire, appear in part to be what they are not. These women frequent dark and obscure places, which are also described as enclosed. The enclosure subcode thus joins the preceding ones through the mechanism of shared semantic juxtaposition. La Chevalière, always dressed in men's clothing, gives nocturnal parties behind closed doors. Love itself, in this context, creates a "dead-end atmosphere" (p. 78), whose air is enclosed and dull.

The enclosure subcode can signify opposing values, depending upon which semantic features are emphasised within a given context. In the case of Renée Vivien, enclosure becomes suffocation: her dimly lit house is filled with dark, heavy furniture, and the windows are nailed shut. (Ironically, Renée Vivien's associates are distinguished from La Chevalière's group, the former being described as "dazzling," the latter as "subterranean.") But Renée Vivien represents an extreme case: she is one of those types the narrator describes as "going too far." The notion of refuge is most often associated with the idea of enclosure: the dark, enclosed spaces frequented by La Chevalière and her friends are also places of safety, an observation made clear in the description of these places as "harbors."

Colette stresses the refuge subcode and introduces the subcode of identity in the chapter on the Ladies of Llangollen. It opens with a description of the pairs of women who construct a "sentimental refuge" (p. 110), where fidelity grows not from passion (elsewhere equated with flames) but similitude: desire is rendered more voluptuous by resemblance. In this section of the text, then, Colette makes explicit the concept of identity which has been implicit in the preceding discussions of pairs of women. At the same time, she contrasts the darkness of identity with the "dazzling difference" (p. 112) of the intruding male who threatens the refuge.

The Ladies, whose sheltered relationship is the most "successful" of the entire work, inhabit a "fantastic" atmosphere behind an "ideal" barrier (p. 119, our translation). They are isolated not only geographically, but temporally as well, since their lives predate the rest of the text by one hundred years. Their impenetrable refuge is admirably suggested in a passage describing the various historical upheavals whose force cannot even touch the house at Llangollen. The passage is worth quoting in its entirety, for it contains numerous semes of the darkness code:

A vow of reclusion descended upon this couple of young girls, separating them from the world, veiling and changing and remaking the universe in their eyes. In the distance would rumble and then die down the storm of no-popery riots in London; the United States would proclaim its independence; a queen and king of France would perish on the scaffold; Ireland would revolt, the British fleet would mutiny; slavery would be abolished...The universal excitement, the conflagration of Europe did not cross the Pengwern Hills that shut in Llangollen, or disturb the waters of the little river Dee. (p. 118)

The passage is further reminscent of the "masculine" rumbling which is reduced to a distant peril by the low ceilings and the dim lights of the places frequented by the women in men's clothes (p. 78). In this way the two groups are brought together and the concept of refuge is extended. But in this case, so perfect is the Ladies' isolation from others, that even Colette cannot completely penetrate their refuge. Limited to the information found in Lady Eleanor's diary (to which Colette does not remain overly faithful), she seems to rage in frustration at their silence. "Beyond time," the Ladies are also "beyond reach" (p. 121). (Significantly, the expression "beyond reach" also occurs in the all-important final paragraph of Le Pur et l'impur.)

We have explored at length the development of the darkness code in order to demonstrate how diverse signs can be textually incorporated into the same code. The water code is differently constituted: instead of a series of integrated subcodes, a single aspect is selected from a larger code. The operating principle here is not one of juxtaposition of shared semantic features, as in the darkness code, but of equation: Colette explicitly places the body in metaphoric relation with various forms of marine life. While there are fewer textual examples of the water code, its importance is stressed by the fact that such references occur in those key passages describing the senses and the human body, and thus promote the figurative expression of Colette's contribution to our knowledge of the senses.

In the first textual reference, the body is compared to a "barrier reef, mysterious and incomprehensible" (p. 19), thereby making the body a metonym of the sea. This relationship is firmly established in the passage on the Inexorable which posits the existence of the Sense. The Sense is compared to a marine creature, and the five senses become its tentacle-like appendages:

She also barred me from the cavern of odors, of colors, the secret refuge where surely frolicked a powerful arabesque of flesh, a cipher of limbs entwined, symbolic monogram of the Inexorable...In that word Inexorable, I gather together the sheaf of powers to which we have been unable to give a better name than "the senses." The senses? Why not *the* sense? That would offend no one and would suffice. *The sense*, dominating the five inferior senses, for let them venture far from it and they will be called back with a jerk — like those delicate and stinging ribbons, part weed, part arm, delegated by a deep-sea creature to. . . (p. 24)

The passage is crucial, for Colette not only adds a new aspect to our concept of the senses by suggesting the existence of a dominating "Sense," she also defines this notion in her own terms by referring to a psychological entity for which no name exists.

The passage reinforces the marine metaphor and adds another element: tentacle-like movement plays a large role in Colette's concept of sensuality. In an important passage comparing the female body with sea wrack, the image repeats the idea of floating tentacles (p. 148). This same idea recurs in the comparison of male homosexuals to cuttlefish (a tentacled, squid-like animal) who obscure their presence by emitting jets of dark ink (p. 131).

Throughout the text, water images are associated with varous parts of the body, reinforcing the relationship between sensuality and water. Many such references describe the eyes: Damien's eyes are bathed in a "false and saline moisture, oyster gray" (p. 41, our translation); Edouard de Max' eyes are like a water salamander, while Charlotte's eyes are "clouded with green like the marine pools the sea abandons at ebb tide" (p. 13, our translation). Images belonging to the water code often contain semes associated with tentacles: sleeves float, hair is compared to that of a drowned person.

In her portrayal of human sensuality, Colette not only explores the semantic potential of various codes, she also adds to it a further dimension by connecting the darkness and water codes at certain points. The richness of *Le Pur et l'impur* is due in part to the extensive incorporation of sensory images into codes, but even more so to the co-presence in given passages of signs belonging to different codes, with the result that more complex dimensions are added to the emerging description of the senses. That water and darkness are essential features of this description is evident if we recall that the sea creature/Sense — the Inexorable — inhabits a "cavern of odors, of colors," a "secret refuge," and that its "arabesque of flesh" recalls the tentacular image of the sensory appendages (p. 24).

The constant interplay of codes finds its best expression at the very end of *Le Pur et l'impur*. The final paragraph can in fact be seen as a microcosm of the entire work, where the juxtaposition of the two codes in a complex relation provides the key to Colette's definition of "pure." Colette clearly suggests that no literal, dictionary definition can describe that which has no expression in ordinary language. Purity for her is sensory, not cognitive or rational. It can however be evoked by combining water images with signs belonging to the various subcodes of the darkness code:

As that word "pure" fell from her lips, I heard the trembling of the

plaintive "u," the icy limpidity of the "r," and the sound aroused
nothing in me but the need to hear again its unique resonance, its
echo of a drop that trickles out, breaks off, and falls somewhere with a
plash. The word "pure" has never revealed an intelligible meaning to
me. I can only use the word to quench an optical thirst for purity in
the transparencies that evoke it — in bubbles, in a volume of water,
and in the imaginary latitudes entrenched, beyond reach, at the very
center of a dense crystal. (p. 175)

As was noted above, darkness and the sea have long been associated with
women, but critics have not always recognized that this traditional association
promotes a limited, if not detrimental, image of women. Darkness may be
enticingly mysterious, but it is also connected with something frightening and
demonic. To equate woman with the sea because of her life-giving properties
seems superficially positive, but in fact limits woman to one function —
reproduction — and her sexuality to a purely utilitarian aspect of her being.

Colette's *tour de force* in *Le Pur et l'impur* consists of taking traditional
metaphors, and, by drawing on semantic elements usually supressed, mod-
ifying radically the basis for metaphorisation in order to create a new conception of female sexuality in its sensual dimension. Women and darkness are
indeed associated in this text, but through techniques of recoding, darkness
here signifies not danger, but refuge; not something strange and mysterious,
but the recognition of identity. Similarly, Colette recodes the sea image: by
using a metonym to replace the sea, Colette substitutes for the concept of
woman as mother (*mer/mère*) a female sensuality that is autonomous, free-
floating, tentacular, and changing.

Because Colette uses the metaphors of darkness and water to define the
Sense and its servants, the five senses, she strongly suggests that sensuality is
essentially feminine in nature. The long section devoted to the culturally
"ideal" male lover, Don Juan, shows his disciples as misogynists. For them,
possession is a lightning bolt — the opposite of darkness and water. In fact,
most male imagery, especially that related to heterosexual males, consists of
words taken from the semantic fields of land and fire. The male homosexuals,
compared to the marine cuttlefish, provide a link between the male earth and
the female water metaphors: Colette also compares them to islands, to an
oasis, and to a shoreline, all images referring to the border where land and
water meet. While Colette explicitly rejects the traditional stereotype of
"effeminate," her image codes suggest that the homosexuals differ from other
male figures in approaching female sensibilities. To describe human sensuality
as feminine does not, however, restrict it to females. The senses, or, better,
the Sense, described in terms of the female darkness and water codes, are
nonetheless shared by all humans.

While we have concentrated in this study on the processes through which

Colette recodes woman and defines human sensuality as feminine, it can also be shown that images belonging to a male code are often associated with women, and vice versa. Such processes negate the superficial impression many readers have of *Le Pur et l'impur* as a set of character portraits only tenuously connected, for Colette has woven a complicated web of associations throughout the text by assigning various elements of her descriptive system to multiple characters. We can thus conclude that for Colette human sensuality is based not on the traditional opposition between males and females, but that instead it constitutes a highly complex spectrum in which her characters represent various gradations. By restructuring the codes which shape our perceptions of the role of the senses in human behavior, Colette provides us with a means of changing the way our culture "sees" the world, and the infinite variety of relationships within it.

Notes

1. *Le Pur et l'impur* was first serialized in the weekly *Gringoire* in 1931 under the title *Ces Plaisirs* ... Its publication was abruptly suspended in mid-sentence, apparently because of the "scandalous" nature of the work. The definitive version appeared in 1941. All page references cited here are taken from the Herma Briffault translation (Colette, *The Pure and the Impure*, New York: Farrar Straus and Giroux, 1966), unless otherwise noted.

2. Elaine Harris, *L'Approfondissement de la sensualité dans l'oeuvre romanesque de Colette* (Paris: Nizet, 1973), p. 41. Although Harris does recognize the existence of the spectrum of sensual behavior, she establishes poles ranging from the most "feminine" to the most "virile" characters, without stressing the importance of the shared characteristics.

3. Colette appears as a character in *Le Pur et l'impur* as well. She participates in the anecdotes and includes passages describing relevant features of her own behavior.

4. For a complete discussion of the concept of node words and their function in the creation of semes, see Diane Griffin Crowder, "Narrative Structures and the Semiotics of Sex in the Novels of Alain Robbe-Grillet" (Dissertation, University of Wisconsin–Madison, 1977), ch. 3.

17 Colette and Signs: A Partial Reading of a Writer "Born *Not* to Write"

CHRISTIANE MAKWARD

Colette might have done an excellent job of producing a "Colette on Colette," as Roland Barthes recently did about himself in the series of monographs for Editions du Seuil titled "Ecrivains de toujours." Barthes dramatized the dilemma of autobiographical writing by warning the reader in the following terms, printed in white on black on the inside cover: "all this must be considered as spoken by a character in a novel." Alain Robbe-Grillet, master-trickster of narrative fiction, is currently concocting his own "Robbe-Grillet by Robbe-Grillet" for the same series. But Colette would probably have refused to devise such an autobiography because she had already done so: it is the script she wrote for Yannick Bellon's film *Colette* (1951). The enterprise is semiologically similar: the verbal discourse constitutes the major system of self-mythification, while bodily language, images, and props make up a de-constructive, demystifying system. This script will therefore be particularly useful in assessing Colette's relationships to the world of signs. Such an enterprise is all the more imperative since this woman without a writer's vocation was thoroughly familiar with modes of expression such as mime and the cinema. Indeed, for Colette, not everything passes through nor can be understood through writing that is part of the complexity of life. As Michèle Sarde deftly demonstrated, the only "real Colette" we can capture is the self-written Colette who is *not* life-size.[1]

Sarde relays an irresistible anecdote recounted in *Claudine en ménage*: it shows Claudine/Colette's first encounter with Marcel/Proust. During his review of Literature at a dinner-table, "Proust" alludes to Claudine's soul only to be cut off with the following words: "'Sir,' said I firmly, 'you are raving. My soul is only full of red beans and bacon bits!'"[2] We know that for this mythical Colette the writer, the reader's sin *par excellence* is to look for her alive between the pages of her books.[3] However, another, no less important Colette has claimed to be starved for the printed word: as a refugee during the Second World War she had to share a scant library with her companions, "some twenty volumes swapped from room to room, going all the way around to start over again. Five or six Prousts, three Balzacs are very much in demand..."[4] Her prevailing self-image is, however, that of an anti-intellectual woman who holds mundane conversation and aesthetic considerations in utter scorn: a woman who does not equate — to refer to the Proustian myth — life and literature.

Some rare remarks that amount to an aesthetic statement can be found in *Journal à rebours*. Inevitably, the setting is the outdoors, the mode is comical: the "hero" is a teenager who appeals to Colette because he does not listen to "adult's language" (*J.R.*, p. 25). Young Tonin seems totally inarticulate when, in fact, he is the true poet: Colette stumbles on him delivering a tirade at the top of his voice, by the river. He has no public; he speaks for no one and he is completely engrossed in his mission, that of the poet: "to forget reality, to promise prodigies to the world, to celebrate victories and to deny death" (*J.R.*, p. 30). This short story probably is the most serious statement on "Art" to be found in Colette's works. She was an expert at eluding questions on the meaning of writing for herself or other writers. She could entertain a reporter for an appropriate period of time and send him off without having told him anything of substance.[5]

In fact, there are numerous remarks throughout Colette's texts on her absence of vocation. No "sacred signs" of it can be remembered by Colette, no youthful poems, no sacrosanct paternal library, no raving or obsession with words but, rather, the very fond memory of a mouldy, battered volume of the New Testament where her first teacher would preserve dried flowers. Un-equivocally, Colette states that as a girl she never felt the desire to write, but rather sensed, every day more clearly, that she was "precisely born *not* to write" (*J.R.*, p. 126) but to climb trees, roam through the woods at dawn and learn the secrets of life, all of which did not depend on verbal communication. Indeed Colette refers to Winter as her "first book" (*J.R.*, p. 124) and constantly applies the key-words of the learning process ("reading," "meaning," "sign-") to her apprenticeship of the natural world. A sky can thus be "unreadable," the flight of swallows has a "meaning" that must be discovered, and Fall can be "read" on the back of a leaf. Not only is the world *the* Book and nature the Temple, but the body as well is perceived as a signifying system, whether it is one's own — enriched with the historical signs of scars and wrinkles (*N.J.*, p. 56) — or the body of the Other, which arouses desire and beckons to the "reader" with its "scattered and mysterious characters" (*N.J.*, p. 183).

It is enlightening to measure the distance between a certain "historical" Colette, that of *Journal à rebours*, and the "mythical" Colette of *La Naissance du jour.* History can hardly be taken into account, Time can hardly be perturbed without the awareness of danger invading consciousness. All that Sido so forcefully represents in later works as well as in *La Naissance du jour* (1928), which can be summarized as the green paradise of childhood, is questioned and presented in a very different light in "Danger," a short non-narrative text of *Journal à rebours.* The word "danger" is carved on a wooden sign nailed on a tree and half blurred but, claims Colette, its meaning is intact and self-generating. In this text, a noteworthy realistic variant of the mythical Sido is described: it is an old woman, beyond Time and history. She stands not as the triumphant keeper of nature's mysteries but as the servant of generations of men, who has peeled her potatoes every day at the same hour for the past seventy-five years. Her silence and submission, her entire presence is a reminder of the warning sign on the tree. The "danger" in question is explained by Colette as the temptation "to forget, to be outside the world, danger to suffer no longer, to be, in spite of oneself, sheltered from what hurts" (*J.R.*, p. 39). Further on, this woman-signifier of "danger" is referred to as "the ultimate sadness": that of "pure vacancy," which is desired by Colette at this point in her life (*J.R.*, p. 41). In other words, Colette creates out of her own spirits depressed by wartime hardships a new signified for "danger." The wooden sign warns passers-by not to walk beyond because the ruins are dangerous. Colette, who is encamped beyond the sign, in the old castle, "reads" her environment as an extension of the signified which is deeply meaningful to her as a writer. She equates "danger" with indifference, numbness, vacancy, and *not* physical death.

The Colette who jealously guarded herself from another sentimental venture in *La Naissance du jour,* the daughter who chanted in *Sido* the vocation to love all creatures rather than one, this mythical Colette is absent from "Danger." Instead, a "historical" Colette speaks, one who is prone to existential vertigo and does not easily accommodate herself to chaos, helplessness, or nature. Beyond the sign is the threat "to perceive ourselves older, intelligent, despondent, unconnected to the serenity that surrounds us" (*J.R.*, p. 42). While the poet's mission is to "deny reality," the real danger for the "real/historical" Colette is to admit — *in writing* and at this time of war — that the "mythical/literary" Colette *is the real Colette.* To achieve this would mean to transgress a certain code of propriety. History makes it indecent for Colette to be and write herself any longer as the one who spurns history and writing, the one who can "retreat" in the heart of Paris, reign over her pets and friends, the one whose serenity was "constructed without spontaneity," that is, *through writing* and by force. The disturbances of war forced Colette out of her Palais Royal queendom to face the ambiguity of her self-mythification under pressure of reality. Michèle Sarde has shed light on this process by pointing out that the paradox of the liar (if a man says he is a liar, etc.) was not at all resolved in *La Naissance du jour.* There, Colette refers to *La Retraite sentimentale* as a web of lies, that is, a *fictional* quest for affective autonomy written and joked about for the benefit of her beloved male companion (Willy presumably). Colette is lying indeed because when she wrote *La Retraite sentimentale* her first husband had long been demystified. In *La Naissance du jour* she admits she had lied artfully in *La Retraite sentimentale* ... yet some twenty years later, while writing *La Naissance du jour*, which deals basically with the same quest for feminine autonomy and the same refusal to let a young man enter her life, she was already deeply involved with Maurice Goudeket, sixteen years her junior and her future husband.

"I am an old monkey," she once said (Virmaux, p. 293): this may be as close to the truth as the reader can ever hope to get in pursuing the "real" Colette. It is not unimportant to know that the famed "pink cactus" of Sido's letter at the opening of *La Naissance du jour* — if it existed at all — did *not* prevent Sido from accepting de Jouvenel's invitation to visit the couple (Sarde, p. 313). Colette's myth-making strategy, the creative substitution of "names of pink cactus" (Colette's own expression) for ordinary objects (referents and their signifier), is a process she labels "exorcising" reality, when in fact it consists in bewitching the reader with her golden pen (*N.J.*, pp. 228, 240). This strategy, also called "art," bars the reader from attempting to unravel myth and reality any further.

In the same manner as Colette carves a *bifrons* Sido (a glorious "savage" garden-face and a care-worn domestic face)[6] but leaves the realistic domestic face in the shadows, she constitutes a *bifrons Colette-on-Colette* in her texts. On the subject of writing and of *herself* writing, Colette-the-person remains in the shadows while she directs the floodlight on Colette-the-writer who did not want to write. On the artful basis of her written statements, it appears clearly that for Colette the art of writing is inessential: it is a marketable craft and the door to freedom from want and men. The "sentimental novel" and melodramatic film ("roman-film" is the term she uses) are particularly despicable genres, but poetry fares no better in her eyes. Colette's indictment of literature, literati, and fiction-writing is consistent. In the family circle and in the "salons de la Belle Epoque" Colette desanctifies writing light-heartedly: Sido is dutifully cleansed of an "accusation" of having had "literary ambitions" made by a desperately underinformed biographer of Colette (*Sido*, p. 22). Poor Juliette, her elder half-sister, is accused in earnest of "Bovary-like" melancholy "haunted by the literary ghosts of heroes" (*Sido*, p. 35). Captain Colette's poetic exercises and their disastrous consequences on the family "country-parties" — namely the reduction of the children's vivacity to unimpressed silence — are ironically evoked by Colette (*Sido*, p. 43). The child Gabri (Colette) mercilessly criticizes a surplus of adjectives in her father's poetry, having imprudently been appointed by him as his first auditor/reader. Then, Sido herself derides the Captain's bookish knowledge and "humane" pragmatism: "You see...you stretch your hand out to know if it is raining"

(*Sido*, p. 47). For Sido has more enchanting ways of telling the weather: she reads it in the way the cat dances, by counting the skins of onions, or by observing the curl of oat-seed hairs. She can also tell the time of day by the scent of plants.

While the father is the failed master of paper and pencils, Sido is the interpreter of natural signs and the dispenser of flowers: sending flowery messages to neighbors, refusing to give up any of her roses to adorn a man's coffin, bestowing her most gorgeous one on a baby "without speech as yet" (*Sido*, p. 210). The child Colette herself is rebuked for "excessive expression" (*Sido*, p. 27) and flittingly praised for "looking stupid" or approved for balking at certain words such as "disease." The association of the father with disastrous literary experiments and that of the mother with irrational or non-verbal communication does not fully account for Colette's portrayal of her parents' relation to communication and signs. The parent's reactions to the idea of death are obviously divergent (*Sido*, p. 50); the father reacts violently to the *tangible* signs of death in Sido's body, while Sido and Colette share a repulsion for the *words* of death. In Colette's eyes, the parents constitute an exemplary couple and the Captain's impotence as a writer is attributed by Sido and Colette to his passion for his companion and proudly discredited as "frivolity" when it was in fact the major source of Sido's strength. A further exchange of the parents' role in her education is Colette's acknowledgement of a debt to the Captain in the emotional realm of music enjoyment. When music moves her, she writes, it is the father in her that lives, and not words, never words. It is as though, beyond the signs, mother and father principles meshed harmoniously. Colette also reports her great astonishment when finding out from a clairvoyante that Sido's spirit is not by her side but "busy elsewhere," while her father's spirit watches her benevolently because she has become what he dreamed of for himself: a writer (*Sido*, p. 53).

On the other hand, far from despising writing, Sido was an assiduous letter writer and a superior one, according to Colette — especially, one might add, when lovingly edited by Colette for her own literary purposes. Whether Sido's ultimate letter is "real" or fictional, the final message of mother to daughter deserves special attention in our investigation of a possible hierarchy of signs for Colette. The last of some two thousand letters to Colette by Sido involves a dramatic transformation of verbal to pictorial discourse: in order to reassure her daughter that she has already freed herself from "the obligation of using our language," Sido had covered two sheets with joyful lines, "vegetal curves," rays and arrows with only a few privileged words such as "she danced" and "my love" (*N.J.*, p. 244). A hieroglyphic language, in short, which is left to the reader to "picture," perhaps in the style of Miro's paintings. This new discourse by Sido seems particularly appropriate to her myth: hieroglyphic language is associated with "primitive" or "savage" cultures or, in the more respectable cases of oriental and middle-eastern civilizations, with polytheistic, non-dualistic symbolic systems: cultures where, to resume Deleuze's pair, Pathos and Logos are not exclusive.[7] Sido's final message therefore constitutes a haunted landscape of plastic signifiers. It is a dream "language" where much love and joy of life can be deciphered by the receptor-Colette who finally sees in this message the metaphor of her own writing. Colette calls out for her "ambiguous friend" (cat-Vial-eros) to "abdicate his form" and to blend perfectly and metamorphose into this scenery, the "haunted scenery" of Colette's vision as created by her pen (*N.J.*, pp. 244–245).

Colette's fascination with non-verbal graphic signs is a recurring theme. She clearly values hieroglyphs and images as being richer in meaning than words. Her sensitivity to the physical-visual-audible aspects of the alphabet is very "contemporary" — or very Proustian. The word "rêche" ("rough") she deems a "good plastic word" (*J.R.*, p. 56); the letter *M* has an unbearable lascivious shape,[8] the letter *S* perfectly signifies "snake" and "diamond" (*N.J.*, p. 112). But the written word is impotent in conveying love, no matter how masterly and inspired the author: Renée Néré complains that "there should be [along with the writing] . . . some fiery drawing, all lit up with colors,"[9] something closer to a tangible, physical representation than mere words. This is Colette's dream as a writer, one she shares with numerous poetically inclined writers. This may be why she considered, or *said* she considered, the best of her work to consist of "the blue of *La Naissance du jour*" or perhaps the Breton scenery of *Le Blé en herbe* (in the script of Y. Bellon's film).

Colette's interest in the cinema as an emerging art form was intense. According to Virmaux, this interest subsided with the advent of sound movies and commercial melodrama. She wrote of the very strong emotional experiences involved in her viewing documentaries and silent educational films on the growth of plants, on landscapes, on insect life (Virmaux, p. 276–278). "We shall never look intensely enough, nor closely enough, nor passionately enough," and she cannot reconcile herself with the public's indifference to natural reality, a reality prodigious enough to keep us enthralled for a lifetime. In view of this preference for the visual, fiction — and particularly novel and film — are considered lowly products of the mind, as despicable as word-games and the "degrading mania of pun-cracking" (Sarde, pp. 114, 154), all "boyish" pastimes associated by Colette with Willy's editorial role on the *Claudine* series. Two decades later, Colette's distrust of words had not abated: fiction writing borders on the ridiculous if the novelist's intent is to capture "real life." "Ink signs," says Colette, are very poor tools to capture reality (*N.J.*, p. 109). The problem can only be alleviated by processing, through the meshes of style, as much color, movement, and line as possible. Several years before the advent of the *nouveau roman*, labelled "the school of the eye," a critic wrote, "Madame Colette has a camera at the tip of her pen" (Virmaux, p. 19).

Echoes of Sido's fundamental teaching "Regarde!" can be traced in particular in *Between Life and Death* by Nathalie Sarraute. While Sarraute's description rarely deals with "objective reality," her poetics rest, like Proust's and Colette's, on the preservation of Life through language. While both Sarraute and Proust have commented substantially on the enormous difficulties and the constant danger of failure, Colette does not attempt to analyze the relationship of reality to language and to writing, other than in the most fragmentary and perfunctory fashion. With fame and success bestowed upon her, a writer without a vocation or an aesthetic, Colette upheld her anti-intellectual role to the end. Was she the dupe of her myth-making machine? On the basis of her cinematic autobiography, I am inclined to answer negatively. What could be more gratifying and reassuring than to both live and die as a myth? What could be more authentic, existentially, than to identify with one's own self-generated myth — winking all the way? Colette was evidently enormously amused by the filming of her self-portrait: it is her final touch — the crown — to herself as a national monument, faultlessly ready for mummification, for the contemplation of those who need mummies.

In Bellon's film, Colette the writer quotes or paraphrases herself on all major components of her literary myth. An enormous bunch of flowers is brought to her; Goudeket reads the card: "It is from a cat, Madame de la Gouttière." Colette acts Sido: "If the swallows and the children are out, it means that the weather is fair." She out-Sidoes Sido when Pauline, her servant, comes back from the market with a basketful of vegetables for Colette's inspection. The sequence is mute but not silent: Colette scrutinizes a head of lettuce, bites into a radish, and sets some aside for herself. She devours an onion, groans ecstatically, chews, nods approvingly — all this without a word, only conniving glances to the camera. When Cocteau pretends to lead her on to discussing her works, she claims that she has, at last, learned the craft of "idleness," defined as being busy with a great many different things. Although her desk and papers have been shown earlier, the last shot is that of Colette at her embroidery-work, with Cocteau's line: "Look at her, Pauline, she is doing embroidery!" as the final words of the script. Only a very attentive reader will remember, seeing the film, that Colette used the needle as a metaphor for her pen: she would not blacken a white page but "embroider it" dutifully (*N.J.*, p. 87).

This biographical picture of Colette on Colette challenges many prevailing myths concerning the writer in 1951: loftiness of thought, engagement, concern with the mission of the writer, coherence of argument, seriousness of purpose, all these "values" are manipulated implicitly in the film: they are glaringly *absent*. As Sido the mythified mother reigned over her natural queendom, Colette rules over her literary myth and her royal p(a)lace. The "happy ending" of her story rests on a lifelong *use* of writing and a proclaimed *distance* from it, doubled by an explicit inability to write about anything but love and self. There is no hierarchy in Colette's realms of signs. The ambivalence of her relationship to language is best epitomized, perhaps, in the adventures of her name. A father's name was degraded by a husband's pen name: when "liberated" at age fifty, this name had become a woman's name and a literary name. In real life, however, Colette was fond of her second husband's name and title, even though she satirized the use of patriarchal names in several of her novels, particularly *La Vagabonde* and *L'Entrave*. In making her father's name her own (and a banal woman's first name), Colette identifies symbolically with *both* her parents: she is "Madame Colette," which was Sido's normal title, and she is "Colette," which was Sido's appellation of her husband. Colette is, after her father and like her father, "the only person in the world to call Sido 'Sido'" (*Sido*, p. 17). While the world identifies Colette as a writer, the writer identifies herself as Sido's daughter: "the daughter of a woman" represented primarily as the green goddess of childhood and of natural signs, lost and regained through writing. Explicitly inessential, the signs of art are separate from the self and from life. For Colette, the pen is neither a sword nor a penis, but a fanciful needle to embroider the feminine way of life and love. Besides verbal discourse, Colette mastered several other languages: that of the silent body in mime, the signs of nature learned from Sido, the "language of animals" and of eros. Denying the essential superiority of the symbolic order of signs over other "languages" *in writing*, Colette only elaborates an important component of her mythical system: born *not* to be a writer and nothing *but* a writer, in the (happy) end.

Notes

1. Michèle Sarde, *Colette libre et entravée* (Paris: Stock, 1978).

2. Ibid., p. 162.

3. Colette, *La Naissance du jour* (Paris: Flammarion, 1928), p. 169. Henceforth referred to in the text as *N.J.* All translations are mine.

4. Colette, *Journal à rebours* (Brouty/Fayard, 1941; Livre de Poche, 1974), p. 48. Henceforth referred to in the text as *J.R.*

5. Alain & Odette Virmaux, *Colette au cinéma* (Paris: Flammarion, 1975), p. 294.

6. *Sido*, followed by *Les Vrilles de la vigne* (Hachette, 1901; Livre de Poche, 1969), p. 14.

7. Gilles Deleuze, *Proust et les signes* (Paris: P.U.F., 1971), p. 116.

8. Colette, *Duo* (Paris: Ferenczi, 1934), p. 222.

9. Colette, *La Vagabonde* (Paris: Ollendorf, 1911; Albin Michel, 1957), p. 205.

Notes on Contributors

ANN COTHRAN teaches at Wittenberg University, and has published studies on Beauvoir, Sarraute, and Sarrazin. Her articles have appeared in *Women's Studies* and *L'Esprit Créateur*.

MARGARET CROSLAND is the author of *Colette: A Provincial in Paris* and *Colette: The Difficulty of Loving*. Her most recent titles are *Women of Iron and Velvet* (1976), and *Beyond the Lighthouse* (1981).

DIANE CROWDER teaches at Cornell College. Her article on semiotics has appeared in the *Bucknell Review*.

CLAIRE DEHON is on the faculty at Kansas State University. She has published on the Symbolists in *Le Flambeau* and *Philological Quarterly*, and is author of an article on Colette's short stories in *La Revue du Pacifique*.

ERICA EISINGER taught at Edgewood College, and is now a law student. Her articles have appeared in *Contemporary Literature, Kentucky Romance Quarterly*, and *Journal of Popular Culture*. She is a contributing editor to the forthcoming *Ecrits de femmes*, and co-editor with Mari McCarty of a special issue on Colette for *Women's Studies*.

ELEANOR REID GIBBARD is Associate Professor Emerita of French at West Virginia University, and has published in the *West Virginia University Philological Papers*.

ANNE DUHAMEL KETCHUM is author of *Colette ou la Naissance du jour* (1968), and is on the faculty of the University of Colorado. Her articles have appeared in *French Review* and *La Revue du Pacifique*.

CHRISTIANE MAKWARD is on the faculty at the Pennsylvania State University. A founding co-editor of *Bulletin de Recherches et d'Etudes Féministes Francophones* (University of Wisconsin), her articles have appeared in *Sub-Stance, La Revue des Sciences Humaines, Poétique,* and *Women and Literature*. She is editor and co-author of *Ecrits de Femmes* (forthcoming).

FRANÇOISE MALLET-JORIS is the author of many novels, among them *L'Empire céleste (Cafe Celeste)* and *Le Rempart des béguines (The Illusionist)*. She is a member of the Royal Academy of Belgium and the Acádemie Goncourt.

ELAINE MARKS is Professor of French, Chair of Women's Studies, and Director of the Women's Studies Research Center at the University of Wisconsin. Her titles include *Simone de Beauvoir: Encounters with Death,* and *Colette*. She is co-editor with George Stambolian of *Homosexualities and French Literature* (1979), and co-editor with Isabelle de Courtivron of *New French Feminisms* (1980).

MARI McCARTY has taught on the faculties of the University of Wisconsin-Madison and Alaska Pacific University. She is the author of *Colette* (University of Wisconsin Extension, 1978), and is the Colette annotator for *Women Writers in Translation* (1980). She and Erica Eisinger are co-editors of a special issue of *Women's Studies* devoted to Colette.

NANCY K. MILLER, on the faculty of Columbia University, is currently a Faculty Fellow at the Bunting Institute of Radcliffe College (1980–82). She is the author of *The Heroine's Text: Readings in the French and English Novel 1722–1782,* and several articles on women's writing.

DONNA NORELL teaches in St. Paul's College at the University of Manitoba. Her work on Colette includes essays in the *Journal of Women's Studies in Literature, L'Esprit Créateur,* and *Women's Studies*. Her current book is *In Search of the Circle: A Synopsis of Colette's Vision*.

SUZANNE RELYEA teaches French at the University of Massachusetts-Boston and is currently preparing a book titled *Women, Writing, and Aristocracy in Seventeenth Century France*. Another of her articles on Colette has appeared in *Women's Studies*.

YANNICK RESCH is on the faculty of the University of Aix-Marseille III in France. She is co-editor of Colette's complete works in the Pléiade edition forthcoming from Gallimard. Resch is author of numerous scholarly articles as well as a book on Colette, *Corps féminin, corps textuel* (1972).

SYLVIE ROMANOWSKI teaches French at Northwestern University. She is author of *L'Illusion chez Descartes: la structure du discours cartésien* (1974), and articles on Malraux, Molière, and préciosité, among others.

MICHÈLE BLIN SARDE's biography *Colette: Free and Fettered* (1980) was crowned by the Académie Française. She has written a novel, *Le Désir fou* (1975), and her book titled *Les Francaises, trop aimées, mal aimées* will appear in 1982.

JOAN HINDE STEWART teaches French at North Carolina State University. She is the author of *The Novels of Mme Riccoboni* (1976), and has also published a critical edition of Riccoboni's *Lettres de Fanni Butlerd* (1979). She is presently writing a book on Colette.

JACOB STOCKINGER teaches at the University of Wisconsin-Madison, where he is an Honorary Research Fellow at the Women's Studies Research Center. He is Contributing Editor of the *San Francisco Review of Books*, and has published articles on the French Enlightenment, Colette, Beauvoir, and Genet.

JANET WHATLEY is on the faculty of the University of Vermont, and has published articles in the *University of Toronto Quarterly*, *The Kentucky Romance Quarterly*, and *Eighteenth-Century Studies*, among others.

Index